Myths
and
Folklore

Myths and Folklore

HENRY I. CHRIST

Amsco School Publications, Inc.
315 Hudson Street / New York, N.Y. 10013

For the typing and preparation of the manuscript; for many valuable suggestions and usable materials; for her good judgment and common sense; and above all for her unwavering and optimistic support, I am, as always, deeply indebted to my wife, Marie E. Christ, who has shared with me a lifetime of schedules and deadlines.

Henry I. Christ

When ordering this book, please specify:
either R 501 H or MYTHS AND FOLKLORE, HARDBOUND.

ISBN 0-87720-784-4

Illustrations by Jeff Fisher

To the Student

The world of myth isn't dead. It isn't a stuffy old antique resting on some forgotten shelf in a museum. It is with us now, living, and playing a role in communication. You will meet that world in everyday words like *atlas, cereal, echo, hygiene, hypnosis, January, martial, music, panic, psychology,* and *volcano.* In your everyday reading, you will be expected to know what a *halcyon* day is, why unpleasant persons are called *harpies,* how an *iridescent* gem shines. All these words have fascinating stories to tell.

Becoming familiar with words like these is only part of the story, however. The old myths are more readable than many novels. There are nature myths, love stories, tales about individuals who outdo the dashing 007, James Bond. There are yarns that read like science fiction. There are monsters galore, too.

These myths do not exist in a vacuum. They are closely related to other forms of literature: legends, folktales, ballads, tall stories, fables, and narrative poetry. All these are pleasantly readable. *Myths and Folklore* provides colorful examples of each type.

The book begins with a study of "the people as creative artists." If you are interested in folk music, folk art, crafts, and folk culture, you will especially enjoy Unit One. This section introduces you to all kinds of folklore and shows how it is connected to myths and legends.

Unit Two concentrates on the myths of Greece and Rome, one of the richest storehouses of tales in the world. Here you will find some of your old favorites, like Hercules and Perseus. You will meet many others who may be new to you, like Tithonus, Psyche, and Daphne. You will brush up on the names of gods and goddesses and discover the kind of part each supposedly plays in human affairs.

Unit Three takes you to the "windy plains of Troy," where Achilles and Hector had their fatal meeting. Then you will leave Troy and wander the world of myth with Odysseus. You will meet monsters to rival the bug-eyed monsters of science fiction. You will find an enduring love story in the the marriage of Odysseus and Penelope.

If you find some of the words strange and difficult to pronounce, just look at the back of the book, in the index. Here the pronunciations of most words have been simplified. Once

you know the accented syllable—printed in capital letters—
you will find the words easy to pronounce, especially with the
simplified guide in parentheses.

Unit Four will leave behind the warm world of the Mediterranean and take you to the icy reaches of Scandinavia. The
gods and goddesses of the Norse people were quite different
from their Greek counterparts. If you are like most readers,
you will be fascinated by the good/bad Loki. He may be
annoying but he's never dull. Thor is another favorite.

Unit Five is a delightful section, with all kinds of folktales
to tickle your fancy and catch your interest. Talking animals,
magic spells, weird voyages, tall stories—all these have been
chosen for their readability. The ballads at the end of the unit
will arouse your curiosity and challenge your imagination.
Don't miss "Get Up and Bar the Door," one of the most
delightful ballads ever passed from generation to generation.

Unit Six is a kind of continuation of Unit Five, but here
the emphasis is upon the magical, the mysterious, the impos-
sible-made-possible. Some of these narratives, like the stories
collected by the Grimm Brothers, are really folktales. Others
have been created by master storytellers like Hans Christian
Andersen and Lewis Carroll. Readers who enjoy *Star Trek* may
find this section especially interesting.

Unit Seven concentrates on the folklore of our own country.
Folk heroes like Paul Bunyan and Davy Crockett share pages
with a touching ballad like "Barbara Allen" and an Indian
legend, "Mon-Daw-Min." One of the best short stories ever
written, "The Devil and Daniel Webster," has a courtroom
scene that makes Perry Mason or Ben Matlock look dull!

Myths and Folklore has been created for your enjoyment.
The stories are readable, among the best of their kind. But
there is more to the book. At the end of each unit there are
sections to improve your reading and your appreciation.
"Reading for Understanding" will challenge you and give you
the satisfaction of knowing that you have mastered the material in the unit. "Words in Context" will help you add to your
vocabulary storehouse by selecting certain words from the
unit and providing four alternatives for each. "Suggested Activities" will provide some ideas for individual and class proj-
ects that will enrich your reading. Then, in Units Two through
Seven, comes a section that deals with allusions. It lists everyday words and expressions that find their roots in the unit
studies. Unit Two adds still another helpful section: "Phrases
from Myths." If, for example, you've ever heard the expression

"The Sword of Damocles" and wondered what it means, you will find its meaning explained here, along with many other phrases.

So you see, *Myths and Folklore* has a twofold purpose. The first is to give you many hours of reading pleasure, of meetings with wild and wonderful creatures and of ordinary people caught up in a whirlwind of unexpected action. The second is to store your memory banks with a great many ideas, sources, and names, so that you will find all your reading and listening enriched.

If you have ever said, "Tell me a story," you will find your wish granted. Here are stories you'll enjoy.

Henry I. Christ

Contents

UNIT SEVEN   American Folklore   273

UNIT · ONE

The People as Creative Artists

In 1879 cave explorers stumbled upon a cave in Altamira, Spain. They were amazed to find inside a world of beauty. Primitive peoples had decorated the walls of the cave. They had painted deer, bison, horses, stags, and ibexes with an artist's loving touch. After a period of about 16,000 years, these paintings still communicate a message of human feeling across the centuries. Since that time other caves have been discovered. Rock paintings in Africa show a similar skill. The purpose of all these drawings may be uncertain, but their beauty is obvious to any observer. They speak to us with strength and reveal our common humanity.

From the beginnings of human history there are clear evidences of human creativity, not only in painting but in all areas of communication like poetry, sculpture, and the dance. The people have expressed their hopes and fears, their joys and sorrows, in some form or other. There is no known culture without some form of art.

One of the most important of all such arts is that of oral communication. Tales have been transmitted through many generations. These tales tell of the achievements of great gods and heroes. They also tell of ordinary people in unusual adventures. These stories may be classified as myths, legends, or folktales. All are important to us today. They show us where we have come from. They reveal common yearnings. They link us to all our ancestors and show us that all human beings belong to one family. The Australian aborigine and the Alaskan Eskimo are kin to the sophisticated Parisian.

The pages that follow will open up the great treasure house of human creativity in the form of myths, legends, and folktales. They will also provide many good stories for sheer enjoyment.

1

I. Myths, Legends, and Folktales

How Do They Differ?

"Where have we come from? What are we? Where are we going?"

The great Impressionist artist Paul Gauguin inserted these questions into one of his paintings. Men and women have always pondered these questions. One way of answering them is through the creation of myths.

Myths are stories intimately bound up with the traditions of a people. They deal with gods, heroes, religious beliefs, and cultural traits. They explain how the world was created, how people and animals came into existence, how important customs were established and preserved. They also explain all kinds of natural phenomena, from rainbows to sunrise.

Three great mythical traditions have greatly influenced the western world: Greek, Roman, and Norse myths. These great classic myths arose in a period before science attempted many of the same explanations. All three are treated in this volume.

There are other stories closely associated with myths. The word *legend* is often associated with *myth*, for example, and the differences between them are sometimes vague. A major purpose of the myth is usually to explain, to show why things are as they are. Mythological characters are often symbols. They represent something else. Apollo represents the sun; Diana, the moon. Thor represents thunder.

A major purpose of the legend, on the other hand, is to entertain with a narrative supposedly based on fact. Legendary characters usually represent themselves as they perform great feats. Legends may have a strong basis in fact. Legendary characters, like Babe Ruth in our own day, actually lived. Babe Ruth legends, like all legends, are told as true. The myth, on the other hand, is told as a story requiring its listeners to believe in the gods who are its characters.

Folktale is a very broad term that includes all kinds of traditional narratives. Sometimes the dividing line between myth and folktale is blurred. Certain creation myths of primitive peoples, for example, are often classified as folktales. In the Zuni Indian myth, for example, Awonawilona existed before the beginning of all things. He made himself into the form of the sun and by his thought created the mists that promote growth. From his activities came all life on earth.

A major characteristic of the folktale is its long and continuing life. It is traditional, handed down from one generation to another. Originality is undesirable. The story is usually preserved intact, most often in oral form.

The folktale is a universal narrative form, characteristic of all peoples. Surprisingly, certain similar ideas keep cropping up in the folktales of peoples around the world. Folktales from Africa to North America, for example, deal with the trickster, the clever animal or person who survives by his wits and confuses both his friends and enemies. A familiar example is given in this text. The folk hero Anansi outwits his old rival, Tiger. Other themes are universal, apparently arising independently in the traditions of various tribes and cultures.

The Narrative Element

"Tell me a story."

"Let me tell you about an amazing experience I had today."

"Did you hear the incredible story of the founding of this town?"

These familiar expressions suggest one thing: everyone loves a good story. Detective novels are extremely popular because they tell good stories. Television programs with good story lines hold listeners. Good storytellers are popular at get-togethers.

It is sometimes difficult to decide whether a particular tale is a myth, a legend, or a folktale. Labels may not really matter. What is important is that all three forms have a common characteristic: they're all good stories. We listeners and readers are interested in what happens next. We want to know whether Thor escapes from the giants, or whether the sorcerer's apprentice is able to undo the magic charm that is proving his downfall.

Common Threads

Though myths, legends, and folktales take widely different forms, they represent certain human yearnings. We want to be protected from the buffetings of bad luck. We want to be secure. We'd like to be healthy, wealthy, and wise. We'd like to survive in a sometimes difficult world. We rejoice in success stories showing that we, too, can do well.

A recurring human need is the yearning for a wise and strong leader. Legendary figures like King Arthur, Charlemagne, and Barbarossa may be ready to return to solve their people's problems. Quetzalcoatal, the legendary god of Middle

America, may have played a role in history. When the Spanish
explorer Cortez landed in Mexico in 1519, the Aztecs thought
he was Quetzalcoatal returning to his people. Their error
paved the way for their downfall, since Cortez was more
interested in conquest than cultural exchange.

Another recurring human need is a closer understanding of
animals. The animal world figures in myths and folktales
everywhere. The centaurs, sirens, and harpies of classical
mythology were part animal. Many of the Egyptian gods were
animal-headed. Characters in the mythology of American Indians were animals. A great many folktales have animal characters: for example, Brer Rabbit of the American Southeast,
Raven of the American Southwest, and Reynard the Fox of
Europe.

II. Ballads

Ballads resemble folktales, though they are more concise
and more specialized. They have been called "a form of narrative folk song." Ballads tend to have certain characteristics.
Of course, they are meant to be sung aloud. They tell a story,
usually focusing on a single incident. The incident is told
impersonally, moving ahead with economy to a quick end.
Dialog is often included. Content and style link ballads to the
world of folklore and demonstrate the ingenuity of the people.

III. Folklore

Folktales are but one part of the larger whole: folklore. It
takes many forms, but all forms reflect the hopes, fears, beliefs, superstitions, skills, customs, and wisdom of the people.

Music and the Dance

Every year, in Asheville, North Carolina, mountain folk
gather for the annual Bluegrass Festival. Three nights of entertainment include musicians, dancers, and storytellers.
Bands, usually of four, play traditional mountain airs in the
dizzying tempo associated with mountain fiddlers and their
partners. The dancers are of two major types: cloggers and
smooth dancers. Both types are variations of the typical

square dance, with squares of four dancers performing intricate patterns alone and in the full group.

Folk music is not restricted to festivals like that in Asheville. It appears in most homes where music is played or just appreciated. Individuals play traditional melodies on the dulcimer or Autoharp, sometimes with vocal accompaniment. Many famous singers like Joan Baez and Arlo Guthrie have popularized traditional folk tunes. Folk music in all its forms has become an important part of world culture. Many great composers, like Antonin Dvořák of Czechoslovakia, have incorporated folk tunes into their major works.

Many children's songs and verses have roots in the distant past. Throughout the world from time immemorial, children have used counting-out rhymes. These are generally used to decide who shall be "it" in a children's game. A leader stands in front of a group and points to each in turn, reciting the rhyme as he points. The child who is pointed to as the verse ends is "it." Here's a fairly recent American counting-out rhyme:

> Engine, engine, number nine,
> Running on Chicago Line.
> If it's polished, it will shine,
> Engine, engine, number nine.

Other rhymes are used by children, like the following to start a race:

> One for the money,
> Two for the show,
> Three to get ready,
> And four to go.

Folk Wisdom

"You never miss the water till the well runs dry."

This proverb, like so many others in common speech, demonstrates folk wisdom at its simplest. It summarizes so much about human nature; yet it does the job in a few words.

Here's another example. People are often dissatisfied, spoiling their lives with dreams of what might have been or should be. A simple proverb sums up the problem and provides practical advice:

"If you don't have what you like, you must like what you have."

Sometimes the wisdom is put into riddle form. Perhaps the most famous riddle is that of the Sphinx, who killed anyone who couldn't solve it.

"What goes on four legs in the morning, on two legs
at noon, and on three in the evening?"
Answer: "Man. As a baby he crawls on all fours.
As a mature adult he walks upright, on two legs.
As an old man, he uses a cane."

Riddles are ancient. They rank with myths, proverbs, and folktales as very early examples of folk thinking. Riddles embody humor and wit. They are universally popular, especially among children and primitive peoples. They are excellent examples of folk wisdom at work.

Folk wisdom is demonstrated in many other ways. Many old folk remedies have been found helpful in handling some medical problems of today. Certain herbs and other plants have medicinal properties that provide relief for sufferers. The juice of the aloe plant, for example, can soothe a burn.

Folk wisdom is also strong in the various rites of passage. Birth, baptism, marriage, and death are all moments worthy of special attention. All are attended by special ceremonies marking the events. Among the most famous are the initiation rites of primitive peoples. These powerful ceremonies mark the end of childhood and the beginning of adult responsibilities. The Jewish bar mitzvah and the Christian confirmation are related examples.

Closely tied to these ceremonies are the special celebrations for birthdays, anniversaries, and holidays. Baby and bridal showers acknowledge important events. Parties for employees taking on new jobs, as well as retirement parties, are all related. All have their roots in the folk wisdom of the past.

"I'm not superstitious, knock wood!"

Though superstitions show a lack of wisdom, they are an important part of folklore. Even those who pride themselves on not being superstitious may worry about the results of breaking a mirror, spilling salt, or walking under a ladder. There are bits of superstitions even in the actions of the most sophisticated. When a person sneezes, we may say, "God bless you." This is just a formula now, but it originally had a deeper meaning. In the Middle Ages people believed the Devil could enter a person's body during a sneeze. The "God bless you" protected the person against that action.

Arts and Crafts

Americans have become interested in preserving their past. Places like Williamsburg in Virginia and Old Sturbridge in Massachusetts reproduce old villages complete with the arts and crafts associated with these places. Amusement parks have craft shops selling the work of local artisans. All across America there are craft shows demonstrating skills that go back to the early years of our country.

People are interested in making things with their hands. Cabinetmakers lovingly create chairs that reflect the simple beauty of an earlier day. Quilters painstakingly sew together traditional patterns to beautify their homes with wall hangings and bed covers. Potters reproduce the shapes and forms of vessels used during the Revolutionary War.

This interest in crafts is part of the renewed attention to our roots. We are interested in knowing where we came from, how we came to act as we do, why we believe as we do. This absorbing interest in folklore is a major subject of this text.

IV. Allusions

Our rich cultural past is with us in many ways. One of the most important and obvious is in the use of implied references called *allusions*. Some allusions are obvious, like *Achilles' heel* for a weakness. Others are concealed, like *cereal* and *martial*, from the Roman Ceres, goddess of agriculture, and Mars, god of war.

Allusions from myths, legends, and folklore abound everywhere. This text will single out allusions in various fields to increase your appreciation of the subject and to enlarge your vocabulary.

READING FOR UNDERSTANDING

Main Idea

1. Which of the following best expresses the main idea of the unit? (a) Folk dancing is the most important area of folklore. (b) Myths, legends, and folklore reflect the collected wisdom of people around the world. (c) Myths deal with gods, heroes, religious beliefs, and cultural traits. (d) Folklore contains such diverse elements as crafts and music, folktales and children's counting-out rhymes.

Details

2. Paul Gauguin was a   (a) musician   (b) potter   (c) writer
   (d) painter.
3. Gods and goddesses are most likely to appear in   (a) fables
   (b) folktales   (c) myths   (d) legends.
4. All the following were mentioned as animal characters EXCEPT
   (a) Hathor   (b) Reynard   (c) Brer Rabbit   (d) Raven.
5. Cloggers are   (a) square dancers   (b) cobblers   (c) fiddlers
   (d) potters.
6. Animal-headed gods appear in the mythology of   (a) Greece
   (b) Ireland   (c) Rome   (d) Egypt.

Inferences

7. When Cortez first arrived in Mexico, the Aztecs probably   (a) left
   for the mountains   (b) greeted him warmly   (c) called him a
   traitor   (d) tried to kill him.
8. "You never miss the water till the well runs dry" can be
   interpreted as: (a) You should plan ahead so that you won't be
   left without water.   (b) Problems arise in unexpected places, in
   unexpected ways.   (c) You never know how wonderful something
   is until it's gone.   (d) You should have regular checkups of your
   water supply to avoid shortages.
9. In the riddle of the Sphinx, the cane is considered   (a) the third
   leg   (b) a useful tool   (c) a child's toy   (d) a mark of style.
10. "I'm not superstitious, knock wood" suggests that the speaker
    (a) is a sound, no-nonsense person   (b) is really superstitious
    (c) hates superstition   (d) is a student of superstitions.

WORDS IN CONTEXT

1. Men and women have always *pondered* these questions.
        Pondered (page 2) means   (a) doubted   (b) challenged
   (c) wrote about   (d) thought about.
2. They also explain all kinds of natural *phenomena*, from rainbows
   to sunrise.
        Phenomena (2) means   (a) things seen   (b) accidents   (c) beliefs
   (d) unexpected events.
3. Originality is undesirable. The story should be preserved *intact*,
   usually in oral form.
        Intact (3) means   (a) colorful   (b) unchanged   (c) humorous
   (d) clear.

4. We want to be protected from the *buffetings* of bad luck.
   Buffetings (3) means (a) unexpected events (b) appearances (c) blows (d) repeated experiences.
5. Others are concealed, like *cereal* and *martial*, from the Roman Ceres, goddess of agriculture, and Mars, god of war.
   Martial (8) means (a) warlike (b) godlike (c) childlike (d) friendly.

THINKING IT OVER

1. Why do you think there are such amazing resemblances between the folklore in one part of the world and that in another?
   Hint: are people basically alike?
2. Why does magic often play a part in folklore? What is the basic appeal of magic? How does magic differ from science?
3. Why is it important to have some knowledge of myths and folklore? How can such knowledge enrich lives?
4. Why are people becoming so interested in folk dancing, folk music, folk arts and crafts? What is the appeal of such subjects?
5. Why are superstitions so hard to eliminate? Why do even intelligent people sometimes show traces of superstitions?

SUGGESTED ACTIVITIES

1. Ask some younger people in your area whether they use counting-out rhymes like the one quoted in this unit. Write the rhymes and bring them to class.
2. Look for examples of folklore in your daily life, using some of the clues presented in the preceding section.
3. Take a census of the class members to find out how many students are interested in the following subjects:

   folk dancing   proverbs and folk wisdom
   folk music   folk celebrations
   folk arts and crafts   folk medicine

   Perhaps one or more students can bring crafts to class or perform folk music.
4. Have you ever attended a gathering of the clans (Scottish) or a neighborhood block party honoring some ethnic group: Italian, German, or Chinese, for example? Tell of the experience.
5. If you live in the city, find out where at least one large ethnic group lives. Perhaps your class can plot an ethnic map of your city. Why do such groups keep their cultural identity even while being good American citizens?

UNIT · TWO

Myths of Ancient Greece and Rome

I. Myths and the World of Today

In 1930 a new discovery excited the world of science. An astronomer had discovered—as a tiny pinpoint on a photographic plate—a new planet. Far out beyond the orbit of Neptune, this new planet moves around the sun, making the trip once in about 249 of our years. Out in the darkness, nearly four billion miles from the source of light, it pursues its lonely way. The sun as seen from the planet would be one-fortieth the size that it appears to us. The naming of this new planet, oddly enough, is very much tied up with the theme of this book.

The planet is called *Pluto*, a name taken directly from the myths and legends of ancient Rome. It is a remarkably fitting name for the planet. Do you know why?

Do you know why a strong man is called a *Hercules*? Why should a handsome young man be called an *Apollo*, or a beautiful woman a *Venus*? What is a *titanic* struggle, *martial* music, a *jovial* mood? Why was quicksilver called *mercury*? How did a *volcano* come to acquire its name? Why do we call certain grains *cereals*? Why is *Cupid* on St. Valentine cards?

The pages that follow will answer these questions and many others. The answers come from magnificent stories, tales you'll enjoy reading. All are bound up with the gods and goddesses of ancient times. To the storytellers who have given us the literature we call myths and legends these gods and goddesses (and, later, godlike human beings) were very real. For us today they live in the everyday words that we have

11

derived from their names, in the many allusions to them and
their exploits found in our own literature, and in paintings
and other works of art for which they were "models."

The Space Age has brought a renewed interest in mythology
as scientists have dipped into the old myths for names—for
example, the Thor, Atlas, and Saturn rockets; the Apollo and
Gemini flights. Thus, the old myths live on in many forms.

II. Similarities Between Greek and Roman Myths

The Greek Myths

The origins of Greek myths go far back into the past. By the
time of Homer (page 61), the list of gods and goddesses was
already rich and full. The poet Hesiod, who probably lived in
the eighth century B.C., wrote a lengthy poem about the gods
and their origins. Many of the stories that we know today
come from his writings.

Greek mythology is colorful and detailed. It has been the
inspiration for much of our art and literature. No education is
complete without some knowledge of a mythology that has
captured the imagination of the world.

The Roman Myths

By the time Rome was founded in the eighth century B.C.,
Greek mythology was already well established. Greek influence upon the new state was strong. Greeks settled in Sicily
and southern Italy. Undoubtedly Greek thought influenced the
earliest Romans.

The Romans did develop a mythology of their own for a
time. There is one Roman god, for example, who appears in
no other mythology: Janus, the god of all gates and doorways.
He had two faces, which enabled him to observe both the
exterior and the interior of a house. He was also, naturally,
the god of departure and return. As the god of beginnings, he
gave his name to January, a month that begins the new year
and looks back at the old.

Throughout the centuries Greek thought continued to
change Rome. Though the Romans were conquerors, the ideas
of their subject peoples often conquered them. The Romans
were hospitable toward foreign ideas and foreign religions.
From the third century B.C., Romans equated Greek gods with

their own gods and adopted Greek mythology. The Greek gods were given new names.

There is no major Greek god who corresponds to Janus. All other major Roman gods, however, have Greek counterparts. Jupiter, ruler of gods and men, is identified with the Greek Zeus. His wife Juno is identified with the Greek Hera. On page 15 you will find a helpful chart that presents the names of the gods and goddesses in pairs for easy reference. Since the Roman name in each pair tends to be more familiar than the Greek name, the Roman names, with a few exceptions, will be used in this chapter. Remember, though, that the Greek versions are more ancient.

III. The Beginnings

Origin Myths

In ancient mythology there are many explanations of the creation of the world. One of the most dramatic says that in the beginning there was *Chaos*—a great, dark, confused mass in which air, earth, and water were all mixed together. Then *Gaea*, or Earth, came into existence and later *Uranus*, or Heaven. Gaea and Uranus were the parents of the mighty gods we call *Titans*. Among the Titans were *Hyperion*, god of the sun; *Oceanus*, god of the waters; *Cronus*, or Saturn, father of the great Olympian gods; and *Iapetus*, father of *Prometheus* and *Epimetheus* (who were chosen by Jupiter to help him complete the creation of beasts and man). Iapetus was also father of *Atlas*, who later had to bear the heavens on his shoulders (page 30). There were also female Titans: among them, *Rhea* (who became the wife of Cronus); *Themis* (the mother of the three *Fates*); and *Mnemosyne* (the mother of the nine *Muses*).

Cronus wrested control of earth and heaven from his father, Uranus. For untold ages, Cronus ruled, until his own overthrow. During his reign he learned of a prophecy that he would be dethroned by one of his own children. Accordingly, he proceeded to swallow each child as soon as it was born. The queen, his sister *Rhea*, tricked Cronus by substituting a stone for the sixth child. This last child, Jupiter, or Zeus, proved indeed to be his father's downfall. He forced Cronus to restore to the light his five brothers and sisters and then warred upon his father. In the terrible battle that followed, Jupiter and his comrades were victorious.

Jupiter called upon his two brothers, *Neptune* and *Pluto*, to assist him in governing the world. Neptune became ruler of the seas, and Pluto was given the shadowy land of the dead. Jupiter himself ruled the earth and heavens. He took his sister *Juno* as his wife. He had two other sisters, *Ceres* and *Vesta*. Ceres became goddess of grain and the harvest, and Vesta became goddess of the hearth and domestic life.

Mount Olympus, in Thessaly, was the abode of the gods. Here neither rain nor snow was known. A gate of clouds, kept by four goddesses, the Seasons, was opened whenever a god left to go down to the earth, or returned from there. Each of the gods had his own dwelling, but, when called, all went to Jupiter's palace. There they feasted on ambrosia and nectar, and listened to music made by Apollo on his lyre, with the Muses singing the refrains. The whole day might be spent thus, but when the sun went down, each god returned to his own dwelling.

The Children of Jupiter

As you probably know, there were more than just these six Olympian gods and goddesses in the Greek and Roman heavens. Most of the other important deities were children of Jupiter. *Minerva*, who sprang from his brain full-grown and armed, was goddess of wisdom and one of the most powerful of all the deities. Jupiter's children by Juno were *Mars*, god of war; *Vulcan*, god of fire; and *Hebe*, goddess of youth. His children by others included *Apollo*, god of the sun (also of archery, music, and prophecy); *Diana* (Apollo's twin sister), goddess of the moon; *Venus*, goddess of love; *Mercury*, god of speed; *Bacchus*, god of wine; *Hercules*, god of strength; and the nine *Muses* (goddesses of music, dance, literature, and science).

Greek and Roman Gods and Goddesses

The following chart has been devised for convenient reference. It gives both the Roman and the Greek name of each of the most important gods and goddesses, along with a brief and simplified statement of their functions. Greek and Roman deities do not always correspond exactly, but this classification is generally accepted.

CHILDREN OF CRONUS

Roman Name	Greek Name	Identification
Jupiter (or Jove)	Zeus	Ruler of all gods and men
Neptune	Poseidon	God of the seas
Pluto	Hades	Ruler over the land of the dead
Juno	Hera	Wife of Jupiter; queen of the gods
Vesta	Hestia	Goddess of the hearth and domestic life
Ceres	Demeter	Goddess of grain and harvests

CHILDREN OF JUPITER; OTHER GODS

Minerva	Athena (or Pallas Athena)	Goddess of wisdom
Apollo	Apollo (or Phoebus Apollo)	God of the sun; god of archery, prophecy, music
Diana	Artemis	Goddess of the moon
Venus	Aphrodite	Goddess of love and beauty
Mars	Ares	God of war
Vulcan	Hephaestus	God of fire
Mercury	Hermes	God of speed; messenger of the gods
Hercules	Heracles	God of strength
Bacchus	Dionysus	God of wine
Proserpine	Persephone	Wife of Pluto; queen of the dead
Cupid	Eros	God of love; son of Venus
Aurora	Eos	Goddess of the dawn

IV. Mythology and Nature

The stories in this section were favorites among the primitive Greeks about 4000 years ago. These people knew nothing about "the laws of nature," but they were inquisitive and they were imaginative. Who makes the echo? they asked. Who

causes the rainbow? Who brings the dawn? Who drives the
sun across the sky every day? Notice that they asked *who*
causes these natural happenings, not (as we do) *what* causes
them, for to these people nature was personal and intimate.
They answered these questions and many others by telling
colorful, imaginative stories.

Echo, they said, was a beautiful nymph condemned by the
gods to haunt the mountainsides, where she could not speak
except to repeat the words of the person speaking. The rainbow was the trail left by the many-colored gown of *Iris*,
Juno's messenger, as she sped between earth and Mount
Olympus. The dawn was made by the rosy fingers of *Aurora* as
she opened the gates of morning for Apollo, the sun god. The
sun was the flaming chariot of Apollo. Thunder was caused by
Jupiter as he hurled his great bolts at insolent mortals. The
many "eyes" on the peacock's tail were taken from Argus, a
giant with a hundred eyes.

For thousands of years these and other myths have been
kept alive. Generation after generation has enjoyed the fanciful explanations found in these stories.

The first two tales that follow are magnificent examples of
the mythological interpretation of nature. The third, about
Pandora, is the explanation, according to ancient mythology,
of the origin of all the world's evils.

How Deserts Were Formed

In summer, when the earth is parched and dry, you may
think of the sun god Apollo and his headstrong child *Phaëthon*. Once upon a time, according to the myth in which these
two characters figure, the sun came close to the earth and
nearly burned everything to a cinder. This is how it happened.

Phaëthon was the son of Apollo and a nymph. One day he was
laughed at by his friends because he claimed the sun god as his
father. He complained to his mother and asked her to give him proof
that Apollo was really his father. She told him that Apollo alone
could provide such proof and advised him to make a visit to the sun
god. Phaëthon traveled to the East, to the Land of the Sunrise, and
made his way toward the throne of Apollo. He stopped at a distance,
unable to come closer because of the dazzling splendor of Apollo's
presence.

Apollo called to him to ask why he had come. Phaëthon cried out
for proof that Apollo was indeed his father. Moved by the boy's plea,

Apollo put aside his dazzling beams and approached his son. He embraced the boy and promised that, as proof of his devotion, he would grant Phaëthon whatever request he might make. Phaëthon had the same ambition as many a modern boy. He asked permission to drive the family chariot—which in this instance *was* a chariot, the chariot of the sun.

Apollo immediately realized what a rash promise he had made. "My son," he said, "I pray you, ask any request but this. No one but I can drive the chariot of the sun—no, not even Jupiter himself. The first part of the way is steep as the chariot ascends the sky. The middle part is so high that sometimes even I am almost overwhelmed by dizziness. The last part is a steep descent that requires skillful driving of the fiery horses before I enter the portals of night. My son, do not insist."

Phaëthon, foolishly stubborn, asked once again to drive the chariot. He knew that Apollo had given his promise, and he knew that the word of a god is binding. Apollo reluctantly led his son to the flaming chariot. Even as they stood there, Aurora, or Dawn, threw open the purple doors of the East and revealed the pathway of the sun. The stars withdrew. The fiery steeds were led to their places in the chariot harness. They pawed impatiently, eager to be off on their daily journey.

Apollo smeared the face of the boy with a powerful oil to protect him from the sun's rays. "Hold tight the reins," he said. "Keep in the pathway; go neither too high nor too low."

Phaëthon sprang gaily into the chariot, thanking his father for indulging him. Apollo looked sadly out toward the pathway in the sky and then, again reluctantly, gave the signal for the start. As the steeds started, they recognized the difference immediately, for their load was lighter than usual and the reins hung more loosely about their necks. Off they dashed; almost at once they left the well-worn ruts and veered out of control.

Phaëthon grew pale with terror. He lost all self-command and forgot the warnings his father had issued. His courage failed, and the reins dropped from his hands. Over pathless places the horses dashed—at first too high, and then too low. Soon they were galloping on a course close to the earth—so close that the earth was scorched by the heat. Forested mountaintops first smoldered and then burst into flame. The fertile fields of northern Africa were scorched and turned into a desert. The earth cracked open with the heat. Men prayed aloud to Jupiter for relief.

Jupiter realized that all would be lost unless he acted quickly. He grasped one of his terrible thunderbolts and hurled it straight at the careening chariot. Phaëthon, struck by the bolt, toppled from his chariot and fell dead to the earth he had almost destroyed. Quickly Apollo gained command of his chariot and brought the steeds back under control.

But it was too late; the damage had been done—and now the desert wastelands are a reminder of the time when a mortal tried to drive the chariot of the sun.

Why We Have Seasons

Pluto, ruler of the lower regions, one day sought a bride to share with him the lonely duties of his reign. Driving his chariot drawn by great black horses, he came upon Ceres' daughter *Proserpine* as she and some companions were gathering flowers. At once he fell in love with her and carried her off. Terrified, Proserpine called to her mother. Ceres ran to help her but Pluto soon outdistanced his pursuer and carried Proserpine down to the darkness of Hades, land of the dead.

Ceres knew not where to look for her daughter. She wandered over the land, vainly seeking her beloved child. But nowhere on the surface of the earth could Proserpine be found. Grieving for her lost daughter, Ceres neglected her regular duties and no longer concerned herself with the harvest. Grain withered; droughts and famine followed; men hungered and died.

Finally, Ceres discovered where her daughter was being kept captive, but in the land of the dead her power was of no avail. She implored Jupiter to use his power to restore Proserpine to her. Jupiter was moved by the pleas of his sister. He consented to restore her daughter to her—on one condition: that Proserpine had taken no food during her stay in Hades.

Meanwhile Proserpine was bearing her captivity sorrowfully. She mourned for her goddess mother. She refused to smile. She ate nothing. At last, in desperation, Pluto offered his captive bride a pomegranate. If you have ever seen a pomegranate you know that it is filled with small red seeds. Proserpine opened the fruit and ate six of the seeds. Pluto rejoiced, although this was seemingly but a minor victory.

Mercury, Jupiter's messenger, was sent to Pluto's kingdom to claim Proserpine. When he arrived, he learned about the pomegranate seeds that she had eaten. According to Jupiter's condition, she could not, therefore, be taken away from Pluto. But finally a compromise was made. It was arranged that Proserpine should spend six months of every year with Pluto—one month for each seed she had eaten—and the rest of the year with her mother.

In those months when Proserpine is with her mother, Ceres is happy and attends diligently to all her duties; but during the other six months of the year, Ceres retires to a cold, lonely cave where she grieves and mourns for her absent daughter. That is why we have spring and summer (six months when plants grow and bloom), and fall and winter (six months when they are withered and dead).

Why Troubles Came

According to one story, Prometheus and his brother Epimetheus were assigned the task of creating man. In addition, they were to provide for man and all animals the skills and abilities needed for their survival. Epimetheus gave to the various animals courage, strength, speed, wisdom, and armor, but Prometheus created a higher being in godlike form.

Taking some clay and water, he formed it into the image of a god. He gave to the new creature, man, an upright stature, so that he could keep his eyes turned on the stars. Seeking gifts to bestow upon his creation, Prometheus found that his brother had lavishly given everything away to the animals. Since he had no gift to bestow, he decided to steal some fire from heaven. With fire in his possession, man might almost be a god.

When Jupiter learned what Prometheus had done, he was very angry. But once man had fire, Jupiter could not take it back. However, he could punish Prometheus. He ordered his son Vulcan, the god of the forge, to fasten Prometheus with chains to Mount Caucasus. Then he decreed that every day a vulture should devour Prometheus' liver, but that at night the liver should grow again—to be devoured once more the following day.

Jupiter also resolved to bring misery upon mankind. Prometheus had feared this. He had warned his brother, Epimetheus, not to accept any presents from the chief deity, for fear Jupiter might be planning some indirect, clever form of retaliation.

His fear was well-founded but his advice was not followed, for Epimetheus was not able to refuse a gift that Jupiter offered him. This irresistible gift was a bride, a mortal woman, *Pandora* by name.

("Pandora" means "all-gifted," for upon her the gods, commissioned by Jupiter, had bestowed their choicest treasures.) She was the sum of all the virtues—charming, accomplished, and beautiful. But she also had curiosity.

As part of Jupiter's plan, the gods gave to Pandora a box, which, they warned her, she was not to open. Though she was happy as the wife of Epimetheus, Pandora occasionally allowed her glance to wander to the mysterious closed box. Since she had been forbidden to open the lid, she had an irresistible—and human—urge to do so. One day her curiosity could be contained no longer.

Resolutely she strode over to the box, threw back the lid, and peered in. There was a hurry and a scurry; then from out the box came all kinds of misery to afflict mankind. Envy, discontent, pain, anger, hunger, plague, crime, desolation—these and many other ills flew out over the earth before Pandora could slam down the lid. Horrified at the evils she had let loose, she wept for the harm that she had done to man. But to no avail—she could not call back the ills.

However, the lid had been shut down just in time to prevent the escape of one thing—*hope*. Therefore, despite all the ills, troubles, and problems of mankind, there is always hope.

How the Planets Were Named

Because the Arabs were such excellent astronomers, many of the stars have Arabic names, like *Achernar*, *Rigel*, *Altair*, *Betelgeuse*, and *Aldebaran*. Other stars, however, have Greek or Roman names, like *Antares*, *Sirius*, *Castor*, and *Pollux*. In planet names, there is no contest. All are of Greek or Roman origin. Even earth has a Greek name associated with it: Gaea, goddess of the earth. Gaea is recalled in words like *geology*, *geometry*, *geography*, and *geophysics*.

The nine major planets, in the order of their distance from the sun, are Mercury, Venus, Earth, Mars, Jupiter, Saturn, Uranus, Neptune, and Pluto. Each one was named for a god in the Greek-Roman heavens. Let us take these in order to see whether each name is appropriate.

Mercury, the planet nearest the sun, is named for the god of speed. It seems to "race" around the sun, making a complete revolution in only 88 days. This compares with our year of 365¼ days. For earthly astronomers, Mercury seems to hug the sun. On a few occasions during the year, it can be seen shining clearly near the horizon just after sunset or before sunrise. Within a few days it is lost in the mists again, speeding from our vision.

Venus, whose orbit is next inside the earth's, is named for the goddess of love and beauty. To the naked eye, Venus is the most beautiful of all the planets. Almost everyone has seen Venus shining brilliantly in the morning or evening sky. But many people see Venus without realizing it. The planet is so bright it is often mistaken for an airplane's taillight or a beacon.

Mars, whose orbit is next outside the earth's, is named for the god of war, associated with destruction, blood, and the color red (for blood); Mars the planet is unmistakably red, too.

Thus we see that the earth is bounded on one side by the orbit of love and beauty and on the other side by the orbit of war and destruction.

Sometimes you'll find Mars and Venus close together in the sky. According to one myth, Mars and Venus were in love with each other. As planets, though, they must spend most of the time far from each other in the evening or morning sky.

Between the orbits of Mars and Jupiter, there is a group of minor planets, called *planetoids* or *asteroids*. Many of these planetoids are also named after the gods and goddesses of ancient mythology: for example, *Ceres, Vesta,* and *Juno.* The members of one asteroid group are named after heroes of the Trojan War (page 61), including Achilles, Agamemnon, Hector, Priam, Patroclus, and Nestor.

Jupiter, which revolves in kingly majesty beyond the orbit of Mars, is named after the king of the gods. It is larger than all the other planets combined; and, except for the sun, the moon, and Venus, it is the brightest object in the sky.

Attendants and lesser gods waited on Jupiter the king; similarly, many satellites turn around Jupiter the planet. Even a pair of binoculars will reveal the four largest moons of Jupiter, named Europa, Io, Callisto, and Ganymede. The first three were beloved of Jupiter (page 14). Ganymede was the cup-bearer of the gods, one who waited on Jupiter as the satellite waits on the planet.

Saturn, the second largest planet, is appropriately named after a god who was the Roman counterpart of Cronus (page 13). Among Saturn's satellites are Iapetus (page 13), Titan (page 13), Rhea (page 13), and Janus (page 12). Saturn has given his name to our Saturday, "Saturn's day." The photographs from the spacecraft Voyager flight have provided new insights into the majesty of Saturn, with its puzzling rings. The same flight has provided new informaton about the moons of Jupiter.

Uranus, the next planet, is named for the old god of the heavens. The astronomer Herschel, who discovered it in 1781, tried to give it the name *Georgium Sidus*, in honor of George III, but the name finally assigned was Uranus. Which do you think is more appropriate?

Neptune, the eighth planet from the sun, was named after the god of the seas, perhaps because it reigns over the "seas of space" almost 3 billion miles from the sun. Invisible to the naked eye, it requires 164 of our years to complete one journey around the sun. Most of us are born, live, and die before Neptune has gone halfway around. Two of Neptune's moons are appropriately named *Triton* and *Nereid*. Triton was a son of Neptune. The Nereids were sea nymphs.

Pluto, the outermost planet yet discovered, was named for the god of the dead (page 14), who reigns over shadows and darkness. Pluto moves far in the outer darkness, where even the sun's rays would seem pallid and weak. It is ordinarily 40 times as far from the sun as is the earth. What an appropriate name for this mysterious planet!

The Constellations

The constellations are clusters of stars. Ancient peoples saw in these clusters definite shapes. Just as the planets have names from classical mythology, so do a great many constellations. Hercules (page 11), Pegasus (55), and Orion are found in the heavens. The twins Castor and Pollux (page 35) are in the constellation Gemini, which means *twins*. The beautiful Andromeda (page 26), who was rescued by Perseus (page 24), is in a star group near him. Fittingly, her mother and father, Cassiopeia and Cepheus, are also nearby. Other constellations, as well as individual stars, have names associated with mythology.

V. The Hero in Myth

One of the important threads in all mythologies is the story of the hero—the mighty person who has a series of challenging adventures. All these myths have many elements in common. Scholars have divided the path of the hero into three sections: separation, initiation, and return. These three sections are a kind of reflection of life. They resemble the rites of passage (page 7), especially the rites preparing young people for adulthood. In the typical hero myth, the leading character is required to go out into the world to face many challenges, often supernatural. He bravely ventures forth and meets many difficult antagonists. He vanquishes all and returns home with new powers to help his fellows.

This theme appears in many mythologies. One of the earliest examples is the Sumerian epic of Gilgamesh. This mighty hero is challenged to fight a supernatural warrior, Enkidu. He overcomes Enkidu and becomes his friend. He goes on to fight all kinds of monsters and survive many dangers. He eventually returns with new knowledge, sadder but wiser. This tale, already 5,000 years old, has counterparts in myths of other lands.

In many ways, Gilgamesh resembles Beowulf, a hero of the Anglo-Saxons, who overran England more than a thousand years ago. Like Gilgamesh, Beowulf fights monsters and overcomes terrible dangers. Similarly, both Odysseus (page 77) and Aeneas (page 88) face terrible dangers on their travels to their goals. Odysseus at last comes home to Ithaca. Aeneas at last ends his travels to found Rome.

Most mythologies have similar myths of great heroes on great quests. These include the Eskimo Raven, King Arthur of ancient Britain, Gautama Buddha of Nepal and India, Lemminkainen of Finland, Siegfried of Germany, Rama of India, and Roland of medieval France.

The myth of the hero is alive and well, with many counterparts today. Characters like Superman, Conan, James Bond (007), and Indiana Jones are modern versions of the indomitable hero. Legendary western heroes, played by actors like John Wayne and Gary Cooper, keep alive the mythology of the American West. All these characters face challenges that would overwhelm an ordinary person. They conquer evil and emerge triumphant after facing impossible odds.

The selections that follow trace the fortunes of five Greek heroes. All of them are larger than life. All face challenges and prevail. Sometimes the final chapter of their lives is tragic, but their magnificent achievements live on.

Perseus

When Danäe, daughter of the king of Argos, bore Jupiter a son, she was banished from her native land by her father. In Seriphus, their country of exile, Danäe and her son, *Perseus*, were at first treated with kindness. But when Perseus was grown to manhood, the king of Seriphus fell in love with Danäe and, wishing to get Perseus out of the way, gave him a seemingly impossible task. Perseus' task was to conquer the *Gorgon Medusa*, a terrible monster that had laid waste much of the country.

Medusa had a weapon—her face—that men could not combat. Her face was so horrible that it turned into stone anyone who looked at her. Her hair was composed of hissing serpents. All around her were the petrified bodies of those who had looked upon her.

Perseus started out on the hopeless quest. Fortunately, he obtained some help from Minerva and Mercury. Minerva lent him her bright shield; Mercury, his knife.

He first came to the cave of the *Three Sisters*, old hags who had but a single eye and a single tooth among them. These they passed from one to another at need. Perseus bided his time and, at a favorable moment, snatched both the eye and the tooth as they were being ·passed from one of them to another. As the price of their restoration he demanded that the sisters guide him to the helmet of Pluto, which makes its wearer invisible. He also requested the winged shoes and pouch of Mercury. These they secured for him.

Fully equipped at last, he set off to meet the monster herself. Advancing unseen, he held up Minerva's bright shield as a mirror. Thus, avoiding a direct look at the monster and looking, instead, at her reflection on the shield, he beheaded her with one quick slash of Mercury's knife. He put the hideous trophy in his pouch and, fastening the winged sandals, flew like a bird in the direction of Seriphus, the land of the tyrant king.

The death of Medusa had two different results. From her blood sprang two quite opposite mythological characters: Pegasus and Chrysaor. Pegasus was the famous winged horse who helped his master Bellerophon conquer the Chimaera, a fire-breathing monster. Pegasus is often pictured on advertising. Chrysaor became the father of Geryon, a monster who appears in the labors of Hercules (page 26). Thus do various myths tie together.

As for Perseus, his great adventure was by no means ended.

On his way he passed over the country of the Ethiopians. It seemed that *Cassiopeia*, wife of King *Cepheus*, had offended the sea nymphs by her excessive vanity, and they in turn had sent a sea monster to

ravage the coasts. To appease the nymphs, Cepheus had agreed to
sacrifice his daughter *Andromeda* to the monster. Accordingly, she
was chained to a rock on the shore to await her doom.

Flying high above the land, Perseus saw the unfortunate maiden
and rushed down to rescue her. At first Andromeda refused to discuss
her plight, but finally she explained how she had come to be chained
to the rock for a sacrifice. As she finished speaking, a horrible sound
announced the arrival of the sea monster. Perseus rushed to the
attack, plunging his sword again and again into the furious beast.
Finally he dealt a death blow, and the monster sank into the sea.

As a reward for his bravery Perseus demanded Andromeda as his
bride. To this request her parents willingly consented. While the
wedding banquet was taking place, a former suitor of Andromeda
arrived to claim her as his own. The king pointed out that the suitor
had lost all claim by his obvious reluctance to battle with the sea
monster to save her. But the suitor refused to yield. Since he had
brought with him a host of warriors, he decided to settle the matter
by force of arms. The newcomers attacked the wedding party, and
soon, because of their superior numbers, were in a fair way of gaining
victory. When Perseus saw this, he took the head of Medusa out of
his pouch and held it up before the attackers. All motion ceased. The
attackers became rooted to the spot, stone monuments to treachery.

Returning to the land of the tyrant king to rescue his mother,
Perseus used the Gorgon's head once more. After he had turned his
enemies into stone, he returned the knife, the shoes, and the shield
to Mercury and Minerva. Medusa's head he presented to Minerva.
Ever afterward, she bore the head upon her shield to recall the great
deeds of Perseus.

Hercules

Like Perseus, *Hercules* was required to perform the miraculous. But instead of having to bring only one mission to a
successful close, Hercules was ordered to complete twelve
great tasks, which are often referred to in literature as "the
labors of Hercules." This is how the challenge came about.

Hercules was the son of Jupiter and Alcmene, daughter of the king
of Mycenae. When Hercules was born, Juno in a jealous anger sent
two serpents to destroy him in his cradle. But Hercules, even then
showing the strength for which he later became famous, strangled

them. Juno's hatred, however, was not easily appeased. She waited until Hercules reached manhood and had achieved some fame; then she placed a spell on him that made him insane. In his fit of madness he slew his wife and children. But he was cured by Minerva and saved by her from shedding more blood. In payment for his crime, for which he had really not been responsible, he was made the servant of his cousin, King *Eurystheus* of Argos, whose commands he was compelled to obey. (Juno's hand was in this, too.) Eurystheus thought up twelve tasks that seemed clearly impossible of fulfillment.

The Nemean Lion. Eurystheus first ordered Hercules to kill the Nemean lion, a terrible beast that had defied all would-be captors. The combat between Hercules and the lion was brutal and cruel. Seeing that his club and arrows were of no avail in the battle, Hercules grasped the lion in his hands and strangled it to death. He returned to Eurystheus, wearing the skin of the lion as a cloak and the head as a helmet.

The Hydra, or Water Serpent. Hercules was ordered next to slay the Hydra, a many-headed water serpent that had taken a heavy toll in the country of Argos. The middle head of the Hydra was immortal, indestructible. Hercules attacked the monster valiantly, but as he struck off one head, two others grew in its place. Hercules realized that he must change his plan of attack. With the assistance of his faithful nephew, he built a huge fire and burnt away the many heads before they could multiply further. The middle head, which was immortal, he buried under a rock.

The Arcadian Stag. Eurystheus commanded Hercules to capture the Arcadian stag, a magnificent beast with antlers of gold and hoofs of brass. Its speed was far beyond that of the swiftest beast known. Hercules pursued it in vain for a year before he succeeded in inflicting a slight wound. Thus handicapped, the stag was captured by Hercules, who carried it, on his shoulders, to his tyrant cousin.

The Boar of Erymanthus. Like the Hydra and the Nemean lion, a huge boar had been laying waste the peaceful countryside. Eurystheus commanded Hercules to capture the beast. He pursued the boar relentlessly, finally captured it in a huge net, and carried it to his cousin.

The Augean Stables. For thirty years the stables of Augeas, king of Elis, had been neglected. Hercules was commanded to clean these stables, which housed three thousand oxen. He succeeded in doing so—in a single day. How? He simply diverted two rivers so that they

would pass through the stables, cleansing them thoroughly by the flow of clean water. After the stables had been cleaned in this way, he redirected the rivers to their beds.

The Man-Eating Birds. In Arcadia there lived a strange flock of birds. Their wings, claws, and beaks were of brass and they used their feathers as arrows. Their favorite food being human flesh, they preyed upon the hapless inhabitants of the country. Eurystheus ordered Hercules to destroy these man-eating birds. As the renowned hero approached the flock, he made a noise with a great rattle. The birds took flight, and Hercules, whose prowess as a marksman evidently equaled his strength, was able to slay them as they flew.

The Cretan Bull. The Cretan bull was a magnificent but terrible brute owned by King Minos of Crete. When it got out of control, Hercules was ordered to capture it. Once again, having used his great strength and skill to advantage, Hercules entered the halls of Eurystheus with a huge beast draped over his broad shoulders!

The Horses of Diomedes. Diomedes, the cruel king of Thrace, fed his horses on human flesh. They were swift, beautiful beasts, but violent and difficult to restrain. Hercules was ordered to snatch them from their owner. He succeeded in capturing them, but Diomedes and his men pursued him. Hercules turned on his pursuers. They fought, and he was victorious. He threw the body of Diomedes to the horses. After they had eaten their master, they became tame, and Hercules had no trouble leading them back to Eurystheus.

The Girdle of Hippolyta. Hippolyta was the queen of the Amazons, a band of warrior women whose reputation for courage was untarnished. Among the Amazons only female children were raised; the boys were either put to death or given to neighboring tribes. Hercules was ordered to secure the girdle of the warrior queen. Because of Hercules' great reputation, Hippolyta received him with respect and kindness. She promised to help him by presenting him with the girdle. But again Hercules' chief foe, Juno, seized an opportunity to cause Hercules difficulty. Disguising herself as an Amazon, she spread a rumor among Hippolyta's subjects that Hercules was planning to carry off their queen. Enraged by this story, the Amazons attacked Hercules, who, in turn, suspected Hippolyta of treachery. He repulsed the attacks of the warrior women, slew Hippolyta, seized her girdle, and set out for home, once more victorious against great odds.

The Oxen of Geryon. Geryon was a frightful monster with three heads (or, as some accounts put it, three bodies). Armed with mighty weapons and assisted by another giant and his two-headed dog,

Geryon tirelessly guarded his famed oxen. Hercules was ordered to secure these cattle, which were kept on an island far to the west, under the setting sun.

On his way there, Hercules had many adventures. According to one account he split a mountain in two by a blow of his club and placed the twin mountains on opposite sides of what is now known as the Strait of Gibraltar. (These two promontories—the Rock of Gibraltar in Europe and the Abyla in Africa—are called the *Pillars of Hercules*.) The journey to the island was a long one, but finally Hercules reached his goal. The guardian monsters, terrible enough to ordinary mortals, were easily vanquished by Hercules. Back went the oxen to King Eurystheus.

The Golden Apples. For his eleventh task, Hercules was ordered by Eurystheus to bring back the golden apples of the *Hesperides*. (The Hesperides were the daughters of *Hesperus*, god of the West. They were charged by Juno with the care of certain golden apples that had been given her as a wedding present. The apples hung on a tree in the Hesperides' garden, where they were watched over by a dragon.) Now this task was the most difficult set so far, for Hercules did not know in what part of the world these apples were to be found.

He wandered far and wide, seeking information from everyone. In the course of his travels, he came upon Prometheus, chained to the mountain (see page 20), and set him free. In gratitude, Prometheus directed him to *Atlas*, who, he said, knew where the apples were. (Atlas was one of the Titans who had been on the losing side in the battle with Jupiter—page 13. As a penalty he had been ordered to support the heavens forever on his shoulders.) Atlas promised to fetch the golden apples if Hercules would take his place and temporarily bear the weight of the sky on *his* shoulders. Hercules agreed and Atlas went off to keep his part of the bargain. He slew the dragon guarding the apples and plucked them from the tree. While he was returning to Hercules, it occurred to him that freedom was too sweet to relinquish and that it would be nice if someone else were to assume the burden of supporting the heavens, at least for a few centuries. So he stepped up to Hercules and said, slyly, "*I'll* take the apples to Eurystheus for you."

But Hercules was clever, too. Pretending to accept the proposal, he requested Atlas to resume the burden of the sky just for a moment, so that he, Hercules, could adjust his lion skin as a pad. Atlas agreed, dropped the apples, and groaned as he once again bent over to receive the weight of the heavens. When the load was safely shifted, Hercules politely thanked Atlas, picked up the apples, and went on his way.

Cerberus, the Guardian of Hades. Eurystheus was desperate, for there was just one more task to be assigned to Hercules. Therefore he devised one that he was sure Hercules would not be able to perform. He commanded Hercules to descend to Hades and to capture *Cerberus*, the three-headed watchdog of the land of the dead. Undaunted, Hercules set out. Assisted by Minerva and Mercury, he reached the throne of Pluto.

Pluto agreed to permit him to take Cerberus to the upper world, but only on condition that Hercules use no weapons against the monster. Hercules consented; after a terrible battle, he subdued the beast. He carried Cerberus, snarling and frothing, to Eurystheus, who was so terrified when he saw Cerberus that he begged Hercules to restore the monster to Hades.

Other Exploits. Thus Hercules finished his twelve labors and was allowed to roam the earth at will, once again a free man. But he did not return to a life of ease and quiet. Before his death, he had many more thrilling adventures, among them participation in the quest of the Golden Fleece (pages 34–37).

After his death Hercules was made immortal. The constellation of Hercules forever circles through the sky. Among other constellations associated with the legends of Hercules are Hydra (the water serpent), Leo (the Nemean Lion), and Taurus the Bull (for the oxen of Geryon). Indeed one explanation associates the twelve constellations of the zodiac with the twelve labors.

There is an interesting postscript to the Hercules story. One of the most persistent themes in folktales (page 242) is the theme of the fatal gift. Someone sends a gift to a supposed friend, but the gift is actually deadly. Sleeping Beauty falls into a long sleep after pricking her finger with a spindle. Snow White eats a poisoned apple and falls down as if dead. Jason's wife (page 37) dies after putting on a poisoned wedding robe. Hercules, too, suffered from a fatal gift. Here's how it came about.

Hercules and his wife Deianira were crossing a stream. Nessus was a centaur, half man and half horse. He offered to carry Deianira across, but he tried to kidnap her. Hercules shot the centaur and retrieved his bride. Before his death, however, Nessus told Deianira his blood would forever preserve Hercules' love. Later, when Hercules fell in love with another, Deianira gave Hercules a shirt that had been steeped in Nessus' blood. Hercules died in agony but was carried off to be with the immortals.

Theseus

Theseus, a third great hero of classical mythology, was a son of Aegeus, the king of Athens, and of Aethra, daughter of the king of Troezen. Aegeus had returned to Athens before Theseus was born, but before his departure he had placed his sword and sandals under a huge rock and had told Aethra to send Theseus to him when the boy was able to move the rock. At sixteen years of age Theseus easily moved the rock, and so set out for Athens.

On his journey to Athens Theseus had many adventures. On his first day's journey he came to Epidaurus, where he met a ferocious savage, who was in the habit of slaying all travelers who tried to cross the lonely area. Armed with a club of iron, the murderer advanced upon Theseus, but Theseus soon felled him. At Corinth Theseus overcame a robber, whose deeds were the terror of the land. One after another, Theseus slew the petty tyrants and marauders who stood in his way. The most famous of all these villains was *Procrustes*, whose manner of killing his victims was unique. He placed each one of his victims on an iron bed. If the victim was too long for the bed, he lopped off his limbs until he fit. If he was too short, he stretched him until he fit.

After Theseus had slain Procrustes, he proceeded to Athens, to the court of his father Aegeus. His stepmother *Medea* (page 36) jealously tried to bring about his death. When she failed, she fled into exile, and Theseus was acknowledged prince of the royal blood.

The Athenians rejoiced at the arrival of Theseus, but their happiness was tempered by the knowledge that soon another quota of young people was destined for death on the island of Crete. Each year Athens was required to send, in tribute to Crete, fourteen of its finest young men and women as a living sacrifice. These young people were turned loose in the Labyrinth, a maze of passages where the *Minotaur* lived. The Minotaur, a terrible monster, half bull and half man, lived on human flesh. In the winding, twisting passageways of the Labyrinth only the Minotaur was at home. Those who were lost in the Labyrinth would be hunted casually by the monster and destroyed one by one.

Theseus offered himself as one of the young men to be sacrificed. His father Aegeus pleaded with him, but Theseus was resolute. At last his father agreed, and the ship with the customary black sails was made ready for departure. Before Theseus left, he promised to exchange the black sails for white if he were victorious over the monster.

Since Theseus had tremendous strength, there was a good possibility that he would be able to meet the Minotaur on fairly even terms. But there remained the difficulty of escaping from the Labyrinth once he was entrapped. Fortunately for Theseus, *Ariadne*, daughter of the king, gave assistance.

When the ship arrived at Crete, the young people were brought directly to King Minos. Ariadne, who chanced to be standing near when the young men and women were before the king, fell in love with Theseus. To help him in the Labyrinth she gave him a sword and a ball of thread. As he entered the narrow, gloomy passages, Theseus let out the thread bit by bit. Further and further into the maze he wandered, but always he felt the reassuring thread in his hand.

Suddenly, there was a loud bellow, and with a rush the Minotaur was upon him. Wielding the sword in great arcs Theseus fought back until at last the monster lay slain at his feet. Theseus picked up the precious thread, his only link with the outside world, and paced slowly back. Through twistings and turnings, past confusing corridors, Theseus walked, trusting in the slender cord upon which his life depended. Several times he paused as other passages looked more familiar, but he resolved to keep on following the thread. At last he saw a glimmer of light ahead—daylight! He rushed ahead now, rejoicing at his good fortune. Outside Ariadne was waiting.

It was back to Athens now for Theseus and his companions. Ariadne pleaded to go with her beloved. Theseus granted her request, and the ship set sail. Then occurred an event that is difficult to explain, for it seems like gross ingratitude on Theseus' part. When the ship stopped at the island of Naxos, Theseus abandoned Ariadne there, slipping away while she was asleep. He excused himself by insisting that a god had ordered him to leave Ariadne as a bride for *Bacchus*. Tradition says that she was wooed and won by Bacchus. After her death the golden crown that Bacchus had given her was transferred to the sky. The constellation, the Northern Crown (or Corona Borealis) can be found near the star group of Hercules.

Perhaps Theseus was punished for his abandonment of Ariadne, for in sailing to Athens he forgot his promise to his father. The ship that bore him homeward still had the black sails of mourning with which they had set out. When Aegeus, watching anxiously from the shore, saw the black sails on the ship, he thought the worst, and threw himself to his death. Upon his arrival Theseus was grief-stricken to learn of his father's fate.

After this, Theseus had many other adventures as new king of Athens. He undertook an expedition against the Amazons, warrior maidens, and carried off their queen as his bride. He took part in the famous battle between the *Lapithae* and the *Centaurs*, a story you may wish to read more about. With his closest friend he undertook an expedition to the underworld to capture *Proserpine* (page 19), wife of Pluto. This quest failed, but Theseus was rescued by Hercules. He even carried off for a brief time *Helen of Troy*, then a child.

Probably a Theseus actually lived, so that in this he resembles some of the folk heroes of America, as discussed in Unit Six.

Jason

The story of the expedition of the *Argonauts* is one of the great legends that have come down to us. Some investigators believe that there may actually have been a historical basis for the tale. Whether or not there is a foundation of fact under the fiction, our chief interest today lies in the thrilling narrative and the fascinating characters who made the voyage.

The story begins in Thessaly, which was being ruled by *Pelias* during the boyhood and youth of his nephew *Jason*, the heir to the throne. There came a day when Jason, grown up, demanded the crown. But by now, Pelias was reluctant to yield the throne and he thought of a clever plan for getting rid of Jason. He arranged a banquet at which bards narrated many stirring stories about the great achievements of past heroes. All the while, he flattered Jason, telling the young man that he too ought to make a name for himself by embarking on some great adventure. Jason's imagination became more and more inflamed as he listened to the stimulating tales and to Pelias's crafty hints of the great glory awaiting him. Finally, one of the minstrels sang of the fabulous Golden Fleece.

According to the story, there had once been a winged ram whose fleece was made of gold. When the ram was sacrificed, this Golden Fleece was hung on a tree in the land of Colchis, from which it could be obtained by anyone brave enough to slay the dragon guarding it.

By this time Jason's youthful enthusiasm knew no bounds and he swore he would not accept the crown of his country until he returned with the Golden Fleece in his hands. That was exactly what Pelias wanted, for he knew that the journey to Colchis was fraught with all sorts of dangers, and he felt certain that the inexperienced, headstrong youth would lose his life somewhere on the way.

By next morning, Jason realized how rash he had been and regretted the hasty decision he had made, but, having given his word, he resolved to keep it.

At Jason's direction, a huge boat, named the *Argo*, was constructed. It was the largest boat that had ever been built up to that time—so large that it could carry fifty warriors. Among the Argonauts, as the members of the crew were called, were many great heroes, including Castor and Pollux (twin sons of Leda and Jupiter), Idas (page 48), Orpheus, Theseus, and Hercules.

With the most renowned adventurers and the best oarsmen in all Thessaly, the *Argo* began her eventful voyage. The expedition suffered many misfortunes and delays on the way to Colchis. On one of the stops for repairs, a member of the crew was drowned, and Hercules, grieving for him, deserted the ship. On another occasion time-out was taken to pursue the *Harpies*, monsters that were part woman and part bird. Later, many Argonauts were wounded when the ship was attacked by birds that used their brass feathers as arrows.

The greatest danger of all during the journey occurred when the *Argo* came to the place of the Clashing Rocks. These two great rocks floated on the water, guarding an entrance through which the ship had to pass. Whenever a boat attempted to pass between these rocks, they would crash together and crush it. Many a boat had been destroyed by their relentless impact. But fortunately Jason had been warned about this danger and he had a plan all ready. He released a dove, which flew through the passageway between the rocks, losing only a few of its tail feathers as the rocks thundered against each other. As the rocks rebounded from the crash, Jason gave the signal to his oarsmen, and the *Argo* leapt forward through the opening. The rocks crashed together again, but too late to do more than graze the rudder of the speeding ship. The *Argo* was safely through.

The crew rowed on and on until they arrived at last at the land where the Golden Fleece was kept. *Aeëtes*, King of Colchis, did not want to give Jason a chance to secure the treasure but said he would do so if certain conditions were fulfilled. Actually, the king felt that there was little risk of his losing the Golden Fleece, for he was certain

that the conditions he proposed could not be met. Jason was to yoke
to a plow two fierce bulls that exhaled fire from their nostrils. Then
he was to use these harnessed bulls to plow a field, which was then
to be sown with the teeth of a legendary dragon. From these dragon's
teeth, everyone knew, would spring a crop of armed warriors who
would turn on Jason and surely slay him. Then, *if* Jason were able
to yoke the fire-breathing bulls, and *if* he were able to control the
bulls to plow the field, and *if* he withstood the attack of the armed
men arising from the dragon's teeth—then he would be given the
chance to battle the monster guarding the Golden Fleece.

Surely these were obstacles to dismay even the bravest of men.
Fortunately for Jason, *Medea*, daughter of the King of Colchis, had
fallen in love with him. She was well-versed in all the arts of magic
and enchantment. In return for Jason's promise to marry her, she
gave him a charm to help him in the battle to come. With this charm,
Jason was easily able to tame the bulls, yoke them, and plow the
field. Then he sowed the dragon's teeth. While Jason's comrades and
the Colchians watched breathlessly, the armed men sprang up from
the furrows in the field, brandishing their weapons. Fiercely they
rushed at Jason to destroy him. Jason bent down, picked up a stone,
and threw it into their midst. Immediately the warriors, each one
thinking the stone had been flung by his neighbor, began to fight
among themselves. They battled one another with such ferocity that
soon not one of them was left alive.

With Medea's further assistance, Jason lulled to sleep the dragon
that guarded the Golden Fleece. He snatched the great treasure from
the branch where it hung and fled to the *Argo*, accompanied by Medea
and her little brother, *Absyrtus*. The ship, made ready for a quick
start, speeded out of the harbor.

The king, infuriated by the loss of not only the Golden Fleece but
also his son and daughter, set out in swift pursuit. The Colchian
rowers gradually gained upon *Argo*, and Medea saw that the king
would overtake the ship and tear her away from the arms of her
beloved Jason—unless she did something to delay him. The way she
succeeded was indeed cruel. She killed her little brother, Absyrtus,
her father's dearest possession, tore him to pieces, and tossed the
fragments overboard, one at a time. The king, of course, abandoned
the pursuit in order to rescue his son's body.

On the way home the Argonauts passed the island of the *Sirens*,
sea nymphs whose enticing melodies lured sailors to their destruction

against the rocks. But the music of Orpheus on board the *Argo* proved stronger than theirs and the ship continued safely on its course.

Arriving at last in Thessaly, Jason discovered that Pelias, now an old man, was not at all willing to give up the crown, which he had worn so long. Again Medea used her sorcery—or, rather, her reputation for sorcery—to clear Jason's path. This time she had the unwitting assistance of Pelias' own daughters. These girls, learning that Medea knew the secret of rejuvenation, urged her to restore their father's youth. Pretending to be willing to help them, Medea persuaded the credulous girls to kill their father, explaining that this was the necessary first step in the magical process. They followed her instructions and then, of course, discovered to their dismay that their father was dead, not restored to youth.

For all her savage efforts in her husband's behalf, Medea was rewarded a few years later in a way she had not expected, for Jason's affection for her cooled and he decided to abandon her and take another wife. To avenge herself, Medea sent Jason's new bride a poisoned wedding robe, which killed the unfortunate maiden as soon as it was put on. Still burning with resentment against Jason, Medea killed the children she had borne him and fled to Athens. There she married King Aegeus, thus becoming Theseus' stepmother (page 32).

Now a lonely, weary, and remorseful man, Jason spent his days and nights on the deck of the slowly rotting *Argo*, meditating on the glory of his quest of the Golden Fleece and the ferocity of the woman who had helped him attain it. It is said that one day, while he was sitting there in reverie, a rotting beam of the *Argo* fell on him and killed him.

Oedipus

Of all the Greek heroes, probably the most tragic is Oedipus. He was courageous, high-minded, honest. He was a just ruler, beloved by his people. But a strange curse hung over him and eventually destroyed him. This is his story.

When *Jocasta*, Queen of Thebes, gave birth to a son, her joy and that of her husband, King *Laius*, knew no bounds. But their joy was short-lived, for they were informed by an oracle that the boy was destined to kill his father, marry his mother, and bring great misery to his native city.

To prevent these things from happening, Laius ordered one of his herdsmen to take the baby secretly out of the city and destroy it. The herdsman carried the child to a bleak and lonely hill and unsheathed his knife. But he could not bring himself to take the life of the innocent and helpless baby. At the same time he did not dare disobey the king's command. His duty demanded that the child be destroyed; his conscience prevented him from killing the child with his own hands. To satisfy both his duty and his conscience, he tied one end of a short cord to the child's ankles and the other end to the limb of a tree on the hillside, expecting that the infant would die of exposure there or be eaten by wild beasts. Then he left, hurrying away from the cries of the child suspended from the tree in this most painful position.

But the child did not die. Another shepherd, hearing the cries of the baby, found him and took him to *Polybus*, King of Corinth. Polybus and his Queen, having no son of their own, adopted him and called him *Oedipus*. (*Oedipus* means "swollen-footed"; the child's feet had been badly swollen because of the tight cord around his ankles.)

In Corinth young Oedipus was given every advantage. He came to love his "father" and "mother."

Soon after he had reached manhood, Oedipus learned from another oracle that he was destined to kill his father. Now Oedipus loved his supposed father Polybus, and fearing that he might in some way kill Polybus, he left Corinth. Fate moved inexorably, without concern for human wishes. On the road Oedipus met his real father, Laius, attended by a servant. They quarreled over the right of way, and Oedipus, in a rage, slew Laius and the attendant. Though he had fulfilled a part of the prophecy, Oedipus was not yet aware of the terrible fact.

He proceeded on to Thebes. Before he reached the city, he met a terrible monster, the *Sphinx*, who used to waylay all travelers and ask one question: "What animal is it that in the morning goes on four feet, at noon on two, and at night on three?" Those who could explain the riddle were allowed to pass. Those who failed were killed. No one could explain the riddle—until Oedipus came along.

Oedipus boldly approached the monster. Once again she presented her fateful riddle. Oedipus boldly answered, and solved the riddle (page 7). The Sphinx, so the legend tells us, was ashamed that he had guessed her riddle. She threw herself from a rock and perished.

The Thebans were grateful. The prize offered to the destroyer of the Sphinx was the throne of Thebes, as well as the hand of Jocasta, widow of Laius. Oedipus accepted the honor. He became king of Thebes and married his mother. Naturally, neither Jocasta nor Oedipus knew who Oedipus really was, nor that he had already slain his father. So the second part of the prophecy was fulfilled.

The last part of the prophecy was to be acted out later, for after some years the city was afflicted with famine and pestilence. The Thebans consulted the oracle and discovered that the plague would not abate until the slayer of Laius was punished. Oedipus resolved to find the guilty man, not realizing that he himself was the one.

As he inquired, the truth came out bit by bit. He discovered that *he* had slain Laius—worse, that Laius was indeed his own father. The prophecy had come true in every detail. Upon hearing the news, Jocasta committed suicide. Oedipus in an agony of remorse put out both his eyes and left Thebes to wander, accompanied only by his loyal daughter *Antigone*. His two sons, Eteocles and Polynices, stayed on to act out another portion of the tragedy.

A great play, *Oedipus the King*, tells this famous story of Oedipus and his destiny. It was written by Sophocles, ancient Greek tragic writer, who is ranked among the world's most powerful dramatists.

The tragedy of Thebes was not yet ended. True, Oedipus himself at last found peace. In the little village of Colonus, near Athens, he died, comforted by his friend Theseus, King of Athens (page 32). But Antigone returned to Thebes, where she became involved in another tragedy.

When Oedipus left Thebes, his two sons, Eteocles and Polynices, agreed to share the kingdom and to reign alternately year by year. Unfortunately, Eteocles liked power and homage. When his year was up, he refused to yield to his brother. Polynices fled to a neighboring kingdom and raised an army in revolt.

Many bloody battles followed, but at last the opposing forces decided to settle the fight simply. The two brothers met in single combat. Equally matched, they fought long and bitterly. At last each one fell, mortally wounded by the other. After their death, both armies renewed the battle. The invaders were at last forced to flee. *Creon*, uncle of the brothers, became king.

Creon proved to be stubborn, unreasonable, and cruel. He allowed Eteocles to be buried with honor, but he refused honorable burial to Polynices. He went even further. He forbade anyone, on penalty of death, to bury the body of this son of Oedipus.

Antigone heard of this ruling and resolved to make matters right. Just as she had shown devotion to her father in his plight, so now she showed a similar devotion to her unburied brother. Unable to secure help from others, she resolved to act alone and bury the body with her own hands. She was caught in the act.

Creon bitterly reminded her of the law she had broken, but Antigone reminded him of a higher law than his, the law of justice. Creon was unmoved. He ordered that she be buried alive.

Creon was to suffer, too, for his unyielding cruelty. His own son *Haemon*, beloved of Antigone, killed himself in his grief. Too late, Creon realized his mistake, but the damage was done. So tragedy came again to Thebes.

The story of Antigone and her devotion, like the tale of Oedipus, is the subject of a great play by Sophocles.

VI. Men and Women

Since mythology reflects life, love stories abound in the myths of Greece and Rome. There are tales of love between gods and goddesses, as in the story of Pluto and Proserpine (page 19), or Jupiter and Juno. Unfortunately, Jupiter was not always faithful to his spouse, for he loved many mortal women: Callisto, Danae, Europa, Io, Semele, and Leda, among others. Children of these affairs, like Perseus, played an important role in the myths.

Goddesses were less likely to follow the lead of Jupiter. Minerva, for example, is never linked romantically to any god or mortal. Her sisters, however, did fall in love with mortals. Diana loved the handsome youth Endymion. Venus loved Adonis. As we shall see in a story that follows, Aurora loved Tithonus.

Myths tell the story of mortal lovers, too. One of the most touching is the story of the aged lovers, Baucis and Philemon. One of the strangest is the story of Pygmalion and Galatea. These two tales, and other love stories, appear in the pages that follow.

Orpheus and Eurydice

Orpheus, son of Apollo (god of the sun and also of music) and of *Calliope* (the muse of epic poetry), was so marvelous a musician that the wild beasts, and even trees and rocks and rivers, came to listen to him. The beautiful nymph *Eurydice* fell in love with him, and they were married.

Shortly after their marriage, Eurydice was bitten by a snake and died. Inconsolable, Orpheus expressed his grief in music, pleading with gods and men for the return of his wife. But ordinarily, of course, no one can return from the land of the dead. In desperation, Orpheus decided to go down to Hades to seek Eurydice and bring her back, if he could, to the world of light and life.

Finding an opening to the lower regions, Orpheus descended to the land of perpetual night. He saw the pale shadows of the dead and at last reached the throne of Pluto and Proserpine.

He sang his plea, begging that Eurydice be given back to him. It is said that his music was so beautiful that even the ghosts wept. The damned, whose labors were eternal, rested a moment from their endless toil to listen. Proserpine wept, and even Pluto was softened by the music.

Finally, Pluto agreed to permit Eurydice's return to the land of the living.

"Take her," he said to Orpheus. "She shall walk behind you; but if you look at her before you reach the land of light, you will lose her forever."

Orpheus was overjoyed. Keeping in mind the terrible commandment, he led Eurydice through the horrors of Hades. He kept his mind on one thought only: *"Don't look back!"* Step by step they threaded their perilous way. At last the light of the upper world glimmered just ahead of them. In his exultation and impatience, poor Orpheus turned too soon to embrace Eurydice. She cried aloud as she saw him turn around, but her warning was too late. The mists closed in upon her, and once again she took up alone her weary pilgrimage to the land of eternal night.

Tortured by the bitterness of his loss, Orpheus began to rage. His rage turned to madness as he tried to grasp the shadow that had once been Eurydice. Returning to the upper air, he wandered until finally he withdrew to a solitary existence in a cave. He refused to have anything more to do with women. He therefore repulsed the advances of some Thracian maidens who had fallen in love with him.

Infuriated by his lack of interest in them, they killed him. Thus, at last, he rejoined Eurydice, but as a shade, not as a mortal.

After his death, his magic harp was placed by Jupiter among the stars, where as the constellation *Lyra*, it may be seen to this day.

Pygmalion and Galatea

Not every lover in mythology was so unfortunate as Orpheus. The love story of *Pygmalion* and *Galatea* has a happy ending, for Venus (goddess of love) chose to help. This is how it all happened.

Pygmalion was an accomplished sculptor, who won the acclaim of everyone for his perfect statues. He was lonely; yet he didn't marry because he could never find the "perfect girl." In his loneliness he made a marvelous statue of ivory, more beautiful than any living woman. Into the statue he put all his skill and all his desire for companionship. Visitors exclaimed with disbelief and amazement at the perfection of the statue.

"Look! She moves!" cried out one after another, but no, the statue was of lifeless ivory.

Pygmalion fell in love with his own creation. He thought, "If only she were alive!" But the statue gazed unseeingly into space.

At last the festival in honor of Venus came around. Pygmalion, obsessed with love for his statue, strode up to the smoking altar of the goddess. A wild idea came to him. Resolutely he cried out, "O goddess, bid my statue live." A flame shot up from the altar, an omen that the goddess had heard.

Pygmalion rushed home. When he arrived, he found his statue garlanded with flowers. A soft voice called his name. The statue started from the pedestal and walked to him. His beloved statue had indeed come to life, as beautiful as ever, but now a living, breathing woman. She was called *Galatea*. Pygmalion and Galatea were married, and Venus herself blessed the ceremony.

George Bernard Shaw, the great Irish playwright, used the Pygmalion theme in one of his greatest plays, called fittingly enough *Pygmalion*. To win a bet, a professor takes an illiterate flower girl from the streets of London. He teaches her correct speech and good manners. He is so successful that he is able to pass her off as a duchess. However, in the process of learning, the girl falls in love with the professor. He seems not

to return her love. To avoid having to go back to her old life, the girl says she will accept the proposal of a rich young man. To his surprise, the professor is reluctant to hear the news. We feel that he, like Pygmalion, has fallen in love with his own creation. The play hints that he will probably not let her go.

A famous musical version of *Pygmalion* is *My Fair Lady*, originally starring Rex Harrison and Julie Andrews. This version closely resembles the original and suggests, perhaps more strongly than the original, that the professor will not lose Eliza Doolittle, his own Galatea.

Baucis and Philemon

Once upon a time Jupiter and Mercury visited the land of Phrygia. As they did so often, they pretended to be mortals. As evening came on, they sought shelter and rest, but they found all doors closed. The inhabitants did not want to bother with these weary travelers.

Then the two gods came to a small, poor cottage. The owners, Baucis and Philemon, welcomed them inside. Though old and feeble, the couple bustled about to make their guests comfortable. Their love was apparent in the way they spoke and acted toward each other. The guests were touched and fascinated by the example of their devotion.

Baucis cooked a simple but nourishing dinner and set it before the guests. Then she put a pitcher filled with wine on the table. All four enjoyed the meal and the wine, but something astonishing happened. As fast as they drank the wine, the pitcher filled up again.

The old couple were terrified. They realized they were entertaining gods, not mortals. They fell on their knees and begged forgiveness for their poor entertainment. They sought to provide better fare for their divine guests.

They decided to sacrifice to the gods an old goose, guardian of their humble cottage. The goose was too quick for the old couple and took shelter by the side of the gods themselves. The gods did not allow the goose to be slain. Instead they said, "Yes, we are gods. The village will pay for its lack of hospitality toward us, but you shall go free."

Jupiter and Mercury escorted Baucis and Philemon to the top of a hill. They watched as the village was sunk in a lake. Only their own house was spared. As they wondered, the humble cottage was changed into a beautiful temple, with marble and ornaments of gold.

"Worthy old man and woman, tell us what favors you would ask of us."

They asked two favors. First, they wanted to be priests and guardians of the temple. Secondly, they wanted to die at the same time, thus never to be separated.

Their favors were granted. When they had reached a great age, they stood one day before the temple. Baucis saw Philemon beginning to put forth leaves. Philemon saw Baucis changing in the same way. As they said to each other, "Farewell, dear spouse," a leafy crown grew over their heads and bark closed over their mouths. There is a story that these two old lovers still stand side by side, an oak and a linden.

Cupid and Psyche

The princess Psyche was so beautiful that even Venus was jealous of her. Venus instructed her son Cupid to punish the innocent girl. Venus wanted Psyche to be tricked into loving some low, unworthy person.

Cupid found Psyche lying asleep. He may have been overwhelmed by her beauty, or he may have been wounded with one of his own arrows. At any rate he fell in love and whisked Psyche off to a magnificent palace. There Psyche was deeply affected by the beauty of the building. Golden pillars supported the roof. Magnificent paintings and carvings were everywhere.

As she was admiring the interior, an invisible person spoke to her. He said, "Everything you see is yours. I am the husband for whom you have been destined. We shall always be happy, but there is one requirement. You must never look upon my face." The voice was that of Cupid, though Psyche did not know it.

And so Psyche lived happily . . . but not forever after. After a while, she missed her family. She asked that her family be brought to her. Cupid unwillingly agreed. When they arrived, everything went well for a time. Then the sisters asked Psyche about her mysterious husband. They aroused all kinds of suspicions in her. They advised her to take a lamp and a sharp knife into the chamber with her. If the husband proved to be a monster, she could kill him.

Psyche resisted for a while, but at last her own curiosity, like

Pandora's (page 20), got the better of her. When Cupid was asleep, she lit the lamp and cried out. Instead of a monster, her husband was a youth of radiant beauty. In her happiness she happened to spill a drop of hot oil from the lamp. It landed on Cupid's shoulder and awakened him. He reproached Psyche bitterly and vanished.

Psyche traveled the world, seeking her husband, but he was nowhere to be found. At last she came to the temple of Ceres. She won the favor of the goddess and asked her help to find Cupid. Ceres prevailed upon Venus to accept Psyche into her service. Venus was not forgiving. Instead she gave Psyche an impossible task of separating all kinds of grains. Psyche would have failed, but Cupid, seeing her again, could not restrain his love. He commanded the ants to do the separating for her.

Venus was still angry with Psyche and gave her other difficult tasks to perform. Psyche overcame each difficulty with the help of her mysterious helper. Though Cupid had been furious with Psyche, he still loved her. And so he went to Jupiter to ask for permission to rejoin Psyche. Jupiter listened. Venus finally agreed to cease her mistreatment of Psyche. Psyche was made immortal, and the two lovers were united, this time forever.

Aurora and Tithonus

Aurora, goddess of the dawn, often fell in love with mortal youths. Perhaps her favorite was Tithonus, son of Laomedon, king of Troy. She stole him away from his favorite haunts and persuaded Jupiter to grant him immortality.

The two were blissfully happy, but then something went wrong. Tithonus began to get gray hairs. His step became slower. Tithonus was immortal, but he was growing old! He had been given immortality but not eternal youth. When Tithonus's hair turned white, Aurora left his side. He still stayed in the heavenly palace and lived luxuriously, but he was clearly wasting away. When he had lost the power of his legs, Aurora shut him up in his chamber. From inside the chamber his feeble voice might still be heard.

Aurora was sad and puzzled. What could she do with her former lover? He was, after all, immortal. She decided to transform him into a living creature, one whose shrill call would be appropriate to the cries of Tithonus. And so Tithonus became a grasshopper. On quiet evenings, they say, you can still hear the eerie cry of Tithonus in the gathering dusk.

VII. Mortals Against the Gods

Because human beings tend to be an unpredictable lot, they sometimes do surprising things. Though the gods were all-powerful, on a number of occasions ordinary mortals countered the will of the gods or even defied them as did Phaëthon (page 16). You will meet three whose profiles of courage are detailed here.

Arachne

Once upon a time there was a Lydian maiden whose skill in weaving was known the world over. She was so good she surpassed all her rivals and became the acknowledged master weaver. An admirer once said, "You must have been taught your skill by the goddess Minerva herself!"

"Not at all. I could compete with Minerva," she replied boldly.

Since Minerva was skilled as a weaver, she did not look with favor upon this newcomer. And so she appeared to Arachne, disguised as an old woman. She gently suggested to Arachne that she be satisfied to compete with mortals only. "It is unwise to vie with the gods."

"I am not afraid of the goddess," Arachne replied. And then, in a moment of heady confidence, she repeated her boast and demanded that Minerva meet her in person in a weaving competition.

"I am here," replied Minerva, and she revealed herself in all her glory. Arachne was still confident, unafraid. She proceeded to the contest.

Minerva wove a scene of great beauty, showing the gods in all their majesty. The figures were so real they almost seemed ready to step out of the pattern. Minerva also wove into her design a warning to Arachne to stop the contest before it was too late. But Arachne did not yield.

Arachne wove scenes of the gods and goddesses, but her designs did not show the deities in a favorable light. Thus she not only defied Minerva, she also poked fun at the very gods themselves. She wove quickly and beautifully. Her weaving was the equal of Minerva's, but the goddess became furious. She demolished Arachne's work. She touched the forehead of Arachne, and at last Arachne realized the error she had made. Because she felt guilty, she hanged herself.

Minerva would not let her die. As a lesson to all foolish mortals who might follow Arachne and challenge the gods, Minerva turned

Arachne into a spider. And so, forever, Arachne spins and spins and spins her web without rest. And to this day, spiders are called *Arachnids*, after Arachne herself.

Marpessa and Idas

One of the most touching of love stories in mythology is the tale of *Marpessa* and *Idas*. Like many other mortal maidens, Marpessa was loved by one of the gods, in this instance Apollo. Her mortal lover, Idas, carried her off with the aid of a winged chariot furnished by Neptune. But Apollo caught up with the pair and rushed down to separate them.

Idas thrust Marpessa behind him and prepared to engage in combat with the god himself. The fight began, but Jupiter stepped in and separated them.

"Let Marpessa decide," was all he said.

On one side stood Idas, sleepless, weary, with all-too-human fatigue showing upon him. On the other stood Apollo, radiant in his divine beauty.

First Apollo spoke and told Marpessa that he could offer her immortality. If she loved him, she would be like a goddess. Never would she taste of sorrow and death, but always live in peace and happiness.

Then Idas spoke, hesitantly, for what could he offer to match the god's gifts? He told her simply that he loved her not only for her beauty, but for herself. He loved her for her power to bring light to the troubled world. He could not promise her freedom from death and sorrow, but he could promise devotion and a share in human joys and troubles.

Even as he spoke, Marpessa took his hand in her own and turned toward Apollo. She declared she knew how pleasant life with a god might be, but she feared the offer of immortality. She feared, too, to be entirely free of sorrow. She knew that for all mankind sorrow has its place. Men have made beauty from sadness. To choose Idas meant growing old—with him. It meant sharing in the rich and full life that men must live upon earth, with all the griefs and all the joys as well.

Apollo cried out in anger and disappeared. Marpessa looked up for a moment, then took Idas gently by the hand, and together they walked away.

Daphne

One day the god Apollo was taunting Cupid for Cupid's unmanly activities as god of love. Cupid thereupon vowed to show his power. He took two arrows from his quiver, one of gold and one of lead. The arrow tipped with gold excited love. The other arrow repelled love. He went out, seeking a character for his little play.

The beautiful nymph Daphne was the daughter of the river god Peneus. She loved hunting and the woodlands. Like Diana she shunned all men and rejected all suitors for her hand. Her father Peneus pleaded with her to marry, but she refused. Still, many men fell in love with her, to no avail.

Cupid, with his wry sense of humor, decided to play a trick on both Apollo and Daphne. He shot Apollo with the gold-tipped arrow and Daphne with the lead-tipped one. Apollo fell madly in love with Daphne, but she would have nothing to do with him. She fled from him in terror. The more he professed his love for her, the faster she fled from him.

In her flight she at last came to the river Peneus, where her father dwelt. She prayed to be saved from the embraces of Apollo, and her prayers were answered. As Apollo was about to clasp her in his arms at last, Daphne was transformed into a laurel tree. Apollo was thwarted, but his love did not die. He declared that the laurel would always be green. He promised to bind the leaves around his head in memory of his lost love. From then on the laurel wreath became a symbol of victory.

The name *laurel* persists in expressions like "rest on one's laurels." The name *Daphne* persists today in a scientific plant name.

READING FOR UNDERSTANDING

Main Idea

1. The main idea of "The Roman Myths" (page 12) is that (a) the Romans were pioneers in the development of religious thought (b) Janus is as important a god as Jupiter (c) the Romans relied heavily upon the Greeks for the development of their mythology (d) the Romans at first rejected Greek religion and philosophy.

2. The main idea of "Mythology and Nature" (page 15) is that (a) gods and goddesses were only mortals with a little more

power (b) thunder was caused by Jupiter's thunderbolts
(c) primitive Greeks enjoyed a good story (d) some myths try
to explain natural processes.

Details

3. The only truly Roman god is (a) Jupiter (b) Apollo (c) Janus
   (d) Cupid.
4. All the following are mentioned as Titans EXCEPT (a) Neptune
   (b) Cronus (c) Hyperion (d) Oceanus.
5. The god of speed is (a) Apollo (b) Mercury (c) Mars (d) Vulcan.
6. The chariots of the sun were usually driven by (a) Diana
   (b) Phaëthon (c) Apollo (d) Aurora.
7. An overwhelming trait of Pandora was (a) cruelty (b) indiffer-
   ence (c) jealousy (d) curiosity.
8. Triton is mentioned as a moon of (a) Mars (b) Saturn
   (c) Jupiter (d) Neptune.
9. The hero of the Sumerian epic is (a) Beowulf (b) Gilgamesh
   (c) Aeneas (d) Odysseus.
10. The following are correctly paired EXCEPT (a) Cupid and
    Psyche (b) Baucis and Philemon (c) Theseus and Andromeda
    (d) Marpessa and Idas.
11. Both *Pygmalion* and *My Fair Lady* retell the legend of (a) Galatea
    (b) Oedipus (c) Orpheus (d) Perseus.
12. The Argo was a (a) song (b) Greek spear carrier (c) ship
    (d) treasure house.
13. Two major characteristics of Antigone are (a) determination
    and carelessness (b) indecisiveness and charity (c) love and
    loyalty (d) thoughtfulness and greed.
14. All the following are correctly paired EXCEPT (a) Daphne—
    laurel (b) Tithonus—grasshopper (c) Baucis and Philemon—
    trees (d) Psyche—weaving

Inferences

15. Antigone defied Creon, knowing the penalty was death, (a) because
    she loved his son Haemon (b) with the full cooperation of
    Minerva (c) just for the sake of defiance (d) because of her
    principles.
16. Cupid (a) was sorry he had played a trick on Apollo (b) hated
    his mother Venus (c) would have preferred Pandora to Psyche
    (d) overcame his pride in his love for Psyche.

17. The person most guiltless of intentional wrongdoing was (a) Jason (b) Theseus (c) Oedipus (d) Medea.

18. Hercules got rid of the burden of the sky through (a) a magic word (b) a clever trick (c) his hatred of Atlas (d) violence.

Outcome

19. If Proserpine had not eaten the six pomegranate seeds, (a) her mother would not have found her (b) Pluto would have kept her captive all year (c) we might not have seasons (d) she would have starved to death.

20. If Jason has not abandoned Medea, she (a) would not have killed the children (b) would have helped him get the Golden Fleece (c) would probably have left *him* (d) would not have harmed Pelias.

WORDS IN CONTEXT

1. Cronus *wrested* control of earth and heaven from his father, Uranus.

    Wrested (page 13) means (a) stole (b) took by force (c) won by persuasion (d) learned.

2. Apollo *reluctantly* led his son to the flaming chariot.

    Reluctantly (page 17) means (a) cheerfully (b) swiftly (c) unwillingly (d) fearlessly.

3. Phaëthon sprang gaily into the chariot, thanking his father for *indulging* him.

    Indulging (17) means (a) giving in to (b) refusing (c) commenting cheerfully to (d) speaking courteously to.

4. Off they dashed; almost at once they left the well-worn ruts and *veered* out of control.

    Veered (17) means (a) burned (b) sped (c) changed direction (d) slowed down.

5. He grasped one of his terrible thunderbolts and hurled it straight at the *careening* chariot.

    Careening (19) means (a) running ahead of a stiff wind (b) tossing from side to side (c) running in a straight line (d) burning with the heat of friction.

6. Since he had no gift to *bestow*, he decided to steal some fire from heaven.

    Bestow (20) means (a) describe (b) seek (c) discover (d) give.

7. There was a hurry and a scurry; then from out the box came all kinds of misery to *afflict* mankind.

    Afflict (21) means (a) torment (b) encourage (c) amuse
(d) challenge.

8. Pluto moves far out in the outer darkness, where even the sun's
rays would seem *pallid* and weak.
    Pallid (23) means (a) gleaming (b) colorful (c) distant
(d) pale.

9. Characters like Superman, Conan, James Bond (007), and Indiana
Jones are modern versions of the *indomitable* hero.
    Indomitable (24) means (a) inevitable (b) wandering
(c) unconquerable (d) epic.

10. Seeing that his club and arrows were of no *avail* in the battle,
Hercules grasped the lion in his hands and strangled it to death.
    Avail (27) means (a) problem (b) help (c) consequence
(d) importance.

11. The birds took flight, and Hercules, whose *prowess* as a marksman
evidently equaled his strength, was able to slay them as they
flew.
    Prowess (29) means (a) superior ability (b) uncanny in-
sight (c) outstanding patience (d) welcome modesty.

12. The guardian monsters, terrible enough to ordinary mortals,
were easily *vanquished* by Hercules.
    Vanquished (30) means (a) pursued (b) defeated
(c) discovered (d) carried.

13. *Undaunted*, Hercules set out.
    Undaunted (31) means (a) fearless (b) modest (c) wise
(d) terrified.

14. Hercules shot the centaur and *retrieved* his bride.
    Retrieve (31) means (a) lost (b) overlooked (c) regained
(d) pursued.

15. These young people were turned loose in the *Labyrinth*, a maze
of passages where the Minotaur lived.
    Labyrinth (32) means (a) puzzling path (b) decorated gar-
den (c) basement (d) huge room.

16. His father, Aegeus, pleaded with him, but Theseus was *resolute*.
    Resolute (32) means (a) fearful (b) uncertain (c) determined
(d) overconfident.

17. Fate moved *inexorably*, without concern for human wishes.
    Inexorably (38) means (a) inescapably (b) slowly
(c) indefinitely (d) improbably.

18. After some years the city was afflicted with famine and *pestilence*.
    Pestilence (39) means (a) unrest (b) disobedience
(c) turbulence (d) disease.

19. The plague would not *abate* until the slayer of Laius was punished.
    Abate (39) means (a) appear (b) spread (c) lessen (d) be identified.

20. Oedipus in an agony of *remorse* put out both his eyes and left Thebes to wander, accompanied only by his loyal daughter Antigone.
    Remorse (39) means (a) disagreement (b) disorder (c) physical pain (d) regret.

21. *Inconsolable*, Orpheus expressed his grief in music, pleading with gods and men for the return of his wife.
    Inconsolable (41) means (a) somewhat unhappy (b) confused (c) broken-hearted (d) tricky.

22. He therefore *repulsed* the advances of some Thracian maidens who had fallen in love with him.
    Repulsed (41) means (a) accepted (b) approved (c) rejected (d) considered.

23. Pygmalion was an accomplished sculptor, who won the *acclaim* of everyone for his perfect statues.
    Acclaim (42) means (a) praise (b) mistrust (c) prizes (d) trophy.

24. Pygmalion, *obsessed* with love for his statue, strode up to the smoking altar of the goddess.
    Obsessed (42) means (a) amused (b) haunted (c) miserable (d) angry.

25. Apollo was *thwarted*, but his love did not die.
    Thwarted (49) means (a) amused (b) prodded (c) frustrated (d) embraced.

THINKING IT OVER

1. (a) Suppose still another planet were to be discovered beyond the orbit of Pluto. Can you think of a mythological name that would be appropriate for this planet?
   (b) Suppose you were given the task of renaming the two planets between the earth and the sun. What names would you assign to them?

2. A myth of the North American Indians explains night and day in this way: "Once when the sun and the moon were stolen from the sky, the people had only the light of the stars. Then a boy of the tribe went out and restored daylight to the world. He traveled to the south until he found a man tending a large ball of fire. He snatched the ball of fire, tucked it under his coat, and ran until his feet were tired. He fled, with the man in pursuit. To light his

way, at intervals he threw up into the air a portion of the ball of fire. This made daylight. Then he went on in darkness until he repeated the procedure. As he reached his village he threw up the last piece. Thus did day alternate with night."

Does this remind you of a myth you have just read? How did the Greeks explain the alternation of day and night?

3. The idea of fate, or destiny, appears in many old Greek myths. It was thought that the life of each person was determined in advance by three sisters—the Fates—before whose will even the gods had to bow. The Fates were named Clotho, Lachesis, and Atropos. Clotho spun the thread (with its light and dark lines of happiness and sadness); Lachesis twisted it (making it weak or strong); and Atropos wielded the shears (the length of the thread being equivalent to the length of the mortal's life).

(a) How did fate bring Oedipus to his doom? Was he entirely blameless? How did he help the prophecies to come true?

(b) Can you find instances in the stories where even the gods were helpless before destiny?

4. Marpessa felt that life would not be desirable without any sorrow or sadness. Do you agree? Do misfortunes ever bring good results? Can you think of times when something that seemed bad had a happy ending? Is it true that we appreciate something most when it is endangered or lost?

Helen Keller, in an essay "Three Days to See," says that we would enjoy life much more if we lived each day as though it were our last. Do you agree?

5. Some scholars have suggested that certain myths may be interpreted as *allegories*—that is, real historical incidents disguised as fiction. For instance, the "Minotaur" may be interpreted as the Cretan government, which had defeated Thessaly in a war and was receiving, as a result of its conquest, a great amount of tribute from the defeated country. Suppose the story of the rebellion of the American colonists against the British in 1776 were told in mythological form. What animal do you think would be used as a symbol of the British Empire?

SUGGESTED ACTIVITIES

1. Keep a mythology workbook by making a record of all words and expressions you come across in your reading that are derived from mythological characters, places, or incidents. Write down the sentence in which the word or expression appears; for instance: "For Sale—*Hercules* work trousers"; "Lost in the *labyrinth* of bureaucracy, he discovered that *the thread of Ariadne* was made of red tape"; "His business increased by leaps and bounds, for he had *the Midas touch*."

2. Look for mythological allusions in place names. (*a*) Make a list of cities and towns that are derived from names you have come across in mythology; for example, *Corinth* and *Ithaca* in New York, *Aurora* and *Flora* in Illinois, etc. (*b*) Make a list of mythological names of streets that exist in your community or that you see in your reading. For example, if your town is near the seashore, you may have a Neptune Avenue.

3. If you are a stamp collector, make a grouping of stamps with mythological subjects. Greece, of course, is a fruitful field, but many other countries, including the United States, have used subjects from mythology. Present a report on your collection.

4. The Gorgon Medusa is just one of many legendary monsters. The words listed below are names of other strange persons and beasts. List them in your notebook; next to each one, write the definition or explanation. Use an unabridged dictionary, *Brewer's Dictionary of Phrase and Fable*, *Bulfinch's Mythology*, or another book about mythology.

basilisk	halcyon	roc
behemoth	hippogrif	salamander
cockatrice	kraken	unicorn
dragon	mermaid	vampire
griffin	phoenix	werewolf

5. In a book of mythology, look up one of the following. Then tell the story to the class in you own words.

Tantalus and Sisyphus	Pyramus and Thisbe
Cadmus and the Dragon	Ceyx and Alcyone
The Children of Niobe	Echo and Narcissus
Admetus and Alcestis	Daedalus and Icarus
Orion, the Mighty Hunter	The Seven Against Thebes
The Pleiades	Dryope
Atalanta's Race	Clytie
Hero and Leander	Diana and Endymion
Damon and Pythias	Pegasus and Bellerophon

WORDS ASSOCIATED WITH GREEK-ROMAN MYTHS

Word	Definition	Named for
Adonis	handsome young man	Adonis, youth beloved of Venus
aeolian harp	box with strings, played by the wind	Aeolus, god of the winds
ambrosial	deliciously fragrant	ambrosia, the food of the gods (page 14)
Apollo	handsome young man	Apollo, god of the sun
arachnid	spider	Arachne, who defied Minerva in a weaving contest
atlas	book of maps	Atlas, a Titan who carried the heavens on his shoulders
aurora borealis	northern lights	Aurora, goddess of the dawn
calliope	steam organ	Calliope, Muse of epic or heroic poetry (page 41)
cereal	grain, especially breakfast food	Ceres, goddess of grain and harvests
chimerical	fantastic, unreal	Chimaera, a fire-breathing monster
cupidity	strong desire, as for wealth	Cupid, god of love
echo	repeated sound	Echo, talkative wood nymph
halcyon	tranquil, happy	Alcyone, changed into kingfisher
harpy	greedy or grasping person	Harpies, hideous winged monsters (page 35)
helium	element first found on sun	Helios, ancient sun god (also called Hyperion)
herculean	of great size and strength	Hercules, god of strength
hermetic	completely sealed	Hermes, often associated with magic
hyacinth	flower	Hyacinthus, beautiful youth

WORDS ASSOCIATED WITH GREEK-ROMAN MYTHS *(Cont.)*

Word	Definition	Named for
hygiene	science of health	Hygeia, goddess of health
hypnosis	sleep-like state	Hypnos, god of sleep
iridescent	having rainbow colors	Iris, goddess of the rainbow
January	month	Janus, two-headed god of doorways
Janus-faced	two-faced	Janus, two-headed god of doorways
jovial	hearty, genial, cheerful	Jove (Jupiter), king of the gods
Junoesque	stately and regal	Juno, queen of the gods
labyrinthine	complicated, puzzling	Labyrinth, the maze of Crete
March	month	Mars, god of war
martial	warlike	Mars, god of war
May	month	Maia, goddess of increase and growth
mercurial	changeable, fickle	Mercury, god of speed, commerce
music	pleasing sequence of sounds	Muses, goddesses of arts, sciences, literature
nectarine	fruit	nectar, the drink of the gods (page 14)
ocean	body of salt water	Oceanus, a lonely Titan
Odyssey	an extended wandering	Odysseus, Greek warrior against Troy
panic	sudden, hysterical fear	Pan, woodland god who often frightened shepherds
phaeton	four-wheeled carriage	Phaëthon, who unsuccessfully drove the chariot of the sun
procrustean	securing conformity at any cost	Procrustes, outlaw who slew strangers by a strange method (page 32)
protean	changeable	Proteus, sea god who could change his shape at will

WORDS ASSOCIATED WITH GREEK-ROMAN MYTHS *(Cont.)*

Word	Definition	Named for
psychology	science of the mind	Psyche, beloved of Cupid
saturnine	gloomy, sluggish, grave	Saturn, father of the Olympian gods
tantalize	tease and disappoint	Tantalus, forever condemned to seek food and drink just beyond his reach
titanic	huge	Titans, giants before the Olympian gods
volcano	explosive vent in earth's crust	Vulcan, god of fire
vulcanize	apply heat to rubber	Vulcan, god of fire
zephyr	gentle breeze	Zephyrus, god of the west wind

PHRASES FROM MYTHS

Phrase	*Meaning*	*Explanation*
Clean the Augean Stables	clean up something in bad shape, as corruption	One of the labors of Hercules. See page 27.
Throw a sop to Cerberus	offer a bribe	Cerberus was the guardian of Hades. It was a good idea to offer him a piece of meat to keep him busy.
Sword of Damocles	uncertainty of fortune	Damocles enjoyed playing at king until he noticed a sword above his head, suspended by a single horsehair.
Damon and Pythias	unselfish, inseparable friends	Damon was ready to die in Pythias' place.
A Gorgon's stare	a terrible gaze	The story of Medusa is told on page 25.
A Hydra-headed monster	an idea with many phases or aspects	Another of the labors of Hercules. See page 27.
lares and penates	all of one's household goods	The Lares and Penates were Roman household gods.
Climb Parnassus	create poetry	Parnassus was the Greek mountain sacred to Apollo.
Pile Pelion on Ossa	perform great deeds in an impossible cause	In their fight with the gods, the giants piled Mount Pelion on Mount Ossa to reach heaven. They failed.
A Sisyphean task	a never-ending task	Sisyphus was punished in Hades. He had to roll a rock uphill; it always rolled back again once he was near the top.

UNIT · THREE

Tales of the Trojan War

When Norway fell to the Nazis during World War II, news-papers all over the world pointed out that the fall had been brought about by a *Trojan Horse* technique. German soldiers had come to Norway as tourists. When the invasion started, these "innocent tourists" became fighters who undermined the resistance of the loyal Norwegian army. "Trojan Horse" is the name for a method of trickery that goes back many centu-ries. The use of this expression is a tribute to the legends that have lived for so many years. For the Trojan Horse is very much bound up with the fall of *Troy*, as you shall see. Other common expressions, too, have their origin in the legends of the Trojan War.

There are three great epic poems attributed to Greece and Rome. Oddly enough, all three deal with heroes and events connected with the Trojan War. The first, the *Iliad*, tells of events near the end of the great struggle. The second, the *Odyssey*, relates the adventures of one of the Greek heroes, Odysseus, as he struggles to return home to Greece. Both are attributed to a Greek poet, Homer. The third, the *Aeneid*, relates the adventures of the Trojan hero Aeneas after the fall of Troy, and tells how he became founder of Rome. This is the work of the Roman poet, Vergil. All three have as part of their cast the gods and goddesses we became familiar with in the first chapter of this book.

I. Was There a Trojan War? A Homer?

Do you enjoy a good mystery? Here's one that has been debated for thousands of years and is still not completely solved. There are four cities involved with our story: Athens, Rome, Sparta, and Troy. There is no problem about the first

61

three. Athens and Rome have been continuously inhabited for
thousands of years. As for the third, the modern city of Sparti
is not far from the site of ancient Sparta. All of these cities
have never been lost. That leaves only Troy. Is it inhabited
now? Did it ever exist?

Troy is not now inhabited, but we do know that Troy did
exist. For many centuries, Troy was lost, and scholars wondered if there ever was a Troy on that windy plain in Asia
Minor. Thus, they doubted that there ever was a Trojan War.
They felt certain that the story of the Trojan War was as
mythical as the tale of Phaëthon and Apollo.

The first task was to determine whether or not Troy ever
actually existed. In the 1870s Heinrich Schliemann was credited with identifying the site and excavating much of it. He
and later archaeologists have identified not one but nine cities
of Troy, the ruins of one on top of the others. Probably the
seventh layer is that of our Troy.

Yes, there was a city that existed at the period assigned to
the Trojan War, but was there actually a war at that time?
Scholars now answer *yes* again. According to the *New Columbia Encyclopedia*, "The Trojan War probably reflected a real
war (about 1200 B.C.) between the invading Greeks and the
people of Troas, possibly over control of trade through the
Dardanelles." The site of Troy is located only four miles from
the Dardanelles, the narrow strait that separates Europe from
Asia. A glance at the map will show how important such a
city would be.

Though the *Iliad*, the epic of the Trojan War, took place
about 1200 B.C., it was not written down until hundreds of
years later. In his book *In Search of the Trojan War*, Michael
Wood suggests that Homer may have lived in the eighth century B.C. He sees little doubt that a single genius created the
Iliad. Modern computer studies agree with his claim. The
creator of the *Iliad* built upon a long oral tradition about the
Trojan War, but he undoubtedly gave structure and poetry to
many separate tales.

Recent studies have provided more and more evidence that
the Trojan War did indeed occur. Places mentioned in the
Iliad exist. A great many names used by Homer have been
verified in other sources. His description of the location of
Troy fits modern observations.

All these questions are enticing as part of a mystery that
can never be entirely solved. No matter. The important fact is
the existence of both the *Iliad* and the *Odyssey*, the two great

epics that deeply influenced the Western writers who came
afterward. Some time in the years before recorded history
there was probably a mighty struggle between Troy and
Greece. Troy was a prosperous city situated strategically in
what is now Asia Minor. Standing at the crossroads of East
and West, it became wealthy and powerful. The adventurous
and far-ranging Greeks eventually challenged that power. The
war that resulted broke the power of Troy and established the
Greeks all over the known world.

So much for the possible reality. We are not concerned,
however, with the actual war but with the legendary war that
has come down to us through literature. It is this struggle
that has stirred the minds and hearts of listeners and readers
for three thousand years.

II. The *Iliad*

Prologue

"Was this the face that launch'd a thousand ships
And burnt the topless towers of Ilium?"

In Christopher Marlowe's *Dr. Faustus*, the doctor makes a
pact with the devil. As one reward, he is able to call before
him the most beautiful woman in history, Helen of Troy. His
reaction is quoted. How did Helen get the reputation of pos-
sessing beauty that could launch a thousand ships?

In the real world the Trojan War was probably fought over
commerce. In the storybook world of ancient legend, the war
was fought over a woman, Helen. This is how it came about.

According to the legend the trouble started at the wedding of *Peleus*
(a prince of Thessaly) and *Thetis* (a sea nymph), parents of *Achilles*,
the great Greek hero. All the gods had been invited except Eris,
goddess of discord. Enraged at this slight, Eris hit upon a means of
causing trouble. She threw among the guests a golden apple with
the inscription, "To the Fairest." Three goddesses—Athena, Aphrodite, and Hera*—claimed the apple.

Zeus was unwilling to settle this contest himself, so he sent the
goddesses to Mount Ida, where *Paris*, as son of King *Priam* of Troy,

---

* Greek forms of the names will be used in discussing the Trojan War, the
Iliad, the *Odyssey*, and the *Aeneid*.

disguised as a shepherd, was guarding his flocks. Paris was to make a decision. Each goddess sought to influence him in her favor. Athena offered him great fame and success in war. Hera promised him wealth and power. Aphrodite promised him the most beautiful woman in the world as his wife.

Paris forgot his own wife and awarded the prize to Aphrodite. From this moment forward Athena and Hera became the enemies of Paris and of Troy. Their actions later did much to bring about the fall of the city. But Paris was not concerned about them, for he looked to Aphrodite to fulfill her bargain.

There was little question about who was the most beautiful of women. *Helen* had had many suitors before giving her hand to *Menelaus*, a Greek chieftain. They had all vowed to stand by whomever she selected as her husband. It was to the hall of Menelaus that Aphrodite brought Paris in accordance with her promise. Paris made love to Helen and with the help of Aphrodite persuaded her to elope with him to Troy. There she was given sanctuary.

Menelaus immediately called upon all the other Greek chieftains to help him regain the beautiful Helen. Nearly all the others came forward at once. *Odysseus*, however, one of the former suitors, was reluctant to come because he was happy in his island home of Ithaca with his wife and child. He feigned madness by sowing salt instead of grain. To test him, Menelaus' envoy placed his little son Telemachus in front of the plow. Odysseus, of course, turned aside, and so confessed to his sanity.

To keep Achilles from going to the wars, his mother dressed him as a girl and sent him to mingle with the daughters of the neighboring king. But Odysseus, now committed to the expedition, tricked him. He went among the girls dressed as a wandering merchant. The girls, of course, picked up and admired the jewelry and other trinkets. But Achilles picked up the weapons included among the ornaments. So he was discovered and forced to join the expedition.

The Greeks gathered their forces to set sail for Troy under the leadership of *Agamemnon*. Besides those already mentioned, among the heroes were *Ajax*, *Diomedes*, and *Nestor*, the wise old counselor. The Trojans were ready for the attack. Among the Trojan warriors, in addition to Paris, were *Sarpedon*, *Aeneas*, *Deiphobus*, and—the greatest of them all—*Hector*, brother of Paris.

The war raged indecisively for nine years. Fortune favored one side, then the other. Many noble deeds were performed on each side.

Then something happened that made a decisive change. This something was the *wrath of Achilles*. It is the major theme of the *Iliad*.

> Though the Trojan War dragged on for ten years, the *Iliad* is concerned with only a relatively short period—from the wrath of Achilles to the death of Hector. The events preceding and following are told in other sources, like the *Odyssey* and the *Aeneid*.

The Wrath of Achilles

The wrath of Achilles was not without foundation. In despoiling one of the cities neighboring Troy, Agamemnon had taken captive a young girl, daughter of a priest of Apollo. When the priest prayed to Apollo for revenge, Apollo sent a pestilence to ravage the Greeks. Achilles put the blame for this misfortune upon Agamemnon for refusing to yield his captive. Agamemnon at last agreed to give up the girl, but as commander in chief of the forces he demanded in her place one of Achilles' captives. Achilles yielded his captive, but vowed that he would no longer take part in the struggle. He went off to sulk in his tents, taking his followers with him, and he even considered leaving for home.

Achilles' mother went to Zeus to plead that the Greek cause go badly so that Achilles would be partly avenged for his miserable treatment, and the Greeks would be forced to repent their actions. Zeus agreed, for which he was scolded by Hera. He proved himself master, however, and Hera withdrew for a time. There was little or no neutrality among the gods over the Trojan War. As we have seen, Athena and Hera were bitter enemies of Troy. Aphrodite and Ares favored the Trojan cause. The other gods, too, participated on one side or the other. Zeus tried to be impartial, but not always with conspicuous success.

After Achilles had withdrawn, the Greeks went to battle without their strongest fighter. During the battle, Menelaus and Paris met in single combat. It was agreed that this fight should decide the war. If Menelaus won, the Trojans would yield Helen. If Paris won, the Greeks would return without her.

The duel began. Paris threw his spear. It struck the shield of Menelaus, but failed to penetrate. Menelaus threw his spear. It pierced the shield of Paris and cut through his garments, but Paris swerved and saved his life. Menelaus drew his sword but broke it on the helmet of Paris. He then grasped the helmet by the plume and began to drag Paris toward the Greek ranks. Aphrodite saved her favorite by cutting the chin strap and carrying him away from the dust of battle.

Menelaus looked in vain for his opponent. Since he had disappeared, Agamemnon claimed victory for the Greeks. It looked for a moment as though the bloody war was over at last, but Athena refused to let Troy off so easily. She persuaded one of the Trojans to shoot an arrow at Menelaus. The Trojan let fly the arrow. Athena permitted Menelaus to be wounded lightly, and the battle was on again in earnest.

The battle began to go against the Greeks, as Zeus had promised. Agamemnon humbled himself and sent an embassy to try to persuade Achilles to return to the fight. Achilles was still firm. The Trojan attack became so serious that the Greek ships were in peril. One was set on fire. Achilles yielded somewhat and allowed his friend *Patroclus* to enter the battle wearing the armor of Achilles himself.

The deception had some effect. When the Trojans saw the dread armor of Achilles, they began to fall back. Patroclus slew the Trojan warrior Sarpedon, and then was confronted by Hector, the Trojan leader. Hector killed Patroclus and took his armor, as was the custom in those days. There was a battle for the body, but the Greeks succeeded in carrying it back to their ships with Hector and Aeneas in hot pursuit.

When Achilles heard of the death of Patroclus, he was grief-stricken. He had but one thought, revenge. To console him, his mother promised to have the god *Hephaestus* make him another suit of armor for battle the next day. Achilles became reconciled with Agamemnon and went forth to battle equipped with his new armor.

With the raging Achilles in the forefront of the Greek army, the tide turned swiftly against the Trojans. Although the hero Aeneas bravely confronted Achilles, he was soon wounded and put out of action. The terrified Trojans had no heart for the battle. As the ranks began to break, there was a mad dash for the safety of the city walls.

Fortunately for the Trojans, Apollo once again intervened in their favor. He led Achilles astray by assuming the disguise of a Trojan prince. When Achilles discovered the deception, nearly all the Trojan army was huddled safely within the walls. But there was one exception, Hector. The great leader of the Trojans, drawn somehow to the fate that awaited him, remained outside the sheltering walls of the city to meet his terrible enemy.

The scene that follows is one of the most touching and powerful scenes in the *Iliad*. It is the climax toward which events have been rushing. There is a feeling of inevitable doom about the actions of Hector, as he stands alone to contend against the rage of Achilles.

This is how Homer tells the story.

The Death of Hector

So, throughout the city, the men huddled together like fawns, wiping off the sweat and drinking to slake their thirst. Meanwhile the Greeks drew close to the walls, their shields upon their shoulders. But Hector stood fast before the gates, for his evil destiny held him there.

Old King Priam was the first to see swift Achilles speeding over the plain. His armor shone as the star of harvest time, and the bronze gleamed as he ran. The old man groaned and raised his hands in supplication to his son, who stood eagerly awaiting the onslaught of Achilles.

"Hector, my beloved son, I pray you do not await this man alone with no one beside you, or else you will quickly meet your doom, slain by Achilles. He is mightier far, a merciless man! O, if the gods only loved him as I do! Then dogs and vultures would soon devour him on the field, and a great pain would pass from my heart. For he has taken away from me many brave sons, slaying them or selling them to far-off islands. Even now, two of my children—Lycaon and Polydorus—have not yet returned from battle. If they are still alive in his camp, we shall ransom them with bronze and gold. If they are already in the land of the dead, then shall their mother and I weep for them. But the grief will be less lasting to the rest of the people unless you too die at the hands of Achilles.

"Come then within the walls, dear son. Save the men and women of Troy. Don't give great glory to Achilles at the expense of your own life. Pity me, too—an old man. Though I am helpless, I still have emotions—unlucky one that I am. I have seen many misfortunes, my sons killed and my daughters made captive, my chambers destroyed, little children dashed to the ground in bitter strife, my sons' wives dragged away by the harsh hands of the Greeks. As for me—raging dogs will drag me from my own door after I have been slain—the very dogs I have raised and fed from my table. They will drink my blood and lie in the courtyard. A young man dead in war may still be glorious and honored, but an old man slain is a piteous sight."

So the old man spoke and tore the hairs from his head, but Hector would not listen. His mother wept aloud and cried, "Hector, my child, pity me. Fight the enemy from *within* the walls. Don't stand in front to meet him. He is merciless. If he slays you, I shall not be able to weep for you by an honored grave. Far away from us, by the Greek ships, swift dogs will devour you."

Thus the two spoke, wailing and pleading with Hector, but they could not move his heart. He stood fast and awaited the coming of mighty Achilles. Just as a mountain snake coils about its hole, waiting for a victim, so Hector with courage unquenched would not withdraw. He propped his shield against a jutting tower and thought, "If I do retreat within the walls, my friend Polydamas will be the first to reproach me. He had advised me to lead the Trojans back to the city when Achilles rose up. But I would not listen to him. How much better if I had listened! Now I have ruined my people by my rashness. I am ashamed that I might hear someone say, 'Hector brought ruin on his people by blind trust in his own strength.'

"So they'll speak. Thus, it would be better for me to face Achilles and slay him, or die gloriously before the city.

"But suppose I put down my shield and helmet, and lean my spear against the wall, then go out myself to meet Achilles, unarmed. I might promise to return Helen to the Greeks, together with all the spoils my brother took with him. After all, this was the beginning of the quarrel. I might make some other division of our wealth. . . . But why do I even think this? Suppose I did approach him only to have him slay me unarmed, without mercy or honor. This is no time for idle conversation, but a time to fight in anger. Well, let us see to whom Zeus will give the glory."

So he debated with himself and stood his ground. Achilles drew close to him like the very god of war, his terrifying spear brandished above his right shoulder. All around, the bronze on him flashed like a blazing fire or the rising sun.

Suddenly, Hector was overpowered by fear and fled madly away from the gates. As a hawk upon the mountains easily swoops upon a trembling dove, so Achilles drove upon Hector. They passed the watchtower and the windswept fig tree. Out from below the wall they sped along the wagon road until they came to the sources of the Scamander River. Onward they ran, one fleeing, the other pursuing swiftly. Valiant was the pursued, but the pursuer was even mightier. This was no race for a trifling prize; the life of Hector was at stake.

All the gods on Olympus watched this fateful race. Zeus, father of gods and men, was the first to speak. "I'm sorry to see that man whom I dearly love pursued around the walls. He has made many sacrifices to me. Now swift Achilles pursues him around the walls of Troy. What do the rest of you think? Shall we save him from death, or let him be slain—brave though he is—by Achilles?"

Then Athena spoke up quickly, "Father, lord of the lightning and the thundercloud, what are you saying? Do you wish to snatch back from death a mortal long ago doomed by fate? Do it if you wish, but we other gods cannot approve such action."

Zeus answered, "Never fear, my child, I did not speak in earnest. I wish to be kind to you. Do whatever seems best to you; don't hesitate."

After he had spoken, Athena needed no further urging and darted down from the peaks of Olympus.

Meanwhile Achilles drove Hector on relentlessly. Just as a deer's fawn cannot elude the dog, so Hector could not elude swift Achilles. Whenever he headed in the direction of the Trojan gates, hoping that the defenders would help him with missiles from above, Achilles would cut him off, then drive him onto the plain. Thus Achilles contrived to keep himself between Hector and the city. It was just like a race in a dream where one chases another without ever catching him. Achilles could not catch him with his running, but Hector could not escape. Hector could not have escaped his pursuer so far if Apollo had not been with him for the last time to give him strength and speed. Achilles motioned to his soldiers not to shoot at Hector for fear that someone else might win the glory of slaying him.

But when they reached the springs for the fourth time Hector's destiny was sealed. Fate decreed his death, and Apollo left him. The goddess Athena came to Achilles and said, "Now the two of us will slay Hector for all his great courage and bring glory to the Greeks. There is no chance for him to escape now. Apollo can do no more for him. Rest a moment and get your breath. I will go and persuade him to fight you hand to hand."

So Athena spoke, and Achilles rejoiced as he leaned on his ashen spear with its point of bronze. Athena left him and went over to Hector. She assumed the disguise and voice of one of the Trojans, brother of Hector.

"Dear brother," she said, "swift-footed Achilles is running you a hard race. But come, let us make a stand and defend ourselves."

"My brother," replied Hector, "even before this moment you were always the dearest to me. But now I must honor you even more. You have dared, for my sake, to come out of the walls while the others wait within."

"Yes," replied Athena, "our father and mother urged me to stay within, and so did my comrades; for they are all afraid. But my heart was troubled. Come, let us fight with determination to find whether Achilles shall slay us or be slain."

By such trickery Athena led Hector on. When they approached Achilles, Hector spoke first. "Achilles, I will fly no more. Three times have I fled around the walls of Troy. I could not endure your attack. But now my heart tells me to stand and face you. I will either slay or be slain. But come, let us make a solemn bargain. If I win the victory, I will not mutilate you. After I have stripped you of your armor, I will give back your corpse to the Greeks. And you do the same."

Achilles retorted scornfully. "Hector, do not talk to me of agreements. There is no truce between lions and men. There is no harmony between wolves and lambs. It is not possible for you and me to be friends. There can be no pledge between us. Call up all your strength. Now you must indeed be a spearman and a mighty warrior. You shall pay now for all the woes of my comrades whom you slew."

As he spoke he drew back his spear and let it fly, but Hector crouched and the spear flew over him. It fixed itself in the earth, but Athena returned it to Achilles without Hector's knowledge.

Then Hector said, "A miss! Evidently you have not yet heard of my doom from Zeus, even though you thought the day had come. You are cunning of tongue and a deceptive speaker. So you thought I might forget my valor and strength. You will not have the chance to plant your spear in my back, but drive it straight through my chest if Zeus so wills. But avoid my own bronze spear. Oh, if only I might slay you. Then would the Trojan cause be aided, if you were dead, for you are our greatest trouble."

As he finished, he hurled his spear. It struck Achilles' shield in the center, but the spear rebounded away from the shield. Hector was angry that he had cast away his only spear in vain. He called aloud for another to his "brother," who he thought was at his side. But he looked around in vain. Then Hector realized the truth. "Truly, the gods have summoned me to death. I thought my warrior brother was at my side, but he is still within the walls, and Athena has tricked me. Death is near me, and there is no escape. At least I will

not die ingloriously without a struggle, but in some great deed of arms forever famous."

He drew his sharp sword and rushed upon Achilles like some great eagle dropping to the plain to seize a tender lamb. He brandished aloft his great sword, but Achilles attacked, too, with a wild fierceness. The light glinted from his spear as Achilles sought with his eye some vulnerable spot on the body of Hector. Though Hector was well covered by the fair bronze armor he had taken from Patroclus, there was an opening at the throat, where life's destruction is swiftest.

Achilles pierced him there with his spear as he rushed forward. The point tore through the neck but did not cut the windpipe, so that Hector could still speak. As Hector fell to the ground, Achilles boasted, "Hector, you thought when despoiling Patroclus you'd be safe; but you forgot me, a mightier comrade, who was left behind, and now I have slain you. Dogs and birds shall devour *your* body, but *he* shall have a decent funeral."

Half fainting, Hector replied, "I beg you by your soul, by your father and mother, do not leave me by your ships for dogs to maul. Take bronze and gold, gifts that my father and queenly mother will give you. Give them my body that the Trojans and Trojans' wives may give me the rightful due of the dead, the ritual of fire."

Scornfully Achilles said, "Dog, don't pray to me by my parents. I wish my angry heart would let me carve and eat your raw flesh for what you have done to me. None shall keep the dogs from you, not even if I receive ransom ten or twentyfold with promise of more— no, not even if Priam gave your weight in gold. Your lady mother will not lay you on a bed to be mourned; the dogs and birds will devour your body."

Then as he died Hector said, "Well do I know you and see you as you are. I never had a chance to persuade you. Your heart is as iron. Take care that I do not draw upon you the wrath of the gods on the day when you too will be slain—when Paris and Apollo slay you for all your valor at the Scaean gate."

As he said this, the shadow of death came upon him. His soul left his body and fled to the House of Hades, leaving behind strength and youth. Hector was dead, but even so Achilles said, "Die; as for my death, I am ready for it whenever Zeus and the other gods are minded to bestow it."

As he spoke he drew from the body his bronze spear. He set it to one side and stripped the bloody armor from Hector's shoulders. The rest of the Greeks came up and gazed at Hector's stature and noble looks. No one missed the opportunity of wounding him, saying meanwhile, "Hector is far easier to handle now than when he burned our ships with blazing fire."

Thus would many a man speak and wound him as he stood there beside him. But after Achilles had stripped off the armor, he said, "Friends, chieftains, leaders of our nation, gods have allowed us to vanquish this man, who has done more harm than all the other Trojans put together. Let us, therefore, make trial in arms around the city so that we may know what the Trojans intend to do. Will they abandon their fortress, or will they fight on although Hector is dead? But wait, what am I thinking about? Beside our ships lies Patroclus, unwept and unburied. I will never forget him as long as I am alive to remember anything. I'll remember him even in death. And if men ordinarily forget everything in the house of the dead, I'll remember him even there. But come, my countrymen, let us return to our ships singing our song of victory. Let us return with the body of our foe. We have won great glory. We have slain great Hector whom the Trojans worshiped almost as a god."

Then he thought of shameful treatment for the body of Hector. He slit the tendons of both feet and bound the two together with ox-hide. He fastened them to his chariot, leaving the head to drag. He mounted the chariot holding up the famous armor. He lashed his horses to speed, and they willingly sped on. The dust rose around the body of Hector. His dark hair flowed loose. His head was fouled with dirt, for Zeus had given him over to his enemies in his own native land.

As his head lay in the dust, his mother tore her hair and cried aloud bitterly. Hector's father moaned piteously, and around them the other Trojans lamented and wept through the town. It was as though all Troy burned from top to bottom. The people could scarcely prevent the old man from rushing forth out of the gates. He prayed to each in turn, calling him by name. "Stop, my friends; though you love me, let me go forth from the city alone to the ships of the Greeks. Let me beg of this violent man to feel shame before his fellows and have pity on my age. He too has an old father—who raised him to be a terror to the Trojans and to me above all. He has slain many of my sons in the years of their youth. Yet though I grieve for all of them, I mourn them all less than I mourn this one alone. My grief for him will yet be my death. If only he had died in my arms; then we might have wept and mourned our fill, his mother who bore him and I myself."

So he spoke, weeping. All the Trojans wept aloud with him. *Hecuba*, mother of Hector, led the Trojan women in wild lament. "My child, alas for me! Why should I live in my suffering, now that you are dead, you who were my pride night and day! Now death and fate have overtaken you, whom the men and women of Troy hailed as a god. Truly you were their greatest glory while you lived."

So she spoke, weeping. But Hector's wife, Andromache, had not yet heard the news, for no messenger had come to tell her of Hector's death. In one of the inner rooms of the lofty house she was weaving a double purple web, embroidering pretty flowers on it. She called to her handmaidens to put a cauldron to boil on the fire, so that Hector might have a warm bath when he came home from battle. Poor creature, she did not realize that her husband lay dead at the hands of Achilles, far from warm baths. But suddenly she heard shrieks and groans outside. Her limbs quivered, and the shuttle fell from her hands to the floor.

She spoke again to the maids. "Come with me, two of you; let me see what has happened. It was the voice of my husband's mother that I heard. My heart is beating faster. My limbs are weak. I fear that some evil has come to all of us. I am terribly afraid that Achilles has cut off my brave Hector from the city and is driving him toward the plain. Hector always ran out in front of his warriors, yielding to no one in his courage."

After she had finished she rushed through the hall like a mad woman, with beating heart, and the maids followed her. When she reached the tower and the crowd of men, she stood still upon the wall and gazed. She saw Hector dragged before the city. Swift horses dragged him ruthlessly toward the Greek ships. Then the darkness of night came over her, and she fell back in a faint. The women thronged around her and held her. When she had revived somewhat, she began to cry aloud in lamentation.

"Hector, I am lost! We were both born to one fate, you in Troy and I in Thebes. I wish I never had been born. You have gone to the House of Hades and have left me a widow in deep mourning. Our son is still a baby, child of two unhappy ones. You can be no protection for him now, Hector, now that you are dead. Even if he should escape the Greeks, still toil and woe will be his lot from now on. Being an orphan makes a child friendless. He must hang his head, and his cheeks are wet with tears. In his begging he may go to his father's comrades and pluck at their clothing. Someone out of pity may hold up his cup for a moment to wet the boy's lips, but some child at the feast will strike him and abuse him. 'Go away; your father is not dining with us.'

"Then, poor orphan, he'll return in tears to his widowed mother. This will be the fate of our Astyanax, who once ate only marrow and the fat flesh of sheep, and who slept at the end of a day in a good bed, happy and contented, with his nurse's arms around him. Now that he has lost his father he will suffer many ills—poor Astyanax, for you lie naked by the curved ships, a prey to dogs and worms, far from your parents. Here is a great store of fine linen made for you by women's hands. But I'll burn all of it since it can never any longer be of any use to you. Never will you lie in it."

She wept while she spoke, and the women wept with her.

Achilles at last relented, however. After the funeral games held in honor of the dead Patroclus, old King Priam came to Achilles to beg back the body of his son. In a very famous scene between Achilles and Priam, the warrior was softened. He agreed not only to let Priam take back the body of Hector, but he agreed also to a truce during which the rites for Hector might be solemnized.

The very last words of the *Iliad* are,

"Thus was held the funeral for Hector, tamer of horses."

The Greatness of the *Iliad*

From one point of view the *Iliad* can be considered a tale of the heroism of war and the glory of battle. But from another viewpoint it is, in many ways, a fierce condemnation of war. It attacks realistically the brutality of war, the human waste that war inevitably brings. Some of the most famous and touching scenes are those describing the interludes of peace, the beloved homelands from which the heroes came. There is a magnificent scene with Hector, his wife, and his child, before he goes out to the series of battles that bring his death. Hector reaches out to embrace his little boy, but the child draws back in terror at the waving plumes on Hector's helmet. Hector takes off the helmet and kisses the boy.

The scene is doubly touching because we know that Hector is soon to die. The war plumes are a symbol of the devastation to follow. The little child is destined to be slaughtered, thrown from the high towers by the conquering Greeks. His

wife, too, will soon be a widow and an unwilling captive of
the son of Achilles.

The *Iliad* has been called a great war novel, but it is also a
plea for peace when the happiness of men can flower, far from
the dust and blood of the battlefield. Most readers have tremendous sympathy for Hector. That sympathy is a tribute to
Homer's impartiality in telling his tale.

After the *Iliad*

The events that follow the *Iliad* can be found partly in the
Odyssey and partly in other sources. Odysseus finally thought
of a plan to take the city. He persuaded the Greeks to build a
huge wooden horse (the Trojan Horse) in front of the city
walls. After it was completed the Greeks apparently sailed
away—but they did not go far off. When the Trojans saw the
Greeks depart they came from the city rejoicing. But let the
Aeneid (pages 89–97) tell the rest of the story.

In the *Iliad* there are hints of the death of Achilles, but the
account of his death is given elsewhere. At the time that he
killed Hector, Achilles had said, "As for my death, I am ready
for it whenever Zeus and the other gods are minded to bestow
it." But later on, in the *Odyssey*, the ghost of Achilles says to
Odysseus in the Land of the Dead, "Speak not so comfortably
to me of death, great Odysseus. I would rather live above
ground as the servant of another than be ruler of the dead!"

Ironically, he was wounded by Paris in the only vulnerable
part of his body, his heel. After his death his body was rescued by Ajax and Odysseus. Because Athena awarded the
armor to Odysseus, Ajax went mad with rage and killed himself. When Odysseus met him in the Land of the Dead (told in
the *Odyssey*), Ajax still refused to speak to him.

After the fall of Troy (for the city did fall), the Greek warriors raged through the city. Priam was killed. Most of the
women were carried away as captives. Priam's daughter *Cassandra* was taken as captive by Agamemnon, whose story will
be told briefly. The downfall of the city was complete.

The Return of the Heroes

The victorious Greeks set sail for home. Menelaus and Helen
returned home, and we meet them in the *Odyssey* living happily, apparently with the Trojan War forgotten. Agamemnon,
though, met a terrible fate. While he had been at Troy fighting
those ten years, his wife *Clytemnestra* had fallen in love with

another. When Agamemnon returned to his palace, he was slain by his wife and her lover. The unhappy Trojan princess Cassandra was killed with him. The tragedy is the subject of many great plays of ancient Greece.

Odysseus, too, started happily homeward, but his return took him ten long years. He encountered monsters, enchantresses, and misfortunes of many kinds. At last he returned, only to find danger in his own house. The story of his adventures after the fall of Troy is the story of the *Odyssey*.

III. The *Odyssey*

Background

The *Odyssey* does not begin at the beginning. Just as many modern motion pictures do, it provides for a "flashback" to give much of the action. Odysseus does the narrating. He tells a sympathetic audience about most of his wanderings. The action of the *Odyssey* itself, however, takes place during just the last six weeks of the ten years during which he wandered. For purposes of telling here, we shall adopt the natural order of events.

After Odysseus and his men left Troy, they stopped at a city called Ismarus. They plundered the city and in the skirmish lost six men from each ship. When they set sail again the wind blew them safely along to the southern tip of Greece. If Odysseus had been able to go north from here, he would have reached home easily, and the *Odyssey* would never have been written. But a strong wind then blew them off their course. On the tenth day of sailing Odysseus reached the land of the Lotus-Eaters, who ate flowers.

Some of his men ate food offered them by the inhabitants. Immediately they lost all thought of home and wished to stay on in Lotus-Land. Odysseus had the men dragged forcibly away and bound to the ships. He ordered the others to leave at once before they could taste of the lotus.

They next reached a mysterious land where a savage race of people lived, monsters, not men, called *Cyclopes*. The Greeks disembarked on a beautiful wooded island across the harbor and had a great feast. But Odysseus, curious as ever, decided to go to the mainland to see just what kind of men lived there. He and his men decided to explore a cave belonging to one of the Cyclopes named Polyphemus, a giant with one eye in the middle of his forehead, who lived apart from his own people. He was a son of Poseidon, ruler of the sea. Odysseus selected twelve of his best men and went to investigate. The following selection, adapted from Book Nine of the *Odyssey*, tells what they found.

The Land of the Cyclops*

When we reached the cave, we found it empty. The Cyclops was out pasturing his fat flocks. We looked at everything with interest. Food there was in abundance! There were baskets filled with cheeses. Pans were swimming with milk and cream. Lambs and kids were separated according to their size. My men urged me to take some of the cheeses, lead the animals into the ships, and be off. I didn't listen to them. If I only had! I wanted to meet the Cyclops and receive the stranger's gifts from him. As it happened, his gifts were far from pleasant to me or my companions.

We lit a fire and waited, eating of his cheeses. He came in with a great bundle of dry wood for the fire and threw it down with a great shout. We were terrified and hid in the back of the cave. He drove the animals into the cave for milking, and closed off the entrance with a huge rock. After he had milked the animals, he spied us.

"Who are you?" he cried out. "What place did you come from? Are you merchants, or sea-robbers ready to kill and be killed for gain?"

We trembled at his words, for we feared him. His monstrous size and heavy voice were no comfort to us. Yet I had to answer him; so I said, "We are Greeks on our way home from Troy. We have been driven far out of our course by wind and storm. We are proud to be followers of Agamemnon, leader of all the Greeks against Troy. His fame has spread to all corners of the earth. We are here to make a request of you. We ask hospitable treatment and such gifts as are due to strangers. Honor the gods, O noble sir, and treat us well. For Zeus protects strangers and those who need help."

He answered cruelly, "You're a fool, my friend, to think that I would fear the gods. We Cyclopes have no respect for any of the 'blessed' gods. We are much above them. If I wish to lay hands upon you or your companions, Zeus won't stop me. But tell me where you keep your ship. Near here? Let me know."

* From *The Odyssey*, Book IX, adapted by Henry I. Christ (reprinted by permission of the publishers, Globe Book Company).

He thought he could trick me into revealing the hiding place of the ship. But I gave him a deceitful answer.

"Poseidon the Earth-Shaker wrecked my ship against the rocks of your island. These men with me are all that escaped destruction."

He didn't bother to answer. Instead he rushed forward and grasped two of my companions. Snatching them like puppies he dashed them against the ground, crushing their skulls. Their brains oozed out on the earth. Cutting them up, limb by limb, he prepared his supper. He devoured them like a mountain lion, leaving no trace of the poor men.

We wept aloud, raised our hands heavenward and prayed for Zeus' assistance. We were without hope. After the Cyclops had eaten, he lay stretched out in the cave and slept. I drew my sword and approached him, thinking to kill him or at least wound him seriously. I stopped. How would I get out? We could never have moved the stone from the cavern's opening. Despondently we waited for morning.

The Cyclops awoke after many hours. He went about his business systematically, milking his cattle and performing other chores. After he finished, he snatched two more of my men and prepared his meal. He ate them and then proceeded to drive the cattle from the cage. When the last had gone through, he again rolled the stone in front of the cave's mouth.

I considered many plans for getting revenge if Athena would only grant my prayer. One plan seemed to be best. There was a huge club in the cave, which the Cyclops had been preparing as a walking stick. It was as big as the mast of a good-sized ship. I cut off a piece about six feet long and had my companions sharpen it. I charred the end and brought it to a good point. I asked the men to draw lots to see who would have the job, with me, of thrusting the stick into the eye of the sleeping Cyclops. Four good men were chosen.

In the evening he again herded his fine cattle and sheep into the cave. He put his barrier back into place and milked the animals. Again, after his chores were finished, he snatched two men and prepared his supper. I went close to the Cyclops and said, "Here, Cyclops, have a drink of wine after your meal of human flesh. I want you to know what kind of drink we had aboard my ship. I brought it originally as a gift offering, so that you would pity me and help me return home. Now I see you are mad beyond all cure. How can you expect men to visit you? You have behaved so cruelly."

He took the wine and gulped it down. Licking his lips he spoke again.

"Some more, please, and tell me your name. I'd like to give you a present that you'll approve. Our wine is good, but this is fit for the gods."

I gave him another draught, and he drank it quickly. Again I offered, and again he drank the wine. At last, when he began to feel the effect of the wine, I said gently, "Cyclops, did you ask my name? Well then, I'll tell you, but don't forget that gift you promised me. No-man is my name. My mother, my father, and all my companions call me No-man."

"No-man," he replied with a cruel grin, "this is my present to you. I'll eat all your companions first. I'll save you till last!"

As he said this, he lurched over and fell upon his back. Sleep overcame him. He became ill in his drunken stupor and vomited wine and bits of human flesh. I put the olive-wood stick in the ashes until it was warm. I kept encouraging my companions to keep their spirits high.

The stick was green; when it was about to take fire, green though it was, I took it out and approached the one-eyed monster. My companions hesitated a moment, but some god inspired them with courage. They took hold of the stake and thrust the point into his eye. I leaned on it from above and turned it round and round, as a man drills a hole. Taking the white-hot stake we twisted it in his eye, and the hot blood flowed around it. We scorched his eyebrows and eyelids as the eyeball burned with a hissing sound.

The Cyclops howled horribly and we drew away in terror. He drew the stake from his eye and threw it with an anguished cry from his hands. He called aloud to the other Cyclopes who lived around him in caves. They heard him and came to find out what was the matter. They stood around the cave and cried out his name.

"What terrible injury, Polyphemus, has made you cry out so in the middle of the night? Is some man driving away your sheep against your will? Is someone killing you by force or by trickery?"

"O my friends," answered mighty Polyphemus, "No-man is killing me, by trickery and not by force."

"Well then," they said, "if no man is assaulting you, you must be sick, and sickness is heaven-sent. You'd better pray to your father, the great god Poseidon."

They left. I laughed inwardly because my name and strategem had worked. But the Cyclops, groaning and weeping from pain, rolled away the stone from the opening. Taking no chances, he sat within the gate and stretched forth his hands. As his flocks went out to graze, he felt each sheep to make certain that none of us tried to escape this way. He must have taken me for a fool! I had been casting about for some plan to save my companions and me, for the future still looked very dark. At last I hit upon this trick.

The rams were sturdy and large, with rich dark coats. I tied them in threes, putting one of my companions under each middle ram. Thus three sheep carried one man. I chose a different method for myself. I picked out the biggest and heaviest ram. I laid hold of its back and slung myself under its shaggy belly. I hung upside down, holding on to the wonderful wool. Thus we awaited the morning.

At dawn the animals rushed to the pasture. The Cyclops, still suffering greatly, felt the backs of all the sheep as they went out. The fool did not realize that my men were tied underneath the sheep. My own sturdy ram went out last, weighed down by his heavy coat and by me. Putting his hand on the ram's back, Polyphemus said, "Dear ram, why are you the last out today? You are not usually the last. You're usually first out and first back. Now you're way behind. Do you feel sorry for the loss of my eye, which a foul villain has blinded after first making me drunk? Well, No-man has not yet escaped. If you could only speak and tell me where he's hiding, I'd dash his brains out on the spot. Then and then only would I rest again."

At his last words he sent the ram away from him out of the cave. A little further on I dropped from the ram and freed my companions. We quickly drove his cattle on until we came to our ship. We who had narrowly escaped death were a welcome sight to the companions we had left aboard ship, but they began to weep for the men who had died. I gave them little time for weeping, for I ordered them to be off at once. When we were a good distance from the mainland, I couldn't resist a parting insult to Polyphemus.

"Hello there, Cyclops, you thought you had a weakling there in the cave when you murdered my companions. Your sins came home to roost, you monster. Since you didn't hesitate to eat your guests, the gods have had revenge upon you."

He was furious. He tore off the top of a large mountain and threw it in the direction of the voice. The missile landed in front of our boat and drove it back toward shore! I took a long pole and pushed powerfully, meanwhile urging my comrades to row with all their might. Soon we were twice as far away as before. I started to shout again.

My comrades tried to stop me. "Foolish man, why do you try to irritate a fierce monster? Just a moment ago he threw a huge rock into the sea and nearly brought us back to shore and our deaths. If he had heard any of us speaking, he'd have crushed us with a rock. He throws far enough."

I was too stubborn to listen. I spoke up again in my anger.

"O Cyclops, if anybody asks about that unsightly eye you have there, just say that Odysseus, destroyer of cities, son of Laertes, blinded you!"

He answered with a wail. "Alas, the old prophecies are coming true. They said I'd lose my sight through the trickery of Odysseus. I have always been expecting a strong, handsome man. Instead a puny weakling has blinded me after conquering me with wine. Come back, Odysseus, so that I can give you suitable presents. I shall urge my father, illustrious Poseidon, god of the sea, to get you back home safely. He will cure my loss of sight, if he chooses, without the help of any other gods."

"I wish I could kill you," I replied, "and send you to Hades where no one could ever cure you—not even Poseidon."

He stretched forth his hands and prayed aloud.

"Hear me, father Poseidon, see to it that Odysseus, destroyer of cities, never reaches his home. If you can't quite do that, if it is his fate to get there eventually, delay him and destroy all his companions. Arrange matters so that he finds great troubles at home."

So he prayed and his father heard him. But Polyphemus raised a much larger stone and sent it flying. This time it just missed the rudder, landing behind the ship. The sea surged up around us as the rock fell. The waves sent us forward to the little island. There we found the other ships and the rest of our comrades. They had almost given up hope, but were glad to see us. We divided the Cyclops' animals evenly. I sacrificed the ram to Zeus, but he did not listen. For as it turned out he had planned the destruction of all my ships and all my men.

We feasted throughout the whole day, and slept that night by the shore of the sea. In the morning we embarked on our ships, rejoicing at our narrow escapes and grieving at our losses.

Further Adventures

But the worst was not over. They sailed next to the isle of *Aeolus*, god of the winds. Aeolus treated Odysseus and his men hospitably. When they left, he gave them a leather bag. Inside were all the winds that might again blow Odysseus off his course. Aeolus left outside the helpful West Wind to blow the ship back to Ithaca without any possibility of a mishap.

For nine days the ships sailed onward. On the tenth day Odysseus got so close to Ithaca that he could see people on shore tending beacon fires. Overcome with weariness he at last allowed himself to take a brief nap. But the men distrusted Odysseus. They thought he was carrying home some rich treasure inside the leather bag, treasure for himself alone. Besides, they were curious to see what the bag contained. While Odysseus slept, they opened the bag, and all the winds roared forth. The ship was quickly borne away from Ithaca as the winds all contended at once. Odysseus was sick at heart, but he resolved to see it through. The winds blew the vessel back to Aeolus, but this time the god of the winds refused to help.

The ships left the island again, with no helpful wind to blow them westward to Ithaca. On the seventh day they came to the land of the *Laestrygonians*, who were not men, but giants. All of Odysseus' ships sailed into a protected harbor, but for some reason Odysseus decided to anchor his ship outside the harbor—fortunately for him. A scouting party landed and was escorted to the hall of the king, a huge, cruel monster. He snatched one of the party and proceeded to eat him. The others ran off in mad flight. The giants came to the harbor and destroyed every ship in the fleet—all except the ship of Odysseus, which was anchored outside the trap. As Homer says, "They stuck the men like fish and carried home their hideous meal."

Odysseus managed to make good his escape by cutting the anchor rope and urging the rowers to redoubled efforts. After a time they reached another island. They put in to shore and again sent out a scouting party to explore the land. Odysseus stayed by the ship with one half the remaining men. The scouting party reached the home of *Circe*, an enchantress. Around her home were wolves and lions. The beasts acted strangely—they were unusually friendly and romped around the visitors.

The men went inside—all but the leader, who sensed treachery. Circe offered the men food and drink. After they had drunk down the wine offered, she tapped them with her wand and changed them into swine. The leader, seeing this sorcery, returned to the ship grief-stricken. He refused to go back to Circe's home, so Odysseus set off alone to undo the evil, if he could.

On the way Odysseus met *Hermes* (messenger of the gods) in the guise of a young man. Hermes obligingly gave him a drug to help him resist the enchantment of Circe, and told him how to overcome the wily sorceress. Odysseus went onward to the house. He was greeted by Circe, who proceeded to give him the drugged wine. She tapped him with her magic wand, saying, "Go to the pigpen and wallow with your friends." Nothing happened. Instead, Odysseus drew his sword as though to slay her. Terrified, she agreed to disenchant the men.

Circe was as good as her bargain. She proved to be an excellent hostess. Odysseus and his men stayed on and on, forgetting about their homes. A year had elapsed before one of the men reminded Odysseus of his native land. Once reminded, Odysseus was homesick and eager to go back. He begged Circe to help him return.

Before he could return, though, he had to make a visit to the Land of the Dead to see the blind prophet *Tiresias*. With Circe's help he found the dread land. There he met the spirits of many men and women whom he had known, among them Achilles and Ajax (see page 76). Finally he found Tiresias, who told him something of the future. He warned Odysseus above all not to let his men touch the Cattle of the Sun on their journey home. If they did, disaster would be their lot. Odysseus would not get home until many years later, and would lose all his men. Besides, he would find traitors in his house seeking to marry his wife.

With these helpful warnings given by Tiresias, Odysseus returned to the island of Circe, and from there at last set out for home. Circe had given him friendly advice and had repeated the dire warning of Tiresias: "Don't touch the Cattle of the Sun."

First the ship passed the *Sirens*, nymphs whose singing had the power of luring men and ships to destruction on the rocks. Odysseus instructed his men to tie him tightly to the ship. Then he stopped the ears of his men with wax, but left his own unstopped to hear the song the Sirens sang. As they passed the rocks he felt the magnetic power of their voices. He struggled to get loose. He urged his men by cries and signs to set him free. However, they just tied him more tightly to the ship, and so they passed the rocks in safety.

The ship next had to sail past two monsters. *Scylla* was a huge six-headed monster who perched on the rocks and snatched sailors from the vessels that passed her. *Charybdis* was a huge whirlpool that bore vessels into its cavernous depths and destroyed them. Having been forewarned by Circe, Odysseus decided to face the lesser evil. Scylla would take six men. Charybdis would take all. Odysseus of course said nothing to his men. They rowed close to the rocks, keeping an anxious eye on the whirlpool. Suddenly Scylla struck. She seized six men and bore them aloft to her lair. No one could help the poor men who had been snatched as a meal for the monster.

They next reached the Island of the Sun. Here were pastured the Cattle of the Sun. Odysseus gave strict orders to his men to avoid eating the cattle. But they were stranded on the island waiting for a helpful wind. After a while their supplies got low. In desperation, in the absence of Odysseus the men slew some of the cattle and ate them. Odysseus was horrified upon his return, but the evil had been done.

Soon afterward, they sailed from the island, but a terrible storm arose. The ship was destroyed with all the crew. Only Odysseus was able to keep afloat by catching hold of portions of the ship as they were drifting by. He drifted back past Scylla and Charybdis. This time Charybdis was less formidable because Odysseus was a tiny object. His "raft" was sucked down, but he was able to hang onto an overhanging fig tree and thus wait for the whirlpool to spout up his makeshift boat.

After drifting for nine days, he reached the island of the goddess Calypso. She fell in love with him and kept him with her for many years. Finally the gods took pity on him in his homesickness and arranged for his return to Ithaca. He had to endure another shipwreck—through the hatred of Poseidon—and other adventures, but at last he reached his homeland of Ithaca.

He had been gone a total of twenty years—ten at Troy, ten during his wanderings. Many people had given him up for dead. Suitors were urging his wife Penelope to marry again. Odysseus could not reveal himself at once among these hostile strangers, so he disguised himself.

How he eventually avenged himself on the suitors and won back his throne is told excitingly in the *Odyssey*.

This outline has been sketchy to give you a taste of the book and a desire to read more. But you must read this great adventure story yourself. It has been popular for three thousand years. It has all the qualities of great imaginative literature.

Tennyson's "Ulysses"

What happened when Odysseus grew old? Was he content
to reign quietly in Ithaca, or did he yearn once again for the
open sea? The poet Tennyson had an answer. He pictured
Odysseus (here called by his Latin name *Ulysses*) chafing at
the bit, determined to set sail for whatever adventures might
lie ahead. Tennyson used Odysseus for a larger purpose: to
describe that divine discontent that occasionally plagues us
all as we wonder what lies just beyond the horizon.

The poem opens with Odysseus's thoughts, his dissatisfac-
tion with his life. Then he provides the essential clue: "I
cannot rest from travel." As he reflects back upon his rich,
adventurous life, he shows how much he has been influenced
by his experiences: "I am a part of all that I have met." But
that is not enough. The goals keep receding from him, tantalizing him to go onward. And so before his death he resolves
to push outward once again.

He recognizes his responsibilities and leaves his son Telemachus in charge of his island. Telemachus is more suited to
the task. He is different from Odysseus. As Odysseus says of
his son, "He works his work, I mine."

Then he addresses his fellow sailors and urges them to join
him in his unending quest. " 'T is not too late to seek a newer
world." No matter what happens—and there may be deadly
danger ahead—they must push on "to strive, to seek, to find,
and not to yield."

This poem, considered one of the greatest in the English
language, uses the legendary character of Odysseus to make a
profound statement about the meaning of life and one approach to its challenges.

Ulysses

It little profits that an idle king,
By this still hearth, among these barren crags,
Matched with an aged wife, I mete and dole
Unequal laws unto a savage race,
That hoard, and sleep, and feed, and know not me.
I cannot rest from travel; I will drink
Life to the lees. All times I have enjoyed
Greatly, have suffered greatly, both with those
That loved me, and alone; on shore, and when
Through scudding drifts the rainy Hyades

Vext the dim sea. I am become a name;
For alway roaming with a hungry heart
Much have I seen and known,—cities of men
And manners, climates, councils, governments,
Myself not least, but honored of them all;
And drunk delight of battle with my peers,
Far on the ringing plains of windy Troy.
I am a part of all that I have met;
Yet all experience is an arch wherethrough
Gleams that untraveled world whose margin fades
For ever and for ever when I move.
How dull it is to pause, to make an end,
To rust unburnished, not to shine in use!
As though to breathe were life! Life piled on life
Were all too little, and of one to me
Little remains; but every hour is saved
From that eternal silence, something more,
A bringer of new things; and vile it were
For some three suns to store and hoard myself,
And this gray spirit yearning in desire
To follow knowledge like a sinking star,
Beyond the utmost bound of human thought.
This is my son, mine own Telemachus,
To whom I leave the scepter and the isle—
Well-loved of me, discerning to fulfil
This labor, by slow prudence to make mild
A rugged people, and through soft degrees
Subdue them to the useful and the good.
Most blameless is he, centered in the sphere
Of common duties, decent not to fail
In offices of tenderness, and pay
Meet adoration to my household gods,
When I am gone. He works his work, I mine.
  There lies the port; the vessel puffs her sail:
There gloom the dark, broad seas. My mariners,
Souls that have toiled and wrought, and thought
      with me—
That ever with a frolic welcome took
The thunder and the sunshine, and opposed
Free hearts, free foreheads—you and I are old;
Old age hath yet his honor and his toil.

Death closes all; but something ere the end,
Some work of noble note, may yet be done,
Not unbecoming men that strove with Gods.
The lights begin to twinkle from the rocks:
The long day wanes; the slow moon climbs; the
    deep
Moans round with many voices. Come, my friends,
'T is not too late to seek a newer world.
Push off, and sitting well in order smite
The sounding furrows; for my purpose holds
To sail beyond the sunset, and the baths
Of all the western stars, until I die.
It may be that the gulfs will wash us down;
It may be we shall touch the Happy Isles,
And see the great Achilles, whom we knew.
Though much is taken, much abides; and though
We are not now that strength which in old days
Moved earth and heaven, that which we are, we are;
One equal temper of heroic hearts,
Made weak by time and fate, but strong in will
To strive, to seek, to find, and not to yield.

IV. The *Aeneid*

Background

The events of the Trojan War continued to stir the imagination of men. A great Roman poet, Vergil, found in the heroic struggle the raw materials out of which he built another of the world's great epics. The *Aeneid*, though written centuries after the *Iliad* and the *Odyssey*, is in some ways a kind of sequel. The *Iliad* tells of the war itself. The *Odyssey* tells of the difficulties experienced by one of the conquerors. The *Aeneid* tells of the adventures of one of the defeated. It throws light on what happened after the Trojans brought the Wooden Horse into their city.

Aeneas, a Trojan, is mentioned in the *Iliad* as a valiant warrior. Vergil tells of his escape and his eventual arrival in Italy. There he founded a city. His son founded another city, which became the birthplace of Romulus and Remus. Legend tells us that they founded the city of Rome.

The *Aeneid*, like the *Odyssey*, does not begin at the beginning. When the story opens, the ships of Aeneas are being tossed around by a terrible storm. Just as Odysseus had to fear the wrath of Poseidon, so Aeneas has to fear the goddess *Hera* (called in the *Aeneid* by her Latin name, Juno). At last he reaches the shores of Carthage, where he is hospitably received by *Queen Dido*. She invites him to tell the tale of his adventures. He goes back to the fall of Troy. We find out from his lips what happened after the Trojans brought the Wooden Horse into the city. Since Vergil was a Roman supposedly descended from the Trojans, his account favors the Trojan cause. A Greek hero like Odysseus (called Ulysses in the *Aeneid*) doesn't get sympathetic treatment. The following is the tale he tells.

The Fall of Troy*

O Queen, dreadful is the woe you bid me recall, how the Greeks overthrew Troy and what part I played in the story. Still if you wish to know of our disasters, I will try.

Since they had not yet conquered, the Greek leaders devised a huge wooden horse. Within the sides they put chosen soldiers. Then they retreated in their ships stealthily to the far side of an island near Troy. We thought they were gone. Troy opened wide her gate, and men went joyfully to see the deserted Greek camps. Here stayed great Achilles, they pointed out. Here were our battle lines.

Some of the Trojans wondered at the huge Wooden Horse. One counseled us to take the Horse into the city. Another urged us to destroy it at once. People took sides and argued about the Horse. Then *Laocoon*, a priest of Poseidon, ran up to us and said, "Foolish men, are you mad? Do you think that the foe has gone? Do you think any Greek gift is free of treachery? Don't you know Odysseus? Either there are Greeks hidden inside the Horse, or else it has been designed in some other way to destroy us. Don't trust the Horse. I fear the Greeks even when bearing gifts."

After he had spoken he hurled his spear straight at the side of the Horse. The spear quivered, and the Horse sounded hollow. At this moment we might have destroyed the Horse on the spot, and Troy would still be standing. Just then some shepherds dragged before us

* Abridged and adapted from the *Aeneid*, Book Two.

a Greek captive with his hands tied behind his back. This was all part of the Greek plan.

The people jeered at the captive, but he cried out, "Alas, where can I go now? I have no place among the Greeks, and now the Trojans are crying for my blood."

The jeers died down, and we encouraged him to speak.

"I'll tell the truth," he said, "in everything. I admit I'm a Greek, *Sinon* by name. When the Greeks, tired of war, sought to leave Troy behind, a storm always arose to thwart them. The oracle declared that a Greek life must be sacrificed before the winds would abate. Through the evil plotting of Odysseus, I was chosen for the sacrifice. In terror I broke my bonds and hid until the ships at last departed. Now I have no longer any hope of seeing my home, my children, or my father. I beg you to pity these woes so great."

We yielded at his tears and let him live. Priam himself ordered the bonds to be removed and addressed him with gentle words: "Whoever you are, from now on forget the Greeks. You are one of us. Now answer my next question truthfully. Why did the Greeks build this monstrous steed? What was their aim? Is this an engine of war?"

The other replied craftily, "May the gods be my witness: Once Athena favored the Greek cause, but she turned from the Greeks after some of their outrages. This image has been built to appease the goddess. It has been built tall so that you may not be able to drag it into the city. If you succeed in taking it into the city, great success will come to the Trojan cause."

So we were tricked by the lying and treachery of Sinon, we who had not been destroyed in ten years' war with the mighty Achilles against us. Then another sight helped convince us. Laocoon, who was priest of Poseidon, was making customary sacrifices when two huge snakes slithered out of the sea. They made for Laocoon. First they coiled about his two little children and then about Laocoon himself, and killed them. At their death we were all terrified. Men said that Laocoon had been punished for throwing his spear at the image. We cried out that the image must be drawn into the city. We broke down the walls and laid open our defenses. We put rollers under the Horse and dragged it into the city. Boys and girls sang and happily assisted in the task. It moved along and glided into the middle of the town—O native land, O Troy renowned in war! Four times in the gateway it stopped and armor rang inside it. Yet we stupidly pushed it on. We decorated the shrines of gods on this day

that would be our last. Meanwhile night came on. The Trojans went to bed wearied from their exertions.

At this moment the Greek fleet was sailing back to Troy. It easily found those familiar shores. Sinon stealthily let free the Greeks inside the Horse. They streamed out, Odysseus and the rest. They rushed upon the sleeping city. The watchmen were cut down. At the open gates they welcomed all their comrades and united their bands.

In my sleep Hector seemed to come to me, deep in grief and shedding many tears. He appeared as he did when he had been torn by Achilles' chariot, his swollen feet pierced with the thongs. How different he looked from the conquering Hector of other days. Weeping, I seemed to address him mournfully, "O light of Troy! O surest hope of the Trojans! What has kept you from us? From what place have you come, Hector our desire? With what weary eyes I see you, after many of your kin have died? Why do I see these wounds?"

To these questions Hector made no reply, but groaning he said, "Fly at once and rescue yourself from these flames. The enemy holds our walls. Troy is falling. Your country and Priam ask no more of you. If our towers could have been defended by strength of hand, this hand too would have defended them. Take with you Troy's household gods. Seek to find another city far over the seas which you shall at last establish."

Meanwhile the city was in agonized confusion. The noises grew clearer, and the clash of armor swelled. I aroused myself from sleep and climbed to the roof, listening. The situation was clear. The treachery of the Greeks was apparent. Already the house of Deiphobus had crashed in flames. The bay was lit with the fire. The night was split by the cries of men and the blare of trumpets. I madly seized my arms, but there did not seem to be much purpose in arms. My spirit was on fire to gather a fighting band about me and charge for the citadel with my comrades. Rage drove me on as I thought how noble it is to die in battle.

Then I met *Panthus*, priest of Apollo, as he came rushing toward the gates, taking his grandchild by the hand. "How stands Troy, O Panthus?" I asked. "What stronghold can we occupy to make a stand?"

As I finished he said to me, groaning, "The end has come for Troy. The city and the glory of the Trojans are no more. The Greeks are lords of the burning town. The Horse, towering in the middle of the city, is pouring forth armed men. Sinon scatters firebrands, insolent in his victory. Some of the Greeks are at the gates. Others are surging through the narrow streets, with drawn swords ready for the slaughter. The guards at the gates scarcely give battle."

I rushed out into the midst of the tumult. Some of my comrades gathered round me. Seeing them ready for battle, I cried out, "Men, you see what has happened to Troy. All the gods have abandoned us. Though the cause is lost, let us attack the enemy and die in the attempt. There is no safety for a conquered people."

So they were roused to fight. We made our way straight into the town and the weapons of our enemies. Who can tell the horror of that night or measure the grief in tears? The old city fell after her long years of power. Corpses lay all about the streets, houses, and temples. But it was not only the Trojans who fell. Courage returned to conquered hearts, and victorious Greeks died, too. Cruel agony was everywhere, with terror and death.

We first met a troop of Greek invaders. Mistaking us for an allied band, the leader said, "Hurry, men. Why are you delaying? Others have been plundering and burning, and you're just coming into the battle."

As he finished speaking, he realized he had fallen among the foe. He drew back in amazement as a man might who had suddenly stepped on a snake. But it was too late. We rushed upon the terror-stricken Greeks, surrounded them, and cut them down. One of our men, flushed with success, cried, "Let us exchange shields and dress ourselves in the Greek armor."

He picked up the plumed helmet of one of the Greeks and put it on. Then he took the rest of the armor. My other men did likewise. We advanced and mingled with the Greeks. We killed many a Greek that night. Some ran off to the ships. Others in cowardly terror climbed into the Horse for safety.

Then came tragedy. *Cassandra*, daughter of Priam, was being dragged off from the temple of Athena. We charged the Greek captors. Then our people mistook us for Greeks and fired upon us from the temple roof. There was great slaughter among us—by the weapons of our own people. Then the Greeks attacked us too and fell on us from every side, the whole Greek army it seemed. We fell, overwhelmed by numbers. One after another of my comrades died.

A few of us tore ourselves away to help defend Priam's house. Here the fight was raging most fiercely. The Greeks were attacking in force. They had thrown ladders upon the walls and were trying to overrun the house, their shields held up for protection. The Trojan defenders threw down upon them towers and pinnacles of the house, for they realized the end had come. But even at the last they defended themselves. We renewed our resolve to aid the royal dwelling and increase the numbers of the defenders.

There was a blind passageway through Priam's halls. Through this, while Troy still stood, poor Hector's wife would often go to her father-in-law's house with her little son. But now *Pyrrhus*, the son of Achilles, stood before the doorway, with many of the Greeks around him. He grasped an ax and burst through the doorway. He wrenched the bronze-plated doors from the hinges. The house within was open to sight. The halls lay open to the invaders. Armed men stood in front of the doorway.

Inside all was confusion. The court echoed with shrieks and the wailing of women. Fearful mothers wandered about the house and clung to the doors, kissing them. But no barriers could hold out. With his father's strength Pyrrhus pressed on. The passage was forced. The Greeks poured through the entrance, slaughtering those they met. It was like a broken dike. I myself saw Pyrrhus raging with slaughter. The Greeks were now in complete possession of Troy.

What of the fate of Priam? When he saw his city in ruins, the gates of his house broken open, and the enemy inside the palace, he put upon his trembling shoulders his long-forgotten armor. He advanced upon his enemy. His wife and daughters tried to stop him. "What madness, poor husband, has moved you to put on armor and weapons? Where are you going? Not even Hector could save us now. Come back here to the altar. The altar will protect us, or you will share our death." So saying, his wife drew the old man back to the holy altar.

One of Priam's children had escaped from Pyrrhus and came flying down the empty halls. Pyrrhus was pursuing him fiercely, his spear poised. As the boy reached his parents' side, he fell dead in a pool of blood. At this, Priam, though close to death, did not spare a cry of wrath.

"May the gods punish you for this crime and give you the reward you deserve—you who made me see my son's murder. You are not like your father Achilles. He respected an old man's prayers. He restored to me the body of Hector and returned me safely to Troy."

As he finished, the old man hurled his weak spear. But Pyrrhus said mockingly, "Take the message directly to my father, then. Tell him of my evil deeds. Now die."

As he spoke he dragged Priam to the altar and plunged his sword to the hilt in Priam's side. Thus ended Priam's fortunes. Thus his destiny was to see Troy destroyed, her towers sunken before his eyes. The great corpse lay along the shore, beheaded, a body without a name.

Then terror gripped me. I saw in my imagination my own father treated as Priam had been. I thought of my wife, my son, my plundered house. I looked around to see what forces had remained in the struggle. Everyone had given up and jumped to the ground or into the fire. Only I was left.

Then I saw Helen, crouching unseen at the altars. She was terrified of both Greeks and Trojans. I resolved to kill her, the cause of our disasters. I vowed she would never see her own country again, there to be waited upon by Trojan captives. As I advanced in fury, my goddess mother Aphrodite appeared to me and stopped me.

"Son," she said as she caught me by the hand, "Why are you raging so? Think first of your old father, your wife and your child. If I had not helped them, they would long ago have been slaughtered by the Greeks. Don't blame Helen or Paris for the fall of Troy. The gods themselves are to blame. Let me take away the veil from your mortal sight. See how the gods themselves are engaged in tearing down Troy. Hurry away, my son, and end your flight. I will never desert you. I will set you safe in the courts of your father's house."

I saw Troy sinking in flame, falling as an old ash tree might fall when hacked around by axes. It nodded, trembled, and then toppled with one last groan. With the help of my goddess mother I reached home safely. When I reached my house, I found my father. He wished to stay on to die in Troy rather than to prolong his life in exile.

"Your blood is at the prime," he cried. "*You* take flight. If the gods had wished to prolong my life, they'd have preserved my home. We have seen enough devastation, we survivors of a captured city. Say good-by to me. My own hand will bring me death. I am too old to keep living."

My wife and son—all of us—urged him to come away, but he refused. I once again resolved to rush into battle and choose death. What else could I do? I could not leave my father. "Was it for this, O goddess, you saved me from fire and sword—to see my father, wife, and son butchered in one another's blood? To arms, my men, to arms! Return me to the Greeks. We shall not perish unavenged."

As I was putting on my armor, my wife clung to my feet and held up my little son. "If you go to die, take us too. But if there is any hope in arms, make this household our rampart. What have I left, I who was once called your wife?"

She shrieked and filled all the house with her weeping. Suddenly there was an amazing and wonderful sign. A light seemed to play about the head of my son, and it did not burn him. In fright we tried to put out the holy fires with water. But my father cried out, "All-powerful Zeus, if you do relent at prayers, look upon us this once. Give us a sign to confirm this omen."

No sooner had he spoken than it thundered on the left. There was a falling star, too, in the dusk. My father was at last convinced. "No more delay. I'll follow. I'll go where you lead, gods of my fathers. Save my house and my grandchild. My son, I no longer refuse to go with you."

As he spoke the fires were roaring nearer. "Get up on my shoulders, dear father. I shall never carry a more precious burden. No matter how matters fall, we shall stay together. My son will come along with me. My wife will follow. You of my household, listen to what I have to say. There is an old temple outside the city near an ancient cypress tree. We shall all meet there. You, my father, carry the sacred things and the statues of our gods. Since I have just come from desperate battle and slaughter, I will not handle them until I have washed in a living stream."

As I finished, I spread over my neck and shoulders a lion skin. I stooped to pick up my burden. My little son put his hand into mine, and my wife followed. I was uneasy and terrified at every noise, fearing for my companion and my burden. And now as I neared the gates and safety, we heard the trampling of feet. My father, looking back into the darkness, cried, "My son, my son, faster; they are coming closer. I can see the gleam of their shields."

In my hurry and confusion I avoided the beaten path. Alas, I have never seen my beloved wife since that moment. When we reached the mound, I found that my wife had disappeared. I left my son and my father with the men and rushed back into the city, girded in my armor. I retraced my footsteps, and I was dismayed at the silence. I went back to our own home on the chance that she might have gone back. The Greeks had poured into it. I revisited the citadel and Priam's home. The Greeks were everywhere guarding the spoils. Boys and fearful women stood around.

I even dared to cry aloud her name through the empty streets, but there was no reply. Then as I sought her in vain, her spirit appeared to me. I tried to speak, but my voice was choked in my throat. Then she spoke to me and helped to quiet my distress.

"What good is this mad grief, my dear husband? This hasn't

happened without divine interference, I am not fated to go with you into exile. Your wanderings will be long and hard, but at last you will come to a land in the west where the river Tiber flows through rich and populous fields. Prosperity awaits you there, as well as a kingdom and a king's daughter for your wife. Don't weep for me. At least I shall never be a slave in the proud homes of the Greeks. And now, good-by; continue to love our child."

After she had spoken to me, she dissolved into air. Three times I tried to put my arms around her; three times the spirit I tried to hold fled out of my arms. And so at last, I went back to my comrades.

Here I found a great many of my people just come together, ready for exile—truly a pitiful crowd. They had come from all over, ready to follow me wherever I led. Putting my father upon my shoulders, I left with them and sought the mountains.

Thus ended this part of Aeneas' story.

Aeneas and Rome

At last, after many preparations, the Trojans put to sea. They wandered about from place to place. One famous adventure was with the Harpies, disgusting birds with the heads of girls and clawed hands. As the Trojans sat down to eat on one of the islands, the Harpies swept down upon the table and picked up the meat. Aeneas and his men struck at the Harpies with their swords, but they were too agile. Besides, their feathers were as hard as steel. The Trojans left in a hurry.

They had other adventures. They passed the cave of Polyphemus the Cyclops (page 78), now blind. He waded out toward their ships, and they left very promptly. The wanderers were able to avoid the twin terrors of Scylla and Charybdis. A storm arose through the malice of Hera (still prejudiced against the Trojans for the judgment of Paris), but at last the wanderers reached Carthage safely.

At Carthage they were entertained by Queen Dido, to whom Aeneas told his tale as described above. The wanderers spent many pleasant months at Carthage. Dido fell in love with Aeneas, and he seemed to return her affection. But Zeus was displeased at the turn of events. He sent Hermes to Aeneas to recall his high destiny, and command him to resume the voyage.

Aeneas departed despite Dido's urgent pleas. After he had gone, she built a funeral pyre, killed herself, and was consumed in the flames. From his ship Aeneas saw the flames above the city. Though he did not know the reason for the flames, he had an inkling of the tragedy.

Aeneas reached Italy at last. His troubles were by no means over. He had to make a visit to the Land of the Dead to see the shade of his father, who had died soon after leaving Troy. He found this Land with the help of Sibyl, a prophetess. The description of the Land of the Dead is famous. There Aeneas met, among others, the old ferryman Charon, the three-headed dog Cerberus, and the shade of poor Dido. She did not answer his pleadings to speak. He saw too some of the infernal tortures for those who had sinned. Ixion, Sisyphus, and Tantalus were there at their eternal labors. Then he came to the blessed lands, the Elysian Fields, where the virtuous dead stay. He saw his father, who told him that some souls have to be reborn after the memories of their former lives are washed away by the waters of Lethe. His father told him, too, of the battles still to be fought before the state would be founded. From this state would rise the power of Rome, the ruler of the world.

The rest of the *Aeneid* tells of the battles before Aeneas finally is established as a king of Italy. He is to win the hand of the princess *Lavinia*, but she has been sought in marriage by many of the neighboring princes. Foremost among the suitors is *Turnus*, king of one of the Italian peoples. Turnus contests Aeneas' claim, and there is war. At last the two warriors meet in hand-to-hand combat, and Turnus is slain. The *Aeneid* ends with the death of Turnus, but tradition says that the son of Aeneas founded the city that became the birthplace of Romulus and Remus, founders of Rome.

READING FOR UNDERSTANDING

Main Idea

1. Which of the following best expresses the main idea of this unit? (a) Achilles was a greater hero than Odysseus. (b) Tales of the Trojan War have had a great influence on Western literature. (c) Among the Trojans, Hector was the outstanding example of courage and chivalry. (d) Though there have been doubters in the past, Achilles actually existed.

Details

2. On his journey homeward Odyessus met all the following EX-CEPT (a) Circe (b) Calypso (c) the Cyclops (d) the Trojan Horse.
3. Helen's Greek husband was named (a) Menelaus (b) Agamemnon (c) Paris (d) Ajax.
4. The Trojan War lasted for (a) several months (b) a year (c) five years (d) ten years.
5. When he left Troy, Aeneas carried on his shoulders (a) his son (b) his father (c) his wife (d) Priam.
6. Two heroes who tried trickery to avoid joining the expedition against Troy were (a) Achilles and Odysseus (b) Ajax and Agamemnon (c) Patroclus and Achilles (d) Pyrrhus and Ajax.

Inferences

7. Odysseus was able to escape destruction at the hands of Polyphemus by (a) superior strength (b) pure luck (c) trickery (d) cowardice.
8. The cause of Dido's death was (a) illness (b) wound in battle (c) disappointment in love (d) an accident.
9. During the Trojan War the gods and goddesses (a) played favorites on both sides (b) all favored the Greeks (c) all favored the Trojans (d) took no part.
10. On several occasions Odysseus came to grief because (a) Tiresias hated him (b) his men disobeyed him (c) he was a poor sailor (d) his ship was not seaworthy.

WORDS IN CONTEXT

1. These "innocent tourists" became fighters who *undermined* the resistance of the loyal Norwegian army.
   Undermined (page 61) means (a) aroused suddenly (b) studied intensely (c) feared unreasonably (d) weakened by degrees.
2. In *despoiling* one of the cities neighboring Troy, Agamemnon had taken captive a young girl.
   Despoiling (65) means (a) visiting (b) bypassing (c) plundering (d) communicating with.
3. Men huddled together like fawns, wiping off the sweat and drinking to *slake* their thirst.
   Slake (67) means (a) increase (b) quench (c) forget (d) reveal.

4., 5. The old man groaned and raised his hands in *supplication* to his son, who stood eagerly awaiting the *onslaught* of Achilles.

    Supplication (67) means (a) horror (b) pleading (c) terror (d) signaling.

    Onslaught (67) means (a) vigorous attack (b) quiet arrival (c) unexpected appearance (d) insult.

6. "If I do retreat within the walls, my friend Polydamas will be the first to *reproach* me."

    Reproach (68) means (a) greet (b) praise (c) ignore (d) blame.

7. Achilles drew close to him, his terrifying spear *brandished* above his right shoulder.

    Brandished (68) means (a) waved menacingly (b) poised quietly (c) carried fearfully (d) perched unsteadily.

8. Meanwhile Achilles drove Hector on *relentlessly*.

    Relentlessly (69) means (a) encouragingly (b) with periods of rest (c) without yielding (d) in a spirit of friendly competition.

9. Achilles *contrived* to keep himself between Hector and the city.

    Contrived (69) means (a) walked with determination (b) planned cleverly (c) hoped (d) shouted.

10. Achilles sought with his eye some *vulnerable* spot on the body of Hector.

    Vulnerable (72) means (a) unprotected (b) clearly visible (c) injured (d) colorful.

11. "As for my death, I am ready for it whenever Zeus and the other gods are minded to *bestow* it."

    Bestow (72) means (a) discuss (b) postpone (c) withhold (d) give.

12. The women *thronged* around her and held her.

    Thronged (74) means (a) cried (b) talked (c) crowded (d) walked.

13. He agreed also to a truce during which the rites for Hector might be *solemnized*.

    Solemnized (75) means (a) performed with ceremony (b) planned in advance (c) discussed in a forthright way (d) given over to a later time.

14. The war plumes are a symbol of the *devastation* to follow.

    Devastation (75) means (a) events (b) successes (c) quiet times (d) destruction.

15. That sympathy is a tribute to Homer's *impartiality* in telling his tale.

     Impartiality (76) means (a) wisdom (b) skill (c) fairness (d) fame.

16. We could never have moved the stone from the cavern's opening. *Despondently* we waited for morning.

     Despondently (79) means (a) confidently (b) hopelessly (c) expectantly (d) eagerly.

17. As he said this, he *lurched* over and fell upon his back.

     Lurched (80) means (a) leaned to one side (b) recovered an upright position (c) turned his head slightly (d) danced nimbly.

18. He became ill in his drunken *stupor*.

     Stupor (80) means (a) laughter (b) dream (c) daze (d) rage.

19. He drew the stake from his eye and threw it with an *anguished* cry from his hands.

     Anguished (80) means (a) very loud (b) tormented (c) ugly (d) unsympathetic.

20. Hermes told him how to overcome the *wily* sorceress.

     Wily (84) means (a) beautiful (b) homely (c) pleasant (d) crafty.

21. "When the Greeks sought to leave Troy behind, a storm always arose to *thwart* them."

     Thwart (90) means (a) successfully oppose (b) deceitfully encourage (c) enthusiastically assist (d) wickedly arouse.

22. "This image has been built to *appease* the goddess."

     Appease (90) means (a) anger (b) forget (c) pacify (d) invite.

23. The Trojan defenders threw down upon them towers and *pinnacles* of the house.

     Pinnacles (93) means (a) windows (b) shutters (c) shingles (d) spires.

24. "If there is any hope in arms, make this household our *rampart*."

     Rampart (95) means (a) attack (b) protective barrier (c) sword (d) battering ram.

25. Aeneas and his men struck at the Harpies with their swords, but they were too *agile*.

     Agile (97) means (a) swift (b) powerful (c) funny (d) unsightly.

THINKING IT OVER

1. Which of the heroes was your own particular favorite? Why? Which had the qualities you most admire?

2. Life is never simple, and a person's character can never be easily summed up. Everyone is a different person to different people. The three epics demonstrate this truth. How, for example, does Achilles seem to the Greeks? To the Trojans? In what way is his son Pyrrhus like him?

3. Epics have remained popular through the ages because they deal with universal human emotions. Prove this statement by referring to one of the excerpts read.

4. Odysseus gave his name to the epic the *Odyssey*. Aeneas gave his name to the epic the *Aeneid*. Should the *Iliad* really have been called the *Achillead*? Present your point of view.

5. All three epics are filled with exciting events. Things happen. The narrative thread is strong in all three. There are great character studies, but there is always a good story to move things along. Do you look for good stories in the books you read? Tell about your preferences.

SUGGESTED ACTIVITIES

1. Here is a list of some of the world's great epics:

   Gilgamesh (Babylonian)
   the *Ramayana* (Indian)
   the *Kalevala* (Finnish)
   the *Shah-Namah* (Persian)
   the *Mahabharata* (Sanskrit)
   the *Lusiad* (Portuguese)
   Beowulf (Early English)
   the *Nibelungenlied* (German)
   Chanson de Roland (French)

   The epics themselves may make for hard reading, but there are many books about them.

   Choose one of the listed epics and prepare a report telling something about the epic and the major characters. Instead of finding the epic itself, you may consult a book that describes the adventures of the epic's hero.

   The distinction is often made between folk epics like *Beowulf* and literary epics like the *Aeneid*. One of the most famous literary epics is John Milton's *Paradise Lost*. This might be included with the foregoing.

2. Read Chapter IV in *The Wonder Book of Travellers' Tales* by H.C. Adams for a discussion of how the wonders in the *Odyssey* can be explained rationally. Ernle Bradford's *Ulysses Found* tries to identify places in the *Odyssey* with actual places in the known world. Michael Wood's *In Search of the Trojan War* does the same for the *Iliad*. Wood's book was dramatized in a television series.

3. You might enjoy drawing a map of Odysseus's wanderings and tracing his route through the known world and the world of fantasy. The Herbert Bates verse translation of the *Odyssey* has a helpful map, as does the prose translation by Henry I. Christ.

4. Report to your class on one of these persons famous in the Trojan cycle.

Agamemnon	Iphigenia
Ajax	Menelaus
Diomedes	Paris
Helen	Priam

5. Some of the great Greek tragedies are based on events during and after the Trojan War. The three greatest writers of tragedy all tried their hand. Aeschylus created three such plays: *Agamemnon*, the *Choephoroe*, and the *Eumenides*. These three plays became the basis of Eugene O'Neill's *Mourning Becomes Electra*. Sophocles wrote *Philoctetes*, about the archer who slew Paris. Euripides wrote *The Trojan Women*, a bitter play about the aftermath of the war.

Three persons might report to the class about these great writers at the dawn of Western literature.

WORDS ASSOCIATED WITH THE TROJAN WAR

Word	Definition	Named for
Achilles' heel	point of weakness	Achilles, who was unprotected only in his heel
Achilles' tendon	tendon joining calf muscles to heel bone	Achilles
Cassandra	one who predicts disaster	daughter of Priam, destined never to be believed
Cerberus	a vigilant, ill-tempered guardian	Cerberus, many-headed dog, guardian of Hades

WORDS ASSOCIATED WITH THE TROJAN WAR *(Cont.)*

Word	Definition	Named for
sop to Cerberus	bribe	Cerberus
Circe	sorceress	Circe, enchantress visited by Odysseus
cyclopean	huge	the Cyclopes, giants described in the *Odyssey*
hector	to bully	son of Priam, whose name was taken by a gang of bullies in England
Helen of Troy	a beautiful woman	woman taken to Troy by Paris
lethargy	drowsiness, inactivity	Lethe, river in Hades, the river of forgetfulness
lotus-eater	lazy person	Lotus-eaters in *Odyssey* (page 77)
mentor	trusted counselor	teacher of Telemachus, son of Odysseus
myrmidons	loyal followers	soldiers in Achilles' band
nestor	respected leader	wise counselor at Troy
between Scylla and Charybdis	choice between two dangers	two dangers on Odysseus's voyage home
siren	beautiful temptress	singers in *Odyssey* who sang fatal songs
sibyl	female prophet	prophetess who helped Aeneas
Trojan horse	someone or something that betrays from within	the Trojan Horse that caused the fall of Troy

UNIT · FOUR

Norse Myths

Saturn, Roman god of agriculture, gave his name to Saturday. Sunday and Monday are, of course, the days of the *sun* and the *moon*. But what of the other days of the week? There, embedded in our everyday speech, are names from mythology—not Greek or Roman this time, but Norse.

The roots of Norse mythology go back into prehistory, to the Bronze Age. The joys and triumphs, anxieties and defeats of those ancient people found their way into the fascinating stories that have come down to us. From the art that has been discovered, we know that the two major concerns of the Bronze Age people were fertility and the sea. Their lives depended upon the fertility of their crops and animals, as well as the survival of their children. And there was always the sea.

Dark and brooding, the sea always beckoned. Much of the food was harvested from the sea. But the seas nearby were not enough. The Norse began to look beyond. After the Romans abandoned Britain, the Norse invaders began pouring ashore in waves. They didn't stop with Britain. Fierce marauders from Denmark, Norway, Sweden, and northern Germany sailed through the known world, even to the distant ports of the Mediterranean. These were superb fighters, used to hardship, and often merciless in battle. After a time they liked what they saw and began settling in conquered lands. The original Celtic inhabitants of Britain were pushed westward, as the hordes of invaders settled in the fertile east. The Norse left an indelible mark on the culture, the people, and the language of what is now Great Britain.

How did Norse mythology come down to us? The only surviving written statements are short inscriptions on wood, stone, bone, or metal. These inscriptions are written in runic characters, a special kind of alphabet. They are difficult to interpret because they are are so short and compact. There was also an oral tradition preserved by the *skalds*, the poets of ancient Scandinavia. Paintings and sculpture provide other

clues. Most of the myths, however, were written down and
preserved only *after* the arrival of Christianity,

We are indebted to two scholars for the survival of most of
what we know about Norse mythology. In the twelfth century
Saxo Grammaticus included many Norse myths in the first six
books of his history of Denmark. The second writer was
Snorri Sturluson, an Icelandic poet and historian. We owe our
greatest debt to him, for about the year 1220 he created a
handbook for poets. He retold the old myths with affection
and understanding. His enthusiasm for the task shines
through his work. But he was writing more than 200 years
after Christianity was accepted in Iceland. There are many
unsolved problems in Norse mythology. Even Snorri Sturluson couldn't provide all the answers.

Still we are left with a rich legend of magic and ritual, of
hearty narrative and interesting characters. We may have lost
a great deal, but we have a treasure house of inspiration for
poets and opera composers, for novelists and readers. Perhaps
some of the Norse gods are merely extensions of great kings
and military leaders. No matter. Thor, god of thunder, still
awes us by his exploits. Loki, mischief-maker of the gods, still
angers and fascinates us by his trickery.

I. Differences Between Greek-Roman and Norse Myths

There are many ways in which Norse mythology is similar
to that of the Greeks, but there are many points of difference,
too. The Greeks lived in a warm climate, under sunny skies;
nature, to them, appeared genial and generous. The Norse
lived in a cold land, where the winter nights seem endless and
the summers are brief and fleeting; the nature they knew
appeared cheerless and meager, something hard and stern, an
enemy to be mastered only by ceaseless struggle. In view of
their environment, it is not surprising that their mythology is
filled with references to *mist, cold,* and *ice.* The very tree of
life in Norse mythology sinks one root into Niflheim, land of
dreary cold, often identified with the land of the dead.

All peoples tend to ask the same questions. How was the
world formed? Who created life? Who controls the swing of
the seasons? The answers have a certain similarity in different
cultures, but the differences are significant. When the cultures
are widely separated, the differences are more pronounced.

Because the Greeks and Romans intermingled, their cultures blended. The Romans, for example, associated their war god Mars with the Greek Ares, and the two have become almost indistinguishable. For tantalizing comparisons we may associate the Norse god Odin with Zeus, but the resemblance is not as close as that of Jupiter and Zeus. The Norse, in their more isolated northern haunts, had little opportunity to assimilate the classical deities. Their mythology was ultimately transformed by Christianity, rather than by the myths of Greece and Rome.

All the myths so far mentioned do have one important element in common. They have influenced Western literature and provided allusions that have enriched our thought and language.

II. The Beginning of the World

"How did it all start?" Most people cannot help asking this question when they look into the night sky. The Norse were no exceptions. Like the Greeks and other peoples, they wondered about the creation of the world. The explanation they gave is not unlike the one in Greek mythology—but it's much colder! In the beginning, they said, there was only an empty space, to the north of which lay a region of mist, ice, and snow, and to the south a region of warmth and sunlight. Out of the mist formed by the continual interaction between warm air from the south and the ice and snow sprang the huge *Ymir*, ancestor of the frost giants. He was furnished nourishment by a giant cow, which had been created at the same time and in the same way. The great cow obtained her nourishment by licking the frost from the ice all around her.

One day, while the cow was thus engaged, the hair of a being appeared on the spot she was licking with her great tongue. Then appeared the head and finally the whole body. This was a god, *Buri*, from whom were ultimately descended, through marriage with the daughter of a giant, the great gods *Odin*, *Vili*, and *Ve*. These three slew the giant Ymir, and from his body they formed the earth, to be the abode of human beings. From Ymir's flesh they made earth; from his blood they formed the seas. From his bones came the mountains; from his hair, the trees; from his skull, the heavens; and from his brain, the clouds. With Ymir's eyebrows the gods built a fence around the earth. They called the new world *Midgard*, because it was halfway between the land of frost and the land of sun.

Odin, Vili, and Ve also slew all of Ymir's descendants except one, who, with his wife, escaped to *Jotunheim*, the land of the giants. In Jotunheim grew up a new race of frost giants, implacable and evil enemies of the gods. Odin, Vili, and Ve (corresponding, roughly to Jupiter, Neptune, and Pluto) became rulers of the heavens and earth. Odin, like Jupiter, became the supreme ruler. It was he who determined upon the alternation of day and night and placed the sun and the moon in the sky. From the source of fire he took bright sparks and placed them in the sky as stars.

The gods then created two mortals to inhabit and enjoy Midgard. From a piece of elm they created the first woman, *Embla*; from an ashen spar they created the first man, *Aske*. These were the parents of the human race. From the flesh of Ymir came also many nonhuman creatures to live in Midgard: dwarfs, trolls, gnomes, fairies, and elves.

To support the universe Odin created *Yggdrasil*, the great tree of life and of time. The huge tree sank one root down into Niflheim, the land of the dead. A second root was in Midgard; and a third in Asgard, land of the gods. Thus the tree bound together all parts of the universe.

To get to Asgard the gods had to cross the rainbow bridge, Bifrost. Only the god Thor was forbidden to use the bridge, for it was feared that his heavy tread might destroy the span. The watchman of the gods, *Heimdall*, kept guard over the bridge day and night to keep the giants from crossing. Heimdall hardly ever slept, and he could see by night as clearly as he could by day. His sense of hearing was so keen that he could even hear the grass grow, or the wool on a sheep's back.

Asgard was filled with great palaces, of which the most magnificent was Odin's Valhalla. It was to this palace that the souls of dead warriors came. Since the Norse glorified warfare, they believed that those who died in battle would be borne immediately to Valhalla (which means "the hall of the slain"). The Valkyrie, maiden attendants of the gods (their name means "choosers of the slain"), carried the fallen warriors to their new home in the sky. In their Valhalla, the warriors fought one another all day. At night, their wounds were miraculously healed and they banqueted in preparation for another day's fighting. This was the Norse idea of heaven.

III. The Great Gods

Odin, as we have seen, was the supreme god of all. He was the god of wisdom and culture, of battle and victory, and also of the dead. As he sat on his throne in Valhalla, two ravens, Thought and Memory, perched on his shoulders. Each day they flew over the whole world and at night reported to him what they had seen and heard.

Everything associated with Odin was on a grand scale. Valhalla itself had five hundred and forty doors, each one wide enough for eight hundred warriors to pass through shoulder to shoulder. Every piece of furniture in Valhalla was made of silver or gold.

When Odin sent the Valkyrie to Midgard for warriors slain in battle, the shields of these warrior maidens produced great bright lights in the sky—the Aurora Borealis. When Odin took an active part in war himself, he rode his eight-footed gray steed, Sleipnir, and held aloft his marvelous spear, which never missed its mark. When Odin went out to hunt, especially in autumn and winter, the winds swept across the barren plains of Midgard.

Odin's wife, *Frigga,* was a counterpart of Juno in some ways. Like Juno she was the goddess of marriage and the special protectress of women. It is said that she invited to her hall after their death all husbands and wives who had dearly loved each other on earth. There they could live together until the end of time. And like Juno she occasionally outwitted her majestic husband, especially when her favorites among the mortals were concerned. She is often identified with *Eastre,* goddess of spring. It is this goddess who has given her name to our own *Easter,* although the holy day has taken on much wider significance.

Thor, the god of thunder and of strength, and a son of Odin, was one of the most important of all the Norse gods. His famous hammer had the miraculous property of always returning to his hand, no matter how far away he threw it. His wife was the golden-haired *Sif.* It was the theft of her hair that oddly enough gave the hammer to Thor—but more of that later.

Tiu was the god of courage and war, very much like Mars in some ways. He is usually ranked next to Odin and Thor in importance. His sword was a terrible and infallible weapon, like Odin's shield and spear, and Thor's hammer.

Freya was the goddess of beauty and love, best beloved of

all the goddesses. She corresponds to Venus in Roman mythology. Love songs were composed in her honor; lovers addressed their prayers to her; music, springtime, and flowers
were sacred to her. Her brother, *Frey*, was a god of fertility, of
rain and sunshine, and of all the fruits of the earth.

Vidar, Bragi, Balder, and *Hoder* were Thor's brothers, sons of
Odin. Vidar was next in strength to Thor. He was a silent god,
a personification of the quiet forests. Bragi was a god of
poetry. He sang the deeds of Midgard's foremost warriors.
(Bragi's wife, *Iduna*, was in charge of the golden apples of
immortality.) Whenever the gods felt old age approaching,
they had only to taste one of the golden apples and they were
young again. Balder the Good, the god of spring, of gladness,
and of light, was the best beloved of all the gods. To look
upon Balder was to experience divinity. His twin brother
Hoder was gloomy, silent, and blind. He was the god of winter, of gloom and darkness.

Loki is usually listed among the Norse gods, but many
legends say he was really a member of the demon race. Certainly, if we judge by his nature, he did not belong among the
other gods. He was a mischief-maker, in many ways a personification of evil. Although handsome, he was fickle and unreli-
able. His three offspring were the wolf *Fenris*, the *Midgard
Serpent*, and *Hela*, or Death. The gods tried to chain the monstrous Fenris, but he broke every chain as though it were
made of flimsy cord. Finally, the mountain spirits made a
chain that could hold him. It was composed of insubstantial
things, like the footfall of a cat, the roots of stones, and the
breath of fishes. The Midgard Serpent was cast into the ocean.
It was so large that it encircled the earth and the lashing of
its tail caused great tempests and sea storms. Hela was given
rule over Niflheim, the land of the dead—the home of mortals
unfortunate enough to die a natural death away from the field
of battle. These three—Fenris, the Midgard Serpent, and
Hela—will be mentioned again later, for it will be seen that
they helped to bring about the destruction of the gods.

The influence of those Norse invaders is reflected in the
English words *Tuesday, Wednesday, Thursday*, and *Friday*.
Tuesday is "Tiu's day." Wednesday is "Woden's day." Woden
is an alternate spelling for Odin. Thursday is "Thor's day."
Friday is "Freya's day." Mediterranean people, who were less
affected by the Norse influence, chose different names. In
French the word for Tuesday is *mardi*; in Spanish it is *martes*;

in Italian it is *martedi*. All are named for the Roman god Mars.

Some of the world's most memorable tales are to be found in the Norse myths. Among the best known are those given in the following pages, but others equally interesting await the student who wishes to read further. If you enjoy tales of giants, dwarfs, magic, and splendid deeds—and who does not?—then you'll enjoy the Norse myths.

IV. Odin's Search for Wisdom*

The wonderful ash tree, Yggdrasil, made a far-spreading shade against the fierce heat of the sun in summer and a stronghold against the piercing winds of winter. No man could remember when it had been young. Little children played under its branches, grew to be strong men and women, lived to be old and weary and feeble, and died; and yet the ash tree gave no signs of decay. Forever preserving its freshness and beauty, it was to live as long as there were men to look upon it, animals to feed under it, birds to flutter among its branches.

This mighty ash tree touched and bound all the worlds together in its wonderful circle of life. One root it sent deep down into the sightless depths of hell, where the dead live; another it fastened firmly in Jotunheim, the dreary home of the giants; and with the third it grasped Midgard, the dwelling place of men.

Serpents and all kinds of worms gnawed continually at its roots but were never able to destroy them. Its branches spread out over the whole earth, and the topmost boughs swayed in the clear air of Asgard itself, rustling against Valhalla, the home of heroes who had done great deeds or died in battle.

At the foot of the tree sat the three Norns, wonderful spinners of fate, who weave the thread of every man's life, making it what they will; and a strange weaving it often was, cut off when the pattern was just beginning to show itself. And every day these Norns sprinkled the tree with the water of life from the Urdar fountain, and so kept it forever green.

In the topmost branches sat an eagle singing a strange song about

*From *Norse Stories*, by Hamilton Wright Mabie.

the birth of the world, its decay and death. Under its branches browsed all manner of animals; among its leaves every kind of bird made its nest; by day the rainbow hung under it; at night the pale northern light flashed over it; and as the winds swept through its rustling branches, the multitudinous murmur of the leaves told strange stories of the past and of the future.

The giants were older than the gods and knew so much more of the past that the gods had to go to them for wisdom. After a time, however, the gods became wiser than the giants, or they would have ceased to be gods and been destroyed by the giants instead of destroying them.

When the world was still young, and there were still many things which even the gods had to learn, Odin was so anxious to become wise that he went to a deep well whose waters touched the roots of Yggdrasil itself. The keeper of the well was a very old and very wise giant, named Mimir, or Memory, and he gave no draughts out of the well until he was well paid; for the well contained the water of wisdom, and whoever drank of it became straightway wonderfully wise.

"Give me a draught of this clear water, O Mimir," said Odin, when he had reached the well and was looking down into its clear, fathomless depths.

Mimir, the keeper, was so old that he could remember everything that had ever happened. His eyes were clear and calm as the stars; his face was noble and restful; and his long white beard flowed down to his waist.

"This water is only to be had at a great price," he said in a wonderfully sweet, majestic tone. "I cannot give to all who ask, but only to those who are able and willing to give greatly in return," he continued.

If Odin had been less of a god he would have thought longer and bargained sharper, but he was so godlike that he cared more to be wise and great than anything else.

"I will give you whatever you ask," he answered.

Mimir thought a moment. "You must leave an eye," he said at last.

Then he drew up a great draught of the sparkling water, and Odin quenched his divine thirst and went away rejoicing, although he had left an eye behind. Even the gods could not be wise without struggle and toil and sacrifice.

So Odin became the wisest in all the worlds, and there was no god or giant that could contend with him. There was one giant, however, who was called all-wise in Jotunheim, with whom many had contended in knowledge, with curious and difficult questions, and had always been silenced and killed, for then, as now, a man's life often depended on his wisdom. Of this giant, Vafthrudner, and his wisdom many wonderful stories were told, and even among the gods his fame was great.

One day as Odin sat thinking of many strange things in the worlds, and many mysterious things in the future, he thought of Vafthrudner. "I will go to Jotunheim and measure wisdom with Vafthrudner, the wisest of the giants," said he to Frigga, his wife, who was sitting by.

Then Frigga remembered those who had gone to contend with the all-wise giant and had never come back, and a fear came over her that the same fate might befall Odin.

"You are wisest in all the worlds, All-Father," she said. "Why should you seek a treacherous giant who knows not half so much as you?"

But Odin, who feared nothing, could not be persuaded to stay, and Frigga sadly said good-by as he passed out of Asgard on his journey to Jotunheim. His blue mantle set with stars and his golden helmet he left behind him, and as he journeyed swiftly those who met him saw nothing godlike in him; nor did Vafthrudner when at last he stood at the giant's door.

"I am a simple traveler, Gangraad by name," he said as Vafthrudner came gruffly toward him. "I ask your hospitality and a chance to strive with you in wisdom." The giant laughed scornfully at the thought of a man coming to contend with him for mastery in knowledge.

"You shall have all you want of both," he growled, "and if you cannot answer my questions you shall never go hence alive."

He did not even ask Odin to sit down, but let him stand in the hall, despising him too much to show him any courtesy. After a time he began to ask questions.

"Tell me, if you can, O wise Gangraad, the name of the river which divides Asgard from Jotunheim."

"The river Ifing, which never freezes over," answered Odin quickly, as if it were the easiest question in the world; and indeed it was to him, although no man could have answered it. Vafthrudner looked up in surprise when he heard the reply.

"Good," he said, "you have answered rightly. Tell me, now, the names of the horses that carry day and night across the sky."

Before the words were fairly spoken Odin replied, "Skinfaxe and Hrimfaxe." The giant could not conceal his surprise that a man should know these things.

"Once more," he said quickly, as if he were risking everything on one question; "tell me the name of the plain where the Last Battle will be fought."

This was a terrible question, for the Last Battle was still far off in the future, and only the gods and the greatest of the giants knew where and when it would come. Odin bowed his head when he heard the words, for to be ready for that battle was the divine work of his life, and then said, slowly and solemnly, "On the plain of Vigard, which is one hundred miles on each side."

Vafthrudner rose trembling from his seat. He knew now that Gangraad was some great one in disguise, and that his own life hung on the answers he himself would soon be forced to make.

"Sit here beside me," he said, "for, whoever you are, worthier antagonist has never entered these walls."

Then they sat down together in the rude stone hall, the mightiest of the gods and the wisest of the giants, and the great contest in wisdom, with a life hanging in either scale, went on between them. Wonderful secrets of the time when no man was and the time when no man will be, those silent walls listened to as Vafthrudner asked Odin one deep question after another, the answer coming swiftly and surely.

After a time the giant could ask no more, for he had exhausted his wisdom.

"It is my turn now," said Odin, and one after another he drew out from Vafthrudner the events of the past, then the wonderful things of the race of giants, and finally he began to question him of that dim, mysterious future whose secrets only the gods know; and as he touched these wonderful things Odin's eyes began to flash, and his form to grow larger and nobler, until he seemed no longer the humble Gangraad but the mighty god he was, and Vafthrudner trembled as he felt the coming doom nearing him with every question.

So hours went by, until at last Odin paused in his swift questioning, stooped down, and asked the giant, "What did Odin whisper to Balder as he ascended the funeral pile?"

Only Odin himself could answer this question, and Vafthrudner replied humbly and with awe, "Who but you, All-Father, knows the words you did say to your son in the days of old? I have brought my doom upon myself, for in my ignorance I have contended with wisdom itself. You are ever the wisest of all."

So Odin conquered, and wisdom was victorious, as she always has been even when she has contended with giants.

V. Tales of Thor, the Thunderer

The Giant's Bride

One day the giant Thrym stole Thor's hammer and buried it deep in the earth. The gods were shaken. The hammer was one of the major defenses against the frost giants. Not knowing where to look, Thor confided in the clever Loki, who was on good behavior for once. In disguise, Loki visited Jotunheim, the land of the giants. He discovered that Thrym was the culprit, but Thrym was not going to return the hammer unless . . .

The price of the hammer's return was the goddess Freya, whom Thrym wanted to marry. When Loki brought back the news, there was turmoil in Asgard. Freya said that *she* would never go off to marry a giant. She stamped and fumed and shattered her necklace in anger. The situation looked bleak, but then Heimdall had a plan. Thor should go to Jotunheim dressed as a bride. Loki should go as a handmaiden. Thor didn't like this idea one bit, but he reluctantly agreed. He dressed himself in Freya's clothing and veiled his face. Then he went to Jotunheim as Freya, blushing bride of the giant Thrym. The expectant groom enthusiastically welcomed his "bride-to-be."

The giants served a bountiful bridal feast. Thrym was amazed at the appetite of his bride, who downed several oxen and salmon without pausing. To calm Thrym's anxiety, Loki told him that Freya had fasted and gone without sleep for nine days and nights. "Her" nervousness had at last been relieved, and "she" was very happy.

Then the groom tried to kiss his bride, but drew back alarmed at the fire in "her" eye. As usual, Loki came up with an explanation, and the giants were satisfied. To complete the bargain, the hammer was brought in according to custom and laid in the lap of the bride. This was the moment Thor was waiting for. He took his hammer in his hand and slew the bridegroom and assembled guests. He and Loki returned jubilant to Asgard.

A Visit to Giant Land

Upon another occasion Thor and Loki set out to visit Jotunheim. They rode in Thor's chariot drawn by two goats. They rode for a whole day and at nightfall reached a peasant's hut on the outskirts of the giants' world. They decided to spend the night at the hut. Their host was a good man, but very poor. Thor realized that the poor folk could not get together a goodly feast for one of his appetite. Accordingly, he slaughtered both his goats, cooked them and began to eat them. He invited the peasant and his family to share in the feast, but he warned them not to break any of the bones. Instead he ordered them to throw the bones into the skins spread out on the floor.

Loki, mischievous as usual, prevailed upon the young son in the family to break one of the bones and suck out the marrow. The youth, *Thialfi*, did not realize that his crime would be detected. Early on the next morning Thor arose to depart. He struck the goat skins with his hammer, and the goats became whole again as before. One of the goats, though, limped as though a bone had been broken—as indeed it had. Thor was furious and would have slain the entire family. Thialfi confessed his misdeed. It was agreed that Thialfi would serve Thor as penance for his act. Accordingly all three set out on foot for Jotunheim, leaving behind the goats for the return journey.

The travelers walked all day and at night found themselves in a dreary, bleak, misty country. Through the dim night they saw an oddly shaped house. The entrance was as wide as the building. They entered and threw themselves wearily down on the floor to sleep. Not long after, they were alarmed by a mysterious rumbling and shaking of the floor. Fearing an earthquake they withdrew into what seemed like a safer wing of the building. Not far away they could hear a terrible groaning, but in the darkness they could make out nothing.

In the morning they left the building. In a moment they came upon the form of a sleeping giant. It was his snoring that had alarmed them. The giant awoke sleepily and groped around him. Then he picked up the object for which he was searching. It was a huge glove. It was the "house" the travelers had spent the night in. The "safer wing" was the opening for the thumb.

Learning their destination, the giant offered to guide the travelers to Jotunheim. He strode off, and the travelers had to struggle to keep him in sight. At night he offered them the provisions in his wallet before he fell asleep. But even Thor's strength was not sufficient to untie the knots.

The giant snored again so noisily that Thor resolved to destroy him. Grasping his hammer Thor dealt him three fearful blows. Each time the giant sleepily awoke to ask whether a twig or a piece of moss had fallen on him. Thor's hammer made no impression whatever.

On the next day again the giant left the travelers. Before he left, he pointed out the shortest road to the castle of *Utgard-Loki*—not to be confused with Loki himself. Utgard-Loki was king of the giants. His castle was built of great ice blocks. Huge icicles were the pillars of his hall. The travelers presented themselves at once to the monstrous Utgard-Loki. He pretended to be surprised at their small size.

Loki was hungry. He said loudly that he'd be ready to enter an eating contest with any giant. The king ordered a huge wooden trough of meat to be brought in. Then he ordered his cook to sit at one end and Loki at the other. They began to eat. Now Loki was a mighty eater, but when he reached the center of the trough, he had to acknowledge defeat. His opponent had eaten not only meat and bones but the trough itself.

Utgard-Loki smiled and made a belittling comment about the puny appetites of the gods. Thor was angered by this remark and boasted that he could outdrink any giant in the hall. The king ordered a horn to be brought in. Good drinkers, he said, emptied the horn in one draught. Moderately thirsty persons took two draughts, puny drinkers took three.

There was expectant silence in the hall as Thor lifted the horn to his lips. He took one mighty draught, of the kind only a god could take. The liquid scarcely seemed to be lowered in the horn. A second and a third draught brought the same unsatisfactory results. Thor had to admit defeat.

The servant Thialfi, one of the swiftest of men, offered to race any contestant. A youth was chosen from the group. The race began. Thialfi was surprised to find that his opponent had run to the post and back before Thialfi had run more than a few yards. Three times did this happen before Thialfi, too, acknowledged defeat.

Utgard-Loki then commented upon Thor's supposed strength. The king invited Thor to try out a children's game. It consisted of lifting the king's cat from the floor. The task looked simple. Thor put his hand under the cat and strained. Despite his utmost straining he could succeed in lifting only one paw from the ground. The king chuckled and commented once again upon Thor's weakness.

Thor, furious at last, challenged anyone to wrestle with him. Utgard-Loki called forth an old hag. He explained that this was his nurse, the only one who would lower herself to try his strength. Thor was sufficiently enraged not to object. He seized the old woman, but the tighter his grasp, the firmer she stood. After a violent struggle Thor went down on one knee. Again Thor admitted shameful defeat.

The night passed in feasting. On the next day Utgard-Loki escorted the travelers to the edge of Jotunheim. Just before he bade them farewell he told them the truth about their experiences. Because of their power he had been forced to use magic against them. He admitted that he was the giant who had first met them. He had placed a mountain between himself and Thor, or else the hammer would certainly have shattered his skull. As it was, the mountain was nearly cut in two.

Then he explained the events in Jotunheim. Loki's opponent in the eating contest was in reality *Fire*, which had indeed consumed everything. Thialfi's running opponent was *Thought*—and who can outstrip thought in a race? Thor's drinking horn had been connected with the ocean. His draught had indeed lowered the water mark around the world. The cat was in reality the Midgard Serpent, which Thor had nearly pulled out of the ocean. The old nurse was in reality old age, whom no one can overcome.

After he had finished speaking, Utgard-Loki warned them never to return. Other magic would surely be applied against them. Then he vanished. Thor swung his hammer, but Jotunheim also had disappeared. So Thor and Loki returned to Asgard, somewhat wiser for their experiences.

Thor's Fantastic Duel

Thor, who must have been a favorite with early storytellers, is the hero of yet another exploit. One time Thor raced the giant Hrungrir to see who owned the faster horse. Hrungrir galloped so fast he was inside Asgard before he stopped. Graciously the gods allowed the giant to drink from Thor's goblet. Unfortunately, the giant grew boastful, threatening to carry off the goddesses and destroy Asgard.

At this moment Thor arrived in a rage. The giant challenged Thor to a duel, and the fight began. Hrungrir had a head and heart of stone. He was protected by a stone shield. He carried a huge whetstone, a knife sharpener. How could Thor overcome such an opponent? Thialfi, one of the onlookers, advised the giant to stand on his shield to protect himself should Thor attack from below. The simple-minded giant agreed and was not ready when Thor attacked from above. Thor attacked with thunder and lightning, hurling his hammer as he dropped. The giant threw his whetstone in return.

At this point the superiority of Thor's hammer became quickly apparent. The hammer and whetstone met in mid-air. The whetstone was shattered, but the hammer sped on to its goal, the giant's head. Though the battle was over, the giant had fallen upon Thor, pinning his leg. A piece of the whetstone had struck Thor in the head.

Thor's little son Magni, already showing great strength, pulled the giant away from his father. For this action Thor gave him the giant's horse as a reward. But what of that piece of whetstone? According to the legend, a seeress was brought in to perform spells that would remove the stone from Thor's head. Always a great storyteller, Thor unfortunately boasted to the seeress how he had once rescued her husband Aurvandil from Giant Land in a basket. When Aurvandil's toe had frozen, Thor had flung it up into the sky to become a star. The seeress was so enchanted by the story she forgot all about her spells. Alas, the full details of that charming story are lost, leaving us to wonder if a piece of whetstone is still in Thor's head.

VI. Tales of Loki, the Trickster

The Architect of Asgard

After the gods had completed Midgard and had built Valhalla, they took stock of their situation. They realized that the frost giants, while momentarily defeated, could rise up at any time to threaten their rule. Of course, they had their miraculous watchman Heimdall to guard Bifrost, the rainbow bridge to Asgard, but they still felt insecure. They decided to build a fortress that would be unassailable.

While they were planning, a mysterious architect came into their midst. He offered to do the entire job, provided the gods would give him as reward the sun, the moon, and the beautiful goddess Freya. The gods refused at first, but upon urging by Loki they finally agreed. They said the fortress would have to be finished in the course of one winter. The architect could have no other assistants than his horse *Svadilfari*. Loki assured them that the condition was impossible to meet.

The architect agreed and set to work at once. By night he hauled huge blocks of stone. By day he built. The work proceeded rapidly. It soon was apparent that the architect would indeed make good his side of the bargain. Soon the entire job was finished, but for one portal that could be erected in one night. Pouncing upon Loki for his bad advice, the gods threatened to kill him unless he got them out of their difficulties.

Loki was frightened, but his cleverness did not fail him. He changed himself into a mare and lured the great steed Svadilfari into the forest. Without his assistant the architect was lost. He realized that he had been tricked and was furious. He assumed his true form, that of a mountain giant, and would have attacked the gods. But Thor shattered the giant's skull to pieces by one blow of his hammer, and sent him tumbling into Niflheim.

The Theft of the Golden Apples

You have already discovered that Loki was a god of mischief. Though he was often charming he was also selfish, thoughtless, and unscrupulous. In many respects Loki resembles the Trickster (page 212) of folklore, but in some ways he seems more of a demon. Many of the troubles experienced in Asgard can be laid at Loki's door. Here is another of Loki's troublesome exploits.

As you know, Iduna kept the golden apples that guaranteed immortality to the gods. Once when they were stolen, the gods were almost doomed. This is how it came about.

One day Odin and Loki went on one of their excursions to earth. They wandered about in a deserted region and could find no friendly peasant's hut for food and lodging. They became weary and desperately hungry. At last they came upon a herd of oxen. They singled out one of the beasts, slew it, and built a fire for their supper. They put the meat over the fire, but the meat remained raw.

The gods were sufficiently versed in magic to know that some sorcery was afoot. Finally they noticed an eagle in the tree above them. At last the bird addressed them. "Give me as much food as I can eat, and the meat will cook."

The gods agreed to the request, and soon the meat was cooked through. The eagle seized the major portion of the ox and began to fly off with it. Loki, hotheaded as usual, forgot himself and picked up a great stick. He began to beat the bird with the stick. To his

dismay, one end of the stick stuck fast to the eagle's back. He found himself dragged over the ground, through thorny bushes, over hard stones. He begged for mercy, but the bird merely increased his speed. At last he promised anything if the bird would give him peace.

The bird stopped at once. He revealed himself as the storm giant *Thiassi*. He agreed to let Loki go on one condition: that he would lure Iduna out of Asgard, so that the giant could steal the golden apples of immortality. Loki accepted the condition and rejoined Odin, but told him nothing of his bargain.

When they returned to Asgard, Loki planned to fulfill his evil bargain. On a day when her husband Bragi was away from Asgard, Loki enticed Iduna out of the garden on a pretext. He insisted that similar apples grew a short distance away. She took the golden apples along to compare with the imaginary apples described by Loki. As they left Asgard, Loki disappeared. Down from the sky swept the storm giant on his eagle wings. He caught up Iduna in his talons and bore her away to his desolate homeland.

In Asgard the gods did not miss Iduna at first. However, as time passed they found themselves aging, with no way of restoring their youth. It was then that they began to miss Iduna and the golden apples. They were annoyed at first, then alarmed. No longer was there sprightliness in their walk. They began to stoop. Their eyes became dull. Each saw in the next his own fears for the future. What would happen when Freya became gray and old, when Thor could no longer wield the magic hammer? Someone recalled that he had seen Iduna last in Loki's company. The gods pounced on Loki and threatened him. At last he agreed to undo the evil he had brought into their midst.

Loki borrowed the falcon feathers of the goddess Freya and flew off to Thiassi's homeland. There he found Iduna alone, homesick for the sunny plains of Asgard. Changing her into a sparrow, he held her in his strong talons and set off for Asgard. But Thiassi saw the falcon fleeing with the sparrow and set off in pursuit. Never before did Loki show such courage or strength. He beat his wings as powerfully as he could—but the eagle gained steadily.

The gods were watching anxiously from the towers of Asgard. Suddenly they caught sight of the fleeing falcon and the speeding eagle. They began to build a huge fire on the walls. It flared up just after Loki by one last effort was able to clear the walls and sink exhausted in safety. The giant in his eagle guise sped on. He tried to check his speed but could not. The gods lit the fire, which flared up just as the eagle flew over the walls. Singed by the fire and blinded by the smoke, the eagle fell downward. The gods immediately slew him. Iduna had been saved; and the gods were able once again to renew their youth by tasting of the golden apples.

Loki and the Dwarfs

Loki was responsible for another theft that put him into disfavor with the gods. This time out of pure mischief he stole the golden hair of *Sif*, Thor's wife. Naturally Thor was furious and set off in search of Loki. Finally Thor caught up with the culprit and grasped him in his powerful hands. Loki changed form, but Thor held on. Loki was forced to yield, and he pleaded for forgiveness. Thor was sternly unforgiving. At last Loki rashly promised to get for Sif, somehow, a new head of hair as beautiful as her own.

Thor released Loki so that he might fulfill his promise. Loki went directly to the caverns underneath the earth where the dwarfs dwelt. By using his most flattering manner, Loki was able to persuade the dwarf *Dvalin* to fashion hair for Sif. Loki hoped to appease the other gods, too, particularly Odin and Frey. Consequently, he urged the dwarf to construct a marvelous gift for each of them besides.

The dwarf, flattered to extend himself, made three marvelous objects. For Sif he spun the finest golden thread imaginable. This would come to life as soon as Sif put the new "hair" next to her head. For Odin he made a marvelous spear which never missed its aim. For Frey he constructed a magic ship which could sail through air as well as water. It was large enough to to contain the gods and all their company, but it could be folded up small enough to be put into a pocket.

Loki was delighted with the results and openly boasted that the dwarf Dvalin was the cleverest craftsman in all the world or under it. These braggart words were overheard by another dwarf named *Brock*. This second dwarf insisted that his brother *Sindri* could make three objects more marvelous still. Loki scorned this statement and foolishly said that he'd wager his head against Brock's on the outcome of the contest.

Sindri learned of the offer and set to work. He put Brock to work blowing the bellows. He warned Brock to work steadily, or else they would fail. Loki hoped to make Brock fail, of course, and he intended to help failure along. He changed himself into a stinging fly and stung poor Brock hard as he worked. Brock, though in agony, did not leave the bellows. Then Sindri drew out the first object, a huge wild boar, which could radiate light as it sped through the sky.

Sindri set to work at the second object. Brock kept faithfully at the bellows. This time Loki stung him on his cheek. Brock persevered. Sindri drew forth from the flames a magic ring. Every ninth night eight similar rings dropped from it.

Sindri set to work at the third object, throwing a huge lump of iron into the flames. He cautioned Brock once again to mind the bellows. This time Loki stung the dwarf above the eye. The wound was deep enough to start the blood flowing. The stream poured down into Brock's eye so that he couldn't see what he was doing. He raised his hand for a moment to wipe away the blood. Sindri cried out in disappointment as he drew the third object from the fire. It was a hammer but its handle was a bit too short.

Brock and Loki went to Asgard to settle their wager. Loki presented his three gifts as already described. Brock presented the magic ring to Odin, the boar to Frey, and the hammer to Thor. This was the hammer for which Thor was so famous. On the strength of his last gift the gods decreed that Brock had won the wager.

Loki fled in terror to prevent Brock from claiming his head as wagered, but Thor overtook him and delivered him to Brock. Thor insisted, however, that Brock could take Loki's head, but he could not touch his neck, which was not part of the bargain. Brock was disappointed, but he sewed Loki's lips together instead. For a brief period Loki was unusually silent, but at last he cut the strings and was his old self again.

The Death of Balder

Once again, Loki's actions brought disaster to the gods. In the experiences already described, sheer mischief or greed seemed to motivate him. In the tragedy of Balder, jealousy moved Loki to evil action.

Balder was the best loved of all the gods. For that reason, Loki hated him. One day Balder had a foreboding of death. He told the other gods of his terrible dreams. Odin was most dismayed, for he knew that the death of Balder would be the first step in the fall of Asgard itself. To prevent his being injured, the mother goddess, Frigga, went to all things on heaven and earth. She made each promise to do no harm to Balder, but Odin was still uneasy.

Odin decided to consult a prophetess to find out whether their precautions were sufficient. Since the prophetess was dead, Odin had to descend to the abode of Hela, goddess of death. His trip to the underworld reminds us of the journeys made by Orpheus (page 41), Odysseus (page 84), and Aeneas (page 98).

When Odin arrived at his destination, he was dismayed that preparations had already been made to receive Balder. What could be done to prevent this tragedy? Back in Asgard, the gods continued to play a favorite game of throwing darts at Balder. Since all things, supposedly, had promised to do him no harm, the darts were turned aside. Some of the gods would strike at him with swords, but the swords would be mysteriously deflected. It came to be an honor to Balder to throw things at him, since the promise was that nothing could harm him.

It is at this point that Loki came maliciously on the scene. He discovered that Frigga had failed to exact a promise from one thing, a shrub called *mistletoe*. She thought the shrub too insignificant to do any harm. Like Achilles (page 8), Balder was invulnerable—except for one small weakness. Loki secured the mistletoe and returned to the sport. There he found Balder's blind brother, Hoder, standing apart from the others. Loki asked why he too did not throw darts at Balder. Hoder said that because of his blindness he could not participate.

Loki volunteered to help Hoder to take part in the game. He put the mistletoe in Hoder's hand, directed his aim, and urged Hoder to throw. Hoder threw the mistletoe. It pierced Balder, who fell dead on the spot.

Never before had there been such grief as at the death of Balder. Hoder was horrified to learn what he had done. The other gods felt that they should take vengeance on him, but decided that the place was not suitable. Frigga, Balder's mother, cried out in her grief. She asked for a volunteer to go to Hela to offer her a ransom if she would restore Balder to life.

All hesitated to face Hela, grim goddess of death. At last *Hermod*, the Nimble, Odin's son, offered to go. Odin's eight-footed horse, Sleipnir, was led forth to carry Hermod to Niflheim, the land of the dead.

For nine days and nights Hermod rode through dark and gloomy chasms until at last he arrived at the abode of the dead. Touching both spurs to his horse, he leapt over the barred gates until he reached the court of Hela. There sat Balder, mourning for the land of light.

Hermod entreated Hela to let Balder return, for he was indeed beloved of everyone everywhere. Hela made a bargain. She would let Balder return if all things in the world would weep for him. But if one person or thing refused to weep, then Balder would have to stay among the shades. Hermod brought this message back to Asgard.

The gods dispatched messengers all over the world to beg everything to weep for Balder, so that he might be delivered. All things willingly agreed—men, trees, metals, and stones. Then the gods prepared to return to Asgard. Just before they reached their destination, they came upon a skinny hag, toothless and old. She sat in her cave and mocked all those who passed. Some say that Loki himself assumed her person to do further evil.

The gods made the same request of her that they had made of all other things. The hag replied in a mocking voice that she would never weep for Balder. "Let Hela keep her prey," she cried exultantly and fled into the cavern. Thus was Balder prevented from ever returning from the land of death.

The gods mournfully took up the dead body of Balder and made a funeral pyre on board his ship *Hringham*. The body of his wife, who had died of a broken heart when she saw her husband dead, was placed on the pyre. At the last moment his great steed was led to the funeral, to perish with his master's body. So Balder left the company of the immortals, and evil became more powerful in the world.

The gods did not let Loki off easily this time. Though he fled to the mountains and took the guise of a salmon, he was at last captured. The gods bound him with chains and placed over his head a serpent. There, it is said, the serpent's venom falls upon Loki's face, drop by drop. Loki's faithful wife Siguna sits by his side and catches the drops in a cup, but when she carries the venom away to empty it, new drops fall upon the unprotected face of Loki. He writhes in horror, so that the earth shakes. There he waits until the day of Ragnarok, when the gods themselves will be destroyed.

VII. The Tale of the Hero Siegfried

Every year at the Metropolitan Opera House in New York City there is great excitement when four of the most popular operas are scheduled. These are the great Wagnerian operas we call "The Ring Cycle." Wagner based these great operas on the story of *Siegfried*. Siegfried, or Sigurd as he is called in one version, was one of the great heroes in Norse and German mythology. Wagner uses the Norse version of the tale, but introduces many German names and elements. The four separate operas tell successive episodes in the saga. Here we meet the great Norse gods as they become involved in the story of Siegfried.

The four operas are called "The Ring Cycle" because the tale revolves around the fateful Ring of the Nibelung. It is the curse of this Ring that brings destruction to all who have a part to play in the story. Even the gods are not immune to the dread curse, for the last opera depicts the downfall of the gods themselves.

The first opera, *The Rhine-Gold*, lays the groundwork of the action. It tells how the gods became involved with the gold and with the curse traditionally associated with it. The second opera, *The Valkyrie*, introduces the warrior maiden *Brunnhilde*. For her action in trying to thwart the will of Odin she is enchanted, put to sleep in the shade of a huge fir tree until someone comes to awaken her. A ring of fire is placed around her. The third opera in the series, *Siegfried*, introduces the warrior hero. After many adventures, he passes through the ring of fire and awakens Brunnhilde. They fall in love, and Brunnhilde forfeits her immortality to be loved by a mortal. In the last opera, *The Twilight of the Gods*, matters come to a tragic climax. Through sorcery Siegfried forgets his love for Brunnhilde. He is at last slain through treachery. Brunnhilde dies on his funeral pyre. The evil tragedy spreads. The curse eventually destroys the halls of Valhalla itself.

VIII. The Death of the Gods

Wagner did not invent the myth of the destruction of the gods. This is part of the original Norse mythology. Wagner merely modified the elements he found. The Norsemen believed that eventually even the great gods themselves would disappear in a mighty struggle. After their destruction a new greater god would appear, a god of love who would bring eternal happiness. No more would there be the battles of Valhalla, but a period of peace forever. Wickedness, destruction, and death would be known no more.

The final destruction, or Ragnarok, will be foreshadowed by a triple winter, three terrible years with no summers. The frost and ice, which figure so often in Norse mythology, will

encroach upon the green valleys. Three more years of death
and destruction on earth will follow. The forces of evil, always
ready to break forth, will at last slip from their bonds. Loki
will set out as the leader of the evil legions. The wolf Fenris
will increase in strength and break free. The Midgard Serpent
will rise from his bed in the sea. Hela, the frost giants, and all
the forces opposing the gods will range over the earth. Evil
will meet good on the plain of Vigard.

Heimdall will sound the horn as the monstrous legions
approach. Odin will take his place at the forefront of his
warriors, but he will be the first to die, a victim of Fenris.
Vidar will avenge his father's death and slay the wolf. Thor
will once again meet his adversary, the Midgard Serpent. He
will slay the monster but die himself, slain by the serpent's
venom. Loki will attack Heimdall with vicious courage, but
both will fall dead. One by one the gods will fall, dying in
battle with the forces of evil.

The universe itself will be destroyed. The sun and the moon
will be devoured. The stars will fall into the abyss. Gods and
men alike will be destroyed. Perhaps, as some legends say, a
man and a woman will be preserved to repopulate a new
earth; for after Ragnarok will come a new era of peace. Poverty, pestilence, and death will be unknown, and the All-
Father will reign through eternity.

IX. The Myths and Literature

Though the legends of Norse mythology are not so numerous as those of Greece and Rome, many are among the finest
tales we know. There is a greater sternness, a gloomier out-
look in many of the Norse myths. Still, a few are tender and
warm, not without humor. Like the Olympian gods, the gods
of Asgard have their limitations. They are endowed with
many human failings as well as human strengths. They are
interesting in their attributes, but they lack the moral qualities we most admire. To the civilized mind the barbarous
cruelties of Odin and Zeus are distasteful. Even to great civilized minds of old, like the Greek playwright Euripides, the
gods seemed unworthy of worship. But the legends and myths
are valuable as stories and as sources of literary allusions. We
should be the poorer without them.

READING FOR UNDERSTANDING

Main Idea

1. The main idea of the introduction to this chapter (pages 105–106) is that (a) Christian scholars were interested in Norse myths (b) Norse mythology is a reflection of the lives and culture of the Norse people (c) Norse mythology was completely reported in the written materials of the day (d) Norse invaders terrorized much of Europe.

Details

2. Snorri Sturluson was (a) an ancient Norse hero (b) a Christian priest (c) a historian and poet (d) another name for Odin the Wise.

3. According to Norse myths the earth was formed from (a) the body of the giant Ymir (b) the magic wand of Odin (c) the dust from the stars (d) the hard work of the frost giants.

4. Jotunheim is (a) the land of the gods (b) another name for Denmark (c) the land of the giants (d) another name for the earth.

5. The goddess who most closely resembles the Roman Venus is (a) Frigga (b) Sif (c) Freya (d) Hela.

6. All the following are named for Norse deities EXCEPT (a) Saturday (b) Tuesday (c) Wednesday (d) Friday.

7. To gain wisdom, Odin gave up (a) a magic cap (b) Thor's hammer (c) the golden apples (d) an eye.

8. The god who dressed in a bride's clothes is (a) Thor (b) Odin (c) Balder (d) Tiu.

9. When Thor wrestled with an old hag, he was really wrestling with (a) Loki in disguise (b) old age (c) the Midgard serpent (d) thought.

10. In the struggle between Thor and Hrungnir (a) Hrungnir wrestled Thor to earth (b) Thialfi was accidentally killed (c) Thor's horse won a race (d) Thor's hammer broke a whetstone.

11. In the pursuit of Loki, the giant Thiassi was destroyed by (a) Thor's hammer (b) a blinding snowstorm (c) a volcanic eruption (d) a fire on the walls.

12. Thor obtained his marvelous hammer through the handiwork of (a) the dwarf Sindri (b) Loki (c) Balder (d) Iduna.

13. Balder was killed by (a) a sharp stone (b) a spear (c) mistletoe (d) fire.

14. After the death of the gods will come (a) an unending period of wars and destruction (b) complete emptiness (c) a rebirth of the same gods and goddesses (d) a new era of peace.

Inferences

15. If the Norse invaders had not settled in England, (a) the English would have invaded Norse lands (b) the English language would be different (c) Christianity would have arrived later (d) they would have settled in Greece.

16. Which of the following statements best describes Loki? (a) Loki is evil without any redeeming qualities. (b) Loki's difficulty was his love for the goddess Freya. (c) Loki's contradictory personality includes both good and evil. (d) Loki was good at heart, but he was misunderstood by the other gods.

17. The unbending enemies of the gods were the (a) dwarfs (b) people of earth (c) inhabitants of the underworld (d) frost giants.

18. Even Loki's enemies would agree that he was (a) kind (b) handsome (c) gentle (d) resourceful.

19. Despair and death in Norse mythology are often suggested by (a) ice and cold (b) the sufferings of Heimdall (c) the heat of summer (d) the sea.

20. Utgard-Loki defeated Thor and Loki by (a) trickery (b) superior strength (c) greater speed (d) an accident.

WORDS IN CONTEXT

1. The original Celtic inhabitants of Britain were pushed westward, as the *hordes* of invaders settled in the fertile east.
    Hordes (page 105) means (a) relatives (b) leaders (c) crowds (d) enemies.

2. The Norse, in their more isolated northern haunts, had little opportunity to *assimilate* the classical deities.
    Assimilate (107) means (a) absorb (b) study (c) reject (d) envy.

3. Their mythology was *ultimately* transformed by Christianity, rather than by the myths of Greece and Rome.
    Ultimately (107) means (a) moderately (b) completely (c) originally (d) finally.

4. Out of the mist formed by the continual *interaction* between warm air from the south and the ice and snow sprang the huge Ymir, ancestor of the frost giants.
    Interaction (107) means (a) high pressure (b) shared influence (c) constant upset (d) tornado watch.

5. From his body they formed the earth, to be the *abode* of human beings.

    Abode (107) means (a) challenge (b) ship (c) home (d) mountaintop.

6. In Jotunheim grew up a new race of frost giants, *implacable* and evil enemies of the gods.

    Implacable (108) means unable to be (a) refused (b) tested (c) excited (d) calmed.

7. His sword was a terrible and *infallible* weapon, like Odin's shield and spear, and Thor's hammer.

    Infallible (109) means (a) never failing (b) uncertain (c) complicated (d) not valuable.

8. Then Frigga remembered those who had gone to *contend* with the all-wise giant and had never come back.

    Contend (113) means (a) have dinner (b) struggle (c) visit (d) complain.

9. It was agreed that Thialfi would serve Thor as *penance* for his act.

    Penance (116) means (a) punishment (b) reward (c) remembrance (d) defense.

10. The travelers walked all day and at night found themselves in a dreary, *bleak*, misty country.

    Bleak (116) means (a) sunny (b) familiar (c) misty (d) depressing.

11. Utgard-Loki smiled and made a *belittling* comment about the puny appetites of the gods.

    Belittling (117) means (a) small (b) unflattering (c) boring (d) angry.

12. According to the legend, a *seeress* was brought in to perform spells that would remove the stone from Thor's head.

    Seeress (119) means (a) surgeon (b) teacher (c) prophetess (d) peasant.

13. The giant in his eagle *guise* sped on.

    Guise (122) means (a) feathers (b) appearance (c) beak (d) cry.

14. This time Loki stung him on his cheek. Brock *persevered*.

    Persevered (124) means (a) kept going (b) took a brief rest (c) fought back (d) gave up.

15. One day Balder had a *foreboding* of death.

    Foreboding (124) means (a) unwilling acceptance (b) remembrance (c) warning feeling (d) taste.

16. Some of the gods would strike at him with swords, but the swords would be mysteriously *deflected*.
    Deflected (125) means   (a) broken in two   (b) rusted   (c) dulled   (d) turned aside.

17. It is at this point that Loki came *maliciously* on the scene.
    Maliciously (125) means   (a) without preparation   (b) with evil intention   (c) in a cheerful mood   (d) unwillingly.

18. Hermod *entreated* Hela to let Balder return, for he was indeed beloved of everyone everywhere.
    Entreated (126) means   (a) angered   (b) disturbed   (c) begged   (d) lied.

19. "Let Hela keep her prey," she cried *exultantly* and fled into the cavern.
    Exultantly (126) means   (a) gleefully   (b) sadly   (c) pleasantly   (d) boringly.

20. The gods mournfully took up the dead body of Balder and made a funeral *pyre* on board his ship *Hringham*.
    Pyre (126) means   (a) coffin   (b) fire   (c) monument   (d) marker.

21. The four separate operas tell successive episodes in the *saga*.
    Saga (127) means   (a) legend   (b) musical instrument   (c) destruction   (d) short poem.

22. For her action in trying to *thwart* the will of Odin, she is enchanted, put to sleep in the shade of a huge fir tree until someone comes to awaken her.
    Thwart (127) means   (a) declare publicly   (b) explain   (c) keep secret   (d) successfully oppose.

23. The frost and ice will *encroach* upon the green valleys.
    Encroach (128) means   (a) send blizzards   (b) move in   (c) reach the borders   (d) advance and retreat.

24. Thor will once again meet his *adversary*, the Midgard Serpent.
    Adversary (128) means   (a) cousin   (b) friend   (c) neighbor   (d) enemy.

25. Poverty, *pestilence*, and death will be unknown, and the All-Father will reign through eternity.
    Pestilence (128) means   (a) trickery   (b) unhappiness   (c) disappointment   (d) disease.

THINKING IT OVER

1. Which myths did you in general enjoy more, the Norse or the Greek and Roman? Why? What are the differences in tone between the two groups? What are the differences between Odin and Zeus?

2. Loki is certainly not a lovable figure; yet the myths involving him are always favorite reading. Why? What is there about Loki that fascinates readers?

3. How did the Norse myth of creation differ from that of the Greeks? How did the climate of northern lands influence the Norse view?

4. A favorite element in myth and folklore is the idea of invulnerability. We'd all like to be safe from the dangers of life. Magic shields, charms that make wearers invisible, all-powerful weapons—these are the daydreams of children and creators of folklore. How do the legends of Perseus, Achilles, and Balder touch upon the myth of invulnerability?

5. Ragnarok, the Twilight of the Gods, symbolizes the recurring conflict in life of good and evil. Can you think of other books you have read in which the principal conflict is that of good and evil? Perhaps the conflict is between a good individual and an evil one, a good idea and an evil one. Such conflict is often the subject of movies or television programs. Mention at least one example and point out the basic conflict.

SUGGESTED ACTIVITIES

1. If you look at some of the myths from a different viewpoint, you come up with surprising results. In the Norse myths the giants and dwarfs are the villains. But if you look at the myths from their point of view, they were often tricked, deceived, and mistreated by Thor and his fellows. Briefly retell one of the myths, or part of one, from the giants' or dwarfs' point of view.

2. Try your hand at an original myth of your own, preferably humorous. Some suggestions follow, but don't hesitate to make up your own.

> Loki Visits the Land of the Dead
> Freya Challenges Aphrodite to a Beauty Contest
> Loki Stars in His Own TV Series
> Loki Goes to High School
> Odin Comes to Earth in Disguise
> Thor Takes Part in the Olympic Games
> The Travels of Odysseus Take Him to Denmark

3. Valhalla was the Norse conception of an ideal life-after-death. Other peoples have had similar dreams. Some of these idealized lands are listed below, along with their sources. Note that two were invented by writers. Their creations have passed into the language.

Lands	Sources
Arcadia	Greek
Avalon	Celtic
Earthly Paradise	European
Elysian Fields	Greek
Happy Hunting Grounds	American Indian
Lyonesse	British
Islands of the Blessed (also Fortunate Isles)	Celtic
Shangri-la	James Hilton
Utopia	Sir Thomas More

Find out what you can about three or more and report to the class. Perhaps the best source is *Brewer's Dictionary of Phrase and Fable*, Centenary Edition. Another good source is *The Reader's Encyclopedia*. You will also find most of these identified in dictionaries, encyclopedias, and books of mythology.

4. The Wagnerian Ring Cycle has been recorded on audiotapes and records. It has also been preserved on television tapes. If someone can obtain an audio- or videotape of a portion of the Cycle, you will find the music stirring, in keeping with the spirit of Norse myths.

5. Some students may wish to pursue the story of Siegfried even farther. There are two principal versions. The Norse version is called the *Saga of the Volsungs*, with the hero Sigurd. The German version is called the *Lay of the Nibelungs*, with the hero Siegfried. The tales, it must be confessed, are somewhat long and involved. Perhaps two students will condense, simplify, and retell the stories. Both can be found in Gayley's *Classic Myths*.

6. In the field of myth this book is concerned principally with the Greek, Roman, and Norse mythologies. Yet there are many other tales worth knowing, tales from Egypt and India, for example. Murray's *Manual of Mythology* has an interesting chapter on Egyptian mythology, telling about the great gods and goddesses: Osiris, Amun, Thoth, Ra, Bubastis, Anubis, Apis, Serapis, and Isis. The same book has a chapter on the mythology of India and the gods Agni, Surya, Indra, Dyaus, and Varuna. *A Dictionary of Non-Classical Mythology* lists and describes the major deities of these other mythologies. *The Young Folk's Book of Myths* has some stories from the other mythologies.

Perhaps members of your group may wish to follow up these additional references and report back to the class, retelling some of the more famous myths.

WORDS ASSOCIATED WITH NORSE MYTHS

Word	*Definition*	*Named for*
berserk	frenzied, crazed	ancient Norse warriors renowned for their frenzy in battle
Friday	day of the week	Freya, goddess of beauty
thorium	chemical element	Thor, god of thunder and strength
Thursday	day of the week	Thor
Tuesday	day of the week	Tiu, god of courage and war
Wednesday	day of the week	Odin, father of the gods

UNIT · FIVE

Folktales and Ballads

We have already considered the close relationship between mythology and folklore (page 2). Heroic legends and famous epics are similarly indebted to folktales and folk wisdom. Great sagas like the *Odyssey* have borrowed many of the episode tales that go far back in time. For example, the danger on both sides, symbolized by Scylla and Charybdis (page 84), is an old theme in folklore. The journey to the underworld (page 84) is a familiar episode. Enchantresses like Circe (83) and Calypso (85) are popular folk characters. Then there is the seemingly unending task (85) as Penelope never quite completes the weaving. Indeed, the *Odyssey* is a magnificent example of the voyage tale itself, a universal theme in folklore, as in the voyages of Sinbad the Sailor (pages 166–179).

I. Folktales a Part of Folklore

Folklore arises from the folk, the people. As the *Standard Dictionary of Folklore* has put it, "Folklore materials thrive in a society in which there are people of considerable native intelligence, artistic appreciation, memory, imagination, and creative urge, who can comprehend, value, remember, and recreate their native folklore and thus propagate it as living tradition. Folklore lives its fullest, purest, and most natural life away from learned culture."

Picture a scene that was once very common all over the world, and may still be in many areas. Night has fallen. A blanket of cold lies over the land. Outside the snow has begun to sift slowly, lightly down. Inside the peasant's hut the fireplace crackles merrily on. Perhaps a candle or two sputter on the heavy wooden table. The evening meal is over and done with. Everyone sits around expectantly. Then the storyteller

137

says four magic words, and the listeners are off to another world.

What are the magic words? "Once upon a time . . ." or a similar formula. Where is the magic? In the sheer delighted concentration of everyone as the storyteller spins his tale. Thousands, tens of thousands, hundreds of thousands of folktales have circulated among the people since the beginning of time. People, it seems, just can't resist a story, particularly a story that stirs the imagination.

Folktales are exciting examples of pure folklore. In folktales the narrative thread is most important, but characters are often colorful, too. We recognize in these universally admired stories experiences and thoughts that we have had. We experience the world through the eyes of an Ashanti storyteller (140) or a Chinese sage (182).

When we read folktales, we are astonished to find similar story plots in the tales of different peoples. The story of Andromeda (page 26) has its counterpart in folktales from ancient Babylon, from Asia, Canada, and Central Europe. According to tradition, the founders of Rome—Romulus and Remus—were raised by a she-wolf. Similar tales come from places as far apart as Brazil, China, India, Ireland, and Zanzibar.

II. Folktales and Literature

The world's folktales have used just about every plot device possible. They have introduced every type of character. They have illuminated human nature, strengths and weaknesses, in many different settings.

The incredible wealth of folklore has not been lost on poets, short-story writers, novelists, playwrights, screenwriters, and movie directors. Chaucer 600 years ago went back to folklore for one of his most penetrating stories. In "The Pardoner's Tale," he told the story of thieves who die while trying to outwit each other for gold, but the plot was old when *he* used it. Six centuries later Hollywood made a prize-winning film, *The Treasure of Sierra Madre*. In this film, as in Chaucer, gold and human greed bring tragedy.

In *The Taming of the Shrew* Shakespeare tells how a man "tames" his ill-tempered bride by outdoing her in bad temper. The plot is an old one in folklore. On the other side, long before women's lib, folktales often told how women cleverly outwitted those who would dominate them.

There's an old saying that there's nothing new under the sun. Settings have changed. Technological advances have altered our way of looking at the movies. But in all probability the plot of your favorite film is a modern retelling of some old folktale.

The folktales and ballads that follow are characteristic examples of their kind. Here you will find many of the elements and themes that enrich folktales. You will discover that a particular theme is not limited to a certain country. The clever hero is a major element of tales from India, Egypt, Arabia, and Surinam. These tales are fun to read.

III. Talking Objects and Animals

Young children talk to their dolls and teddy bears and imagine that these toys can talk to them. Pet dogs and cats are treated as family members by adults as well. "Our dog (or cat) can almost talk" is a common reaction to the family pet. Deep inside us is a wish that animals *could* talk.

In folktales, animals *do* talk. Indeed, many inanimate objects are also given the power of speech, as the following Ashanti folktale wittily demonstrates. Animals in folktales often prove wiser than their owners.

Humor often characterizes animal folktales. "The Dog That Talked," retold in Katharine Briggs's *British Folktales*, gives a different twist to the story of a talking dog.

As the man enters a village, a sheepdog greets him with "Good morning, sir." The man is dumbstruck. He goes up to the owner and remarks how special the sheepdog is.

"There's nothing special about the dog," replies the owner.

"He said 'Good morning, sir' to me," exclaims the visitor.

The owner asks if there was another dog around when the visitor heard the words. When the visitor mentions a white terrier a little ways off, the owner says, "That explains it. He's a ventriloquist!"

Though the following two stories are factually presented, they demonstrate an exaggeration so common in stories people enjoy. (See also page 215.) They also demonstrate other folktale themes.

Talk—An Ashanti Tale (African)

The rich and varied cultures of Africa have produced folk-tales similar to those of the Western world. Some African stories resemble the creation myths described in Greek and Scandinavian mythology (pages 13, 107). Others are similar to the animal fables of Aesop (pages 262–267). Still others interpret nature and the origin of things as in "Mythology and Nature" (pages 15–23).

Among the most charming of African folktales are those that reflect not only a sense of humor but also a profound insight into human nature. In the following tale you will find ingredients common to folktales in general. For example, you will notice the cumulative repetition of details, as in the old story of "Chicken Little" and the rhyme "This Is the House That Jack Built." You will also find a surprise ending, dear to all good storytellers. Best of all, this legend is a worthy ancestor of all modern talking-dog stories.

Once, not far from the city of Accra on the Gulf of Guinea, a country man went out to his garden to dig up some yams to take to market. While he was digging, one of the yams said to him, "Well, at last you're here. You never weeded me, but now you come around with your digging stick. Go away and leave me alone!"

The farmer turned around and looked at his cow in amazement. The cow was chewing her cud and looking at him.

"Did you say something?" he said.

The cow kept on chewing and said nothing, but the man's dog spoke up. "It wasn't the cow who spoke to you," the dog said. "It was the yam. The yam says leave him alone."

The man became angry, because his dog had never talked before, and he didn't like his tone besides. So he took his knife and cut a branch from a palm tree to whip his dog. Just then the palm tree said, "Put that branch down!"

The man was getting very upset about the way things were going, and he started to throw the palm branch away, but the palm branch said, "Man, put me down softly!"

He put the branch down gently on a stone, and the stone said, "Hey, take that thing off me!"

This was enough, and the frightened farmer started to run for his village. On the way he met a fisherman going the other way with a fish trap on his head.

"What's the hurry?" the fisherman asked.

"My yam said, 'Leave me alone!' Then the dog said, 'Listen to what the yam says!' When I went to whip the dog with a palm branch the tree said, 'Put that branch down!' Then the palm branch said, 'Do it softly!' Then the stone said, 'Take that thing off me!' "

"Is that all?" the man with the fish trap said. "Is that so frightening?"

"Well," the man's fish trap said, "did he take it off the stone?"

"Wah!" the fisherman shouted. He threw the fish trap on the ground and began to run with the farmer, and on the trail they met a weaver with a bundle of cloth on his head.

"Where are you going in such a rush?" he asked them.

"My yam said, 'Leave me alone!' " the farmer said. "The dog said, 'Listen to what the yam says!' The tree said, 'Put that branch down!' The branch said, 'Do it softly!' And the stone said, 'Take that thing off me!' "

"And then," the fisherman continued, "the fish trap said, 'Did he take it off?' "

"That's nothing to get excited about," the weaver said. "No reason at all."

"Oh, yes it is," his bundle of cloth said. "If it happened to you, you'd run too!"

"Wah!" the weaver shouted. He threw his bundle on the trail and started running with the other men.

They came panting to the ford in the river and found a man bathing. "Are you chasing a gazelle?" he asked them.

The first man said breathlessly, "My yam talked at me, and it said, 'Leave me alone!' And my dog said, 'Listen to your yam!' And when I cut myself a branch the tree said, 'Put that branch down!' And the branch said, 'Do it softly!' And the stone said, 'Take that thing off me!' "

The fisherman panted, "And my trap said, 'Did he?' "

The weaver wheezed, "And my bundle of cloth said, 'You'd run too!' "

"Is that why you're running?" the man in the river asked.

"Well, wouldn't you run if you were in their position?" the river said.

The man jumped out of the water and began to run with the others. They ran down the main street of the village to the house of the chief. The chief's servant brought his stool out, and he came and sat on it to listen to their complaints. The men began to recite their troubles.

"I went out to my garden to dig yams," the farmer said, waving his arms. "Then everything began to talk! My yam said, 'Leave me alone!' My dog said, 'Pay attention to your yam!' The tree said, 'Put that branch down!' The branch said, 'Do it softly!' And the stone said, 'Take it off me!'"

"And my fish trap said, 'Well, did he take it off?'" the fisherman said.

"And my cloth said, 'You'd run too!'" the weaver said.

"And the river said the same," the bather said hoarsely, his eyes bulging.

The chief listened to them patiently, but he couldn't refrain from scowling. "Now this is really a wild story," he said at last. "You'd better all go back to your work before I punish you for disturbing the peace."

So the men went away, and the chief shook his head and mumbled to himself, "Nonsense like that upsets the community."

"Fantastic, isn't it?" his stool said. "Imagine, a talking yam!"

Cats Are Queer Articles (Irish)

From talking yams to a talking cat is not a great step! In this charming folktale, an ordinary household cat not only talks but suggests a mystery we cannot solve. Who was Balgury? Why did Balgeary suddenly leave the family hearth? Who is holding the funeral? Could Balgeary be the next King of the Cats upon the death of his predecessor? Where is Balgeary now? We can only guess.

There is a special appeal to this folktale. As in so many folktales, the details are all down-to-earth. The storyteller himself is a very prosaic, no-nonsense farmer. His description of the preparation for the fair, the trip both ways, and his report of the conversation with his wife—all these are realistic and believable. And so, when the cat at the graveyard sticks its head through the railing and talks, the episode all seems quite ordinary. The storyteller doesn't bat an eye when he hears a talking cat.

His arrival at home brings a little masterpiece of sharp dialog. The ordinariness of the conversation doesn't prepare us for the startling conclusion to come. We can deduce some things from these final moments in the story, but we are left with a sense of mystery that contrasts with the sober details.

In the best folktales, the miraculous blends easily with the commonplace. The events in "Talk—An Ashanti Tale" are

both ordinary and miraculous, and they are blended as
though talking objects were run-of-the-mill. In that tale, as
here, the characters are sharply drawn, even if briefly. There
are three main characters in "Cats Are Queer Articles." Which
one will you remember longest?

I tell you, cats are the queer articles. You never know where you
are with them. They seem to be different than every other class of
animals. In the old days there were some foreign peoples who
worshipped them, and it is not to be greatly wondered at, when you
think of the intelligence of cats.

I had a strange thing happen to myself years ago with cats. It was
many, many years ago now. I had a calf to sell, and it was the time
of the November fair in Macroom. I'd borrowed the loan of a crib
and horse from a neighbor, and was ready to set off for the fair about
one o'clock in the morning.

Well, it came to one o'clock and I got up. I opened the door, and
the night was so black that you would scarcely know which foot you
were putting before you. I stirred up the fire and put some sticks
under the kettle to make a cup of tea, and while it was boiling I went
out to tackle up the horse. There was a mist coming down, so that I
was wet enough already by the time that I had that job done.

I made the tea, and while I was drinking it I thought what a foolish
thing it was for me to be getting out of a warm bed and going into
the cold, wet night and traveling for twenty-four miles through the
night. But it had to be done, so I buttoned up a grand frieze coat I
had, and off we set. The horse was as unwilling as myself for the
road, and the two of us were ashamed to look each other in the face,
knowing the class of fools we were. We traveled for hours and hours,
and not much of the first hour had gone before I was wet through
and through.

As we drew nearer to the town I could see the lights in the farms
by the roadside, where the people were getting up for the fair who
had not to lose a night's sleep to get there. There was a regular
procession now on the road of calves and cattle being driven into
the fair, but it was still dark and the daylight was only just coming.

Well, I took my place in the fair, and no one came to me and made
me an offer for a long time. I thought that things were not going too
well with me. Then a few asked me, but were offering only a poor
price. I saw other cattle being driven away, and men I knew told me
to sell, for it was a bad fair and prices were low. So at last I did sell,

for the heart had gone out of me with the loss of sleep, and the long journey and the cold and the long waiting.

I tell you that I was a miserable man, standing there with ne'er a bite to eat and wet to the skin, and with the prospect of the long journey home again, and the poor pay I had for my suffering. When I got the money I had something to eat and made a few purchases, and then I thought that if any man ever earned a drink, it was me. So I met some friends and we had a few drinks together, and then parted and went our different ways.

I let the horse go on at her own pace, with the reins hanging loose. The rain came down again, and the power of the drink soon wore off, and I wrapped myself up in my misery. With the sound and the swing of the crib and the creaking of the wheels and the darkness coming down again I fell asleep, as many a man does on the long way home from a winter's fair.

Now and again someone passed me on the road, but I scarcely heard them at all. For miles and miles I went; now asleep, now awake, with all manner of queer notions running in my head, as does happen to a man when he is exhausted.

As I was passing the graveyard of Inchigeela a cat put his head through the railings and said to me, "Tell Balgeary that Balgury is dead." I paid little heed to that, for my head was full of strange notions. I continued on my way. At last I reached home again, and untackled the horse and watered it and fed it, and then went into the house to change out of my wet clothes.

Herself started on me straightaway. 'Tis wonderful the energy that does be in a woman's tongue and the blindness that can be in her eyes, for I was in no mood for talk.

"Well," she said, "what sort of a fair was it?"

"Ah! the same as all fairs," said I.

"Did you get a good price?"

"I did not," said I.

"Were there many at the fair?" she asked then.

"The usual number, I suppose. Did you expect me to count them?"

"Did ye hear any news while ye were in the town?"

There was no end to her questions.

"Hold your tongue," I said, "and give me the tea."

I drank the tea and had a bite to eat and began to feel better. Still she kept on asking me questions.

"Glory me! Fancy going in all that way and hearing nothing at all," she said, when I had no news for her. "You might as well have stayed at home for all the good that you get out of a fair."

I got up from the table and sat by the fire and lit my pipe, but still she plagued me and pestered me with her questions. Had I seen this one? Was I speaking with that one? Was there any news of the other one?

I suppose that the tea and the fire and the tobacco softened me. News and gossip are almost life to a woman, and she bore the hardness of our life as well, and I had brought her nothing home. Then I remembered the cat.

"The only thing that happened to me today," I said, "that has not happened on all fair days, was that when I was passing the graveyard of Inchigeela a cat stuck his head out of the railings."

"Wisha! there is nothing strange in that," she took me up.

"As I passed it called up to me, 'Tell Balgeary that Balgury is dead.' "

At that, the cat, sitting before the fire, whipped round on me. "The Devil fire you!" said he, "why didn't you tell me before? I'll be late for the funeral." And with that and no more, he leapt over the half-door, and was gone like the wind, and from that day to this we have seen no sign of him.

IV. The Surprise Ending

In some folktales we can guess the outcome. We somehow know that Cinderella will win a handsome suitor. We feel that the ugly frog will some day turn into a prince. We trust that Beauty will somehow transform the Beast into someone worthy of her love. Sometimes, however, the folktale turns the tables. "Talk" (page 140) provides an unexpected last line that delights the reader. "The Salamanna Grapes" also provides a surprise ending.

The Salamanna Grapes (Italian)

The story of a princess with many suitors is common in folklore. Shakespeare's *The Merchant of Venice* uses a choice of caskets to determine the winning suitor. More commonly, a quest is required. The suitors must go out into the world to prove themselves worthy, in one way or another, for the beautiful princess's hand. Douglas Fairbanks's classic movie *The Thief of Baghdad* uses the latter device.

Here's another example. In "The History of Prince Ahmed"
in *The Arabian Nights' Entertainments*, three sons of the Sultan
of India must go out into the world on a quest for the hand of
the Princess Nouronnihar. As in *The Thief of Baghdad* and
"The Salamanna Grapes," they must find the rarest object to
be worthy of the beautiful princess. The quest is familiar, but
in the *Arabian Nights* story the sultan has an unusual plan for
settling the tie. What happens next is completely different
from either tale already mentioned, showing how folktales
may take familiar themes and change them in subtle ways.

For many reasons "The Salamanna Grapes" has a familiar
ring. There is a beautiful princess. Three brothers seek her
hand in marriage. All three brothers have remarkable success
on their quest. The youngest brother, as is often the case,
seems to have a favored position. But it is at the moment of
expectant certainty that the folktale decides to provide something extra.

There was once a king who had a very beautiful daughter of
marriageable age. A neighboring king had three grown sons, who all
fell in love with the princess. The princess's father said, "As far as I
am concerned, you are all three equal, and I couldn't for the life of
me give any one of you preference over the other two. But I wouldn't
want to be the cause of any strife among you, so why not travel
about the world for six months, and the one who returns with the
finest present will be my son-in-law."

The three brothers set out together, and when the road branched
off in three different directions, each went his separate way.

The oldest brother traveled for three, four, and five months without
finding a thing worth taking home as a present. Then one morning
of the sixth month in a faraway city, he heard a hawker under his
window: "Carpets for sale! Fine carpets for sale!"

He leaned out the window, and the carpet seller asked, "How about
a nice carpet?"

"That's the last thing I need," he replied. "There are carpets all
over my palace, even in the kitchen!"

"But," insisted the carpet seller, "I'm sure you have no magic
carpet like this one."

"What's so special about it?"

"When you set foot on it, it takes you great distances through the
air."

The prince snapped his fingers. "There's the perfect gift to take back. How much are you asking for it, my good man?"

"One hundred crowns even."

"Agreed!" exclaimed the prince, counting out the hundred crowns.

As soon as he stepped onto it, the carpet went soaring through the air over mountains and valleys and landed at the inn where the brothers had agreed to meet at the end of the six months. The other two, though, had not yet arrived.

The middle brother also had traveled far and wide up to the last days without finding any suitable present. And then he met a peddler crying, "Telescopes! Perfect telescopes! How about a telescope, young man?"

"What would I do with another telescope?" asked the prince. "My house is full of telescopes, and the very best, mind you."

"I bet you've never seen magic telescopes like mine," said the telescope seller.

"What's so special about them?"

"With these telescopes you can see a hundred miles away and through walls as well."

The prince exclaimed, "Wonderful! How much are they?"

"One hundred crowns apiece."

"Here are one hundred crowns. Give me a telescope."

He took the telescope to the inn, found his big brother, and the two of them sat and waited for their little brother.

The youngest boy, up to the very last day, found nothing and gave up all hope. He was on his way home when he met a fruit vendor crying, "Salamanna grapes! Salamanna grapes for sale! Come buy nice Salamanna grapes!"

The prince, who'd never heard of Salamanna grapes, since they didn't grow in his country, asked, "Just what are these grapes you're selling?"

"They are called Salamanna grapes," said the fruit vendor, "and there're no finer grapes in the world. They also work a special wonder."

"What do they do?"

"Put a grape in the mouth of someone breathing their last, and they will get well instantly."

"You don't say!" exclaimed the prince. "I'll buy some in that case. How much are they?"

"They are sold by the grape. But I'll make you a special price: one hundred crowns per grape."

As the prince had three hundred crowns in his pocket, he could buy only three grapes. He put them in a little box with cotton around them and went to join his brothers.

When they were all three together at the inn, they asked each other what they had bought.

"Me? Oh, just a little carpet," said the oldest boy.

"Well, I picked up a little telescope," replied the middle boy.

"Only a little fruit, nothing more," said the third.

"I wonder what's going on at home right now. And at the princess's palace," one of the boys said.

The middle boy casually pointed his telescope toward their capital city. Everything was as usual. Then he looked toward the neighboring kingdom, where their beloved's palace was, and let out a cry.

"What's the matter?" asked the brothers.

"I see our beloved's palace, a stream of carriages, people weeping and tearing their hair. And inside . . . inside I see a doctor and a priest at somebody's bedside, yes, the princess's bedside. She lies there as still and pale as a dead girl. Quick, brothers, let's hurry to her before it's too late. . . . She's dying!"

"We'll never make it. That's more than fifty miles away."

"Don't worry," said the oldest brother, "we'll get there in time. Quick, everybody step onto my carpet."

The carpet flew straight to the princess's room, passed through the open window, and landed by the bed, where it lay like the most ordinary bedside rug, with the three brothers standing on it.

The youngest brother had already taken the cotton from around the three Salamanna grapes, and he put one into the princess's pale mouth. She swallowed it and immediately opened her eyes. Right away the prince put another grape into her mouth, which regained its color at once. He gave her the last grape, and she breathed and raised her arms. She was well. She sat up in bed and asked the maids to dress her in her most beautiful clothes.

Everybody was rejoicing, when all of a sudden the youngest brother said, "So I'm the winner, and the princess will be my bride. Without the Salamanna grapes she'd now be dead."

"No, brother," objected the middle boy, "if I'd not had the telescope and told you the princess was dying, your grapes would have done no good. For that reason I will marry the princess myself."

"I'm sorry, brother," put in the oldest boy. "The princess is mine, and nobody will take her away from me. Your contributions are

nothing compared with mine. Only my carpet brought us here in time."

So the quarrel the king had wanted to avoid became ever more heated, and the king decided to put an end to it by marrying his daughter to a fourth suitor who had come to her empty-handed.

V. Cleverness Admired

Some of the world's great stories tell of people getting into trouble and then getting out again. The James Bond movies have been successful because James Bond gets into incredibly difficult situations—and then miraculously gets out of them. So with many folktales.

Most people admire cleverness. The characters in the stories that follow are challenged in some way or other. In each story the character surmounts the challenge by cleverness and achieves a happy ending.

The folktales come from four different continents, but the central problem is the same. The central character wins out by using unexpected ingenuity.

Jack and His Master (Celtic)

In many folktales the youngest brother or sister is misunderstood, underestimated, and sometimes mistreated as well. "Cinderella" is a good example. We all enjoy cheering the underdog, and folktales show us the underdog triumphant. In the following folktale the youngest brother, often called the "Fool," proves himself the brightest brother and saves the honor and fortune of his family. By acting a fool, he puts his enemy off guard and wins the day.

A poor woman had three sons. The eldest and second eldest were cunning clever fellows, but they called the youngest Jack the Fool, because they thought he was no better than a simpleton. The eldest got tired of staying at home, and said he'd go look for service. He stayed away a whole year, and then came back one day, dragging one foot after the other, and a poor wizened face on him, and he as cross as two sticks. When he was rested and got something to eat, he told them how he got service with the Gray Churl of the Townland of Mischance, and that the agreement was, whoever would first say he was sorry for his bargain, should get an inch wide of the skin of his back, from shoulder to hips, taken off. If it was the master, he should also pay double wages; if it was the servant, he should get no wages at all. "But the thief," says he, "gave me so little to eat, and kept me so hard at work, that flesh and blood couldn't stand it; and when he asked me once, when I was in a passion, if I was sorry for my bargain, I was mad enough to say I was, and here I am disabled for life."

Vexed enough were the poor mother and brothers; and the second eldest said on the spot he'd go and take service with the Gray Churl, and punish him by all the annoyance he'd give him till he'd make him say he was sorry for his agreement. "Oh, won't I be glad to see the skin coming off the old villain's back!" said he. All they could say had no effect: he started off for the Townland of Mischance, and in a twelvemonth he was back just as miserable and helpless as his brother.

All the poor mother could say didn't prevent Jack the Fool from starting to see if he was able to regulate the Gray Churl. He agreed with him for a year for twenty pounds, and the terms were the same.

"Now, Jack," said the Gray Churl, "if you refuse to do anything you are able to do, you must lose a month's wages."

"I'm satisfied," said Jack; "and if you stop me from doing a thing after telling me to do it, you are to give me an additional month's wages."

"I am satisfied," said the master.

"Or if you blame me for obeying your orders, you must give the same."

"I am satisfied," said the master again.

The first day that Jack served he was fed very poorly, and was worked to the saddleskirts. Next day he came in just before the dinner was sent up to the parlour. They were taking the goose off the spit, but well becomes Jack he whips a knife off the dresser, and cuts off one side of the breast, one leg and thigh, and one wing, and fell to. In came the master, and began to abuse him for his assurance. "Oh, you know, master, you're to feed me, and wherever the goose goes won't have to be filled again till supper. Are you sorry for our agreement?"

The master was going to cry out he was, but he bethought himself in time. "Oh no, not at all," said he.

"That's well," said Jack.

Next day Jack was to go clamp turf on the bog. They weren't sorry to have him away from the kitchen at dinnertime. He didn't find his breakfast very heavy on his stomach; so he said to the mistress, "I think, ma'am, it will be better for me to get my dinner now, and not lose time coming home from the bog."

"That's true, Jack," said she. So she brought out a good cake, and a pint of butter, and a bottle of milk, thinking he'd take them away to the bog. But Jack kept his seat, and never drew rein till bread, butter, and milk went down the red lane.

"Now, mistress," said he, "I'll be earlier at my work tomorrow if I sleep comfortably on the sheltery side of a pile of dry peat on dry grass, and not be coming here and going back. So you may as well give me my supper, and be done with the day's trouble." She gave him that, thinking he'd take it to the bog; but he fell to on the spot, and did not leave a scrap to tell tales on him; and the mistress was a little astonished.

He called to speak to the master in the haggard, and said he, "What are servants asked to do in this country after aten their supper?"

"Nothing at all, but to go to bed."

"Oh, very well, sir." He went up on the stable-loft, stripped, and lay down, and someone that saw him told the master. He came up.

"Jack, you anointed scoundrel, what do you mean?"

"To go to sleep, master. The mistress, God bless her, is after giving me my breakfast, dinner, and supper, and yourself told me that bed was the next thing. Do you blame me, sir?"

"Yes, you rascal, I do."

"Hand me out one pound thirteen and fourpence, if you please, sir."

"One divel and thirteen imps, you tinker! what for?"

"Oh, I see, you've forgot your bargain. Are you sorry for it?"

"Oh, ya—no, I mean. I'll give you the money after your nap."

Next morning early, Jack asked how he'd be employed that day. "You are to be holding the plough in that fallow, outside the paddock." The master went over about nine o'clock to see what kind of a ploughman was Jack, and what did he see but the little boy driving the bastes, and the sock and coulter of the plough skimming along the sod, and Jack pulling ding-dong again' the horses.

"What are you doing, you contrary thief?" said the master.

"An' ain't I strivin' to hold this divel of a plough, as you told me; but that ounkrawn of a boy keeps whipping on the bastes in spite of all I say; will you speak to him?"

"No, but I'll speak to you. Didn't you know, you bosthoon, that when I said 'holding the plough,' I meant reddening the ground?"

"Faith, an' if you did, I wish you had said so. Do you blame me for what I have done?"

The master caught himself in time, but he was so stomached, he said nothing.

"Go on and redden the ground now, you knave, as other ploughmen do."

"An' are you sorry for our agreement?"

"Oh, not at all, not at all!"

Jack ploughed away like a good workman all the rest of the day.

In a day or two the master bade him go and mind the cows in a field that had half of it under young corn. "Be sure, particularly," said he, "to keep Browney from the wheat; while she's out of mischief there's no fear of the rest."

About noon, he went to see how Jack was doing his duty, and what did he find but Jack asleep with his face to the sod, Browney grazing near a thorn-tree, one end of a long rope round her horns, and the other end round the tree, and the rest of the beasts all trampling and eating the green wheat. Down came the switch on Jack.

"Jack, you vagabone, do you see what the cows are at?"

"And do you blame, master?"

"To be sure, you lazy sluggard, I do."

"Hand me out one pound thirteen and fourpence, master. You said if I only kept Browney out of mischief, the rest would do no harm. There she is as harmless as a lamb. Are you sorry for hiring me master?"

"To be—that is, not at all. I'll give you your money when you go to dinner. Now, understand me; don't let a cow go out of the field nor into the wheat the rest of the day."

"Never fear, master!" and neither did he. But the churl would rather than a great deal he had not hired him.

The next day three heifers were missing, and the master bade Jack go in search of them.

"Where will I look for them?" said Jack.

"Oh, every place likely and unlikely for them all to be in."

The churl was getting very exact in his words. When he was coming into the bawn at dinnertime, what work did he find Jack at but pulling armfuls of the thatch off the roof, and peeping into the holes he was making?

"What are you doing there, you rascal?"

"Sure, I'm looking for the heifers, poor things!"

"What would bring them there?"

"I don't think anything could bring them in it; but I looked first into the likely places, that is, the cowhouses, and the pastures, and the fields next 'em, and now I'm looking in the unlikeliest place I can think of. Maybe it's not pleasing to you it is."

"And to be sure it isn't pleasing to me, aggravating goose-cap!"

"Please, sir, hand me one pound thirteen and four pence before you sit down to your dinner. I'm afraid it's sorrow that's on you for hiring me at all."

"May the div—oh no; I'm not sorry. Will you begin, if you please, and put in the thatch again, just as if you were doing it for your mother's cabin?"

"Oh, faith I will, sir, with a heart and a half," and by the time the farmer came out from his dinner, Jack had the roof better than it was before, for he made the boy give him new straw.

Says the master when he came out, "Go, Jack, and look for the heifers, and bring them home."

"And where will I look for 'em?"

"Go and search for them as if they were your own." The heifers were all in the paddock before sunset.

Next morning, says the master, "Jack, the path across the bog to the pasture is very bad; the sheep does be sinking in it every step; go and make the sheep's feet a good path." About an hour after he came to the edge of the bog, and what did he find Jack at but sharpening a carving knife, and the sheep standing or grazing round.

"Is this the way you are mending the path, Jack?" said he.

"Everything must have a beginning, master," said Jack, "and a thing well begun is half done. I am sharpening the knife, and I'll have the feet off every sheep in the flock while you'd be blessing yourself."

"Feet off my sheep, you anointed rogue! and what would you be taking their feet off for?"

"An' sure to mend the path as you told me. Says you, 'Jack, make a path with the foot of the sheep.' "

"Oh, you fool, I meant make good the path for the sheep's feet."

"It's a pity you didn't say so, master. Hand me out one pound thirteen and fourpence if you don't like me to finish my job."

"Divel do you good with your one pound thirteen and fourpence!"

"It's better pray than curse, master. Maybe you're sorry for your bargain?"

"And to be sure I am—not yet, anyway."

The next night the master was going to a wedding; and says he to Jack, before he set out: "I'll leave at midnight, and I wish you to come and be with me home, for fear I might be overtaken with the drink. If you're there before, you may throw a sheep's eye at me, and I'll be sure to see that they'll give you something for yourself."

About eleven o'clock, while the master was in great spirits, he felt something clammy hit him on the cheek. It fell beside his tumbler, and when he looked at it, what was it but the eye of a sheep. Well, he couldn't imagine who threw it at him, or why it was thrown at him. After a little he got a blow on the other cheek, and still it was by another sheep's eye. Well, he was very vexed, but he thought better to say nothing. In two minutes more, when he was opening his mouth to take a sup, another sheep's eye was slapped into it. He sputtered it out, and cried, "Man o' the house, isn't it a great shame for you to have anyone in the room that would do such a nasty thing?"

"Master," says Jack, "don't blame the honest man. Sure it's only myself that was throwin' them sheep's eyes at you, to remind you I was here, and that I wanted to drink the bride and bridegroom's health. You know yourself bade me."

"I know that you are a great rascal; and where did you get the eyes?"

"An' where would I get em' but in the heads of your own sheep? Would you have me meddle with the bastes of any neighbour, who might put me in the Stone Jug for it?"

"Sorrow on me that ever I had the bad luck to meet with you."

"You're all witness," said Jack, "that my master says he is sorry for having met with me. My time is up. Master, hand me over double wages, and come into the next room, and lay yourself out like a man that has some decency in him, till I take a strip of skin an inch broad from your shoulder to your hip."

Everyone shouted out against that; but, says Jack, "You didn't hinder him when he took the same strips from the backs of my two brothers, and sent them home in that state, and penniless, to their poor mother."

When the company heard the rights of the business, they were only too eager to see the job done. The master bawled and roared, but there was no help at hand. He was stripped to his hips, and laid on the floor in the next room, and Jack had the carving knife in his hand ready to begin.

"Now you cruel old villain," said he, giving the knife a couple of scrapes along the floor, "I'll make you an offer. Give me, along with my double wages, two hundred guineas to support my poor brothers, and I'll do without the strap."

"No!" said he, "I'd let you skin me from head to foot first."

"Here goes then," said Jack with a grin, but the first little scar he gave, Churl roared out, "Stop your hand; I'll give the money."

"Now, neighbours," said Jack, "you mustn't think worse of me than I deserve. I wouldn't have the heart to take an eye out of a rat itself; I got half a dozen of them from the butcher, and only used three of them."

So all came again into the other room, and Jack was made sit down, and everybody drank his health, and he drank everybody's health at one offer. And six stout fellows saw himself and the master home, and waited in the parlour while he went up and brought down the two hundred guineas, and double wages for Jack himself. When he got home, he brought the summer along with him to the poor mother and the disabled brothers; and he was no more Jack the Fool in the people's mouths, but "Skin Churl Jack."

The Flying Contest (Surinamese)

Superior strength and ability are valuable qualities. Sometimes, though, using one's head is more successful than using one's brawn, as the following folktale demonstrates.

Now, one time all the birds got together and decided that they needed a king, because all important creatures had a king. So they went to Lion to have him call a council of birds, as Lion was king of all the animals.

When the meeting was called, all the birds came together. Kunibre was the smallest, but he was smart! He thought about the subject, and finally announced that despite his size, he would be king. The others wondered about this, but they didn't really know what to do.

Lion thought about it and asked the birds how they thought it should be settled. They all talked, and Falcon, who knew he could fly high, hoped that they would decide by having a contest to see who could fly highest. But he couldn't suggest this because the other birds would know what he was up to. Luckily, Nightingale said, "I want to say something, but I don't know if it will be agreeable to everyone." They all said, "Speak! Let's hear what you have to say." "I won't suggest that you should choose by who sings most sweetly, because I know that if I raise a note, I should win. But let me say that God gave us all one thing and that is wings. So whoever can fly the highest, he should be made king." Falcon was pleased when he heard this as it had been on his mind for such a long time. He jumped up and said, "I think that is the best plan," and all the others agreed, even Kunibre. What no one knew was that Kunibre had his own plan in mind.

When they began the contest Kunibre sat right down in the middle of Falcon's back. Now Kunibre was so small that Falcon didn't even know he was up there. So they started out, and after a while, when they looked and saw how high Falcon had flown, they said, "Falcon takes first prize and he shall be our king." But when he landed, they saw that Kunibre was there on top. So they had to say, "Well, no, Kunibre was even higher than Falcon, and he shall be our king."

The Mice That Ate Iron (Indian)

The following folktale is a good example of the underdog triumphant. The young man seems to have no way to right the wrong perpetrated by the merchant, but he chooses to fight fire with fire. If the merchant seeks to cheat by an absurdity, the young man will counter with an equal absurdity—and win.

Once upon a time there was a merchant's son who had spent all his father's wealth and had only an iron balance left. Now the balance was made of a thousand *Palas** of iron; and depositing it in the care of a certain merchant, he went to another land. When, on his return, he went to that merchant to get back his balance, the merchant said, "It has been eaten by mice." And he repeated, "The iron of which it was composed was particularly sweet, and so the mice ate it." This he said with an outward show of sorrow, although laughing inwardly at the simple fellow who seemed to believe his story.

Thereupon the merchant's son asked him for some food, and the other one, being in a good temper, consented to give him some. Then the merchant's son went to bathe, taking with him the other's son, a mere child, whom he persuaded to come with him by offering him a gift. After he had bathed, the wise merchant's son deposited the boy in the house of a friend and returned alone to the house of the merchant. The latter said to him, "Where is that son of mine?"

* About 100 pounds.

Whereupon the merchant's son replied, "A hawk swooped down from the air and carried him off."

The merchant in a rage said, "You have concealed my son." And so he took him into the king's judgment hall; and there the merchant's son repeated his original statement. The officers of the court said, "This is impossible. How could a hawk carry off a boy?"

So the merchant's son answered, "In a country where a large balance of iron was eaten by mice, a hawk might easily carry off an elephant."

When the officers of the court heard that, they inquired further and, on being told the entire story, made the merchant restore the balance to the owner, and he, for his part, restored the merchant's son.

The Treasures of Rhampsinitus (Egyptian)

Human nature calls to us across the centuries. Human qualities, both good and bad, appear in the earliest written records, but we can be sure that oral traditions carried them still farther back. Perhaps the earliest folktale in *Myths and Folklore* is this story of greed and ingenuity from ancient Egypt. Once again a powerful person is outwitted by a simple person, a mason's son.

There was once a king of Egypt who was called *Rhampsinitus*. He was very rich and greedy. He tried to get as much money as he could from his people; but the more he had, the more he wanted. His house was full of gold and silver; and his servants every day brought him more, until he was puzzled to know where he should put it.

For a long time he thought how he might hide it, for he could hardly rest by day or sleep by night for fear that thieves might come and take away some of his riches. At last he sent for a mason and told him to build a great and strong room, which should have no windows and only a single door, fastened with iron bars and with strong bolts and locks. So the room was built in a corner of the palace, and the outer wall faced the roadway.

When the room was finished, Rhampsinitus carried all his silver and gold secretly into it; and the whole room was filled with his riches. There were jars full of gold round the walls, and others full of diamonds, and pearls, and rubies, and jaspers; and in the middle of the room there was a great heap of coins, which shone so brightly that they almost made that dismal place look cheerful.

Then King Rhampsinitus thought himself a happier man, and he went to sleep more soundly, because he fancied that no one would be able to steal his money.

Not long after this the old mason who had built the treasure house fell ill, and he called his sons to his bedside and said to them, "I am so weak and ill that I know I shall soon die; but I do not wish to leave you without telling you the secret of the room where King Rhampsinitus has hoarded up his money. I have little to give you myself, for the king tried to make me work hard and to give me as little as he could for all my trouble. But I know a way in which you may get money when you are in need of it. The king does not know that I have placed a mark on one of the stones in the wall of his treasure house on the side which faces the road. This stone can be easily taken out and put back again by two men, or even by one, and his money can be taken without moving the bolts or touching the locks."

Soon after he had told them this secret, the old mason died; and not long afterward his two sons began to think about the treasures of King Rhampsinitus, for the money which the old mason left them was soon wasted in eating and drinking with their friends. But they did not care, for they knew that when they wanted it they could get plenty of money from the treasure of King Rhampsinitus.

So one night, when the moon was shining high up in the sky, they went very softly to the house where the money was hidden; and after looking about for a little while, they found the stone, and they put it aside and went into the room. They were afraid to stay there long; but they filled their clothes with as much gold and silver as they could carry, and when they had put back the stone carefully, they went home and showed their mother all the money which they had stolen from the king.

The next night they went again; and for many nights they kept on going, till at last King Rhampsinitus began to think that some of the heaps of money were smaller than they used to be; and every day when he went into the treasure house he looked at the heaps, and rubbed his eyes, and looked at them again, for he could not make out how it was they seemed to grow smaller and smaller.

And he said, "This is very odd. What can it be that takes away my money? The locks of the treasure house are not touched, and the bolts and bars have not been moved; and still my heaps of gold and silver seem every day to become smaller than they were."

Then he thought that perhaps it might be his own fancy, until he put a heap of coins on purpose in one part of the room; and very soon these were taken away. Then he knew that some thief had found out a way to come in without unlocking the door. But King Rhampsinitus did not care much about it, for he said, "I think I know how to catch the thief who comes to steal my money." So he got a large trap which was big enough to hold a man's leg and put it in the treasure house.

In a day or two after this the sons of the old mason came again, and the younger one went in first and presently stepped into the trap. His leg was terribly hurt, but he did not scream or make any noise, because he was afraid that King Rhampsinitus might hear him. Then he called to his brother who was standing outside, and showed him how he was caught in the trap, so that he could not get his leg out of it; and he said, "Make haste brother and cut off my head, and carry it away. You must do this; for if you do not, the king will come and see who I am, and then he will have your head cut off as well as mine."

His brother was very sorry, but there seemed to be no help for it. So he cut off his head and took it home with him; and when King Rhampsinitus came in the morning to look for gold and silver, he started back and held up his hands in great wonder; for he saw that the two men had come in and that one had carried away the dead man's head, and he knew that there was someone else still alive who might come and rob him of his money.

Then he thought of a way to find him out, and he told his servants to take the body out of the trap and hang it upon the wall, and ordered the soldiers to watch and if they saw anyone crying or weeping near it, to take him and bring him before the king.

Now when the mason's elder son got home, he was obliged to tell his mother that his brother had been caught in the trap and that he had cut off his head and brought it away with him; and his mother was very sorry and very angry too, and she said that he must go and get the body and bury it along with the head. And she was still more angry when in the morning the soldiers hung the body of her son high up on the wall; and she called her elder son and said to him that she would go and tell King Rhampsinitus all that had been done unless he went and brought his brother's body to her.

At first her son was greatly troubled and could not think what to do; but presently he started up from his seat and went out and got five or six donkeys, and on their backs he placed large leather sacks full of wine, which he had bought with the money of King Rhamp-

sinitus. Then he drove the donkeys by the wall on which his brother's body was hung up; and when he came near the soldiers who were guarding it, he loosed the string which was round the mouth of two or three of the sacks and the wine began to trickle down upon the ground.

Then he cried out with a loud voice for all the guards to hear, and tore his hair, and ran about the road as if he did not know which sack to tie up first. Quickly the soldiers came up, and there was such a pushing as was never seen before. Instead of helping him to tie up the leather bottles, they ran for cups to catch up the wine as it streamed out on the ground, and they drank it up as fast as their cups were filled.

Then the mason's son began to scold them and pretended to be dreadfully angry; but the soldiers tried to coax and soothe him, until at last he drove his donkeys off the road and began to put the sacks right again. Then the guards came round him and began to talk and laugh with him; and by and by he gave them one of the bottles of wine to drink. But they said that they would not drink it unless he drank some of it with them. So they poured the wine out into the cups, and they drank and made merry together.

Then he gave them another bottle, and another, and another, till the soldiers fell down to the ground fast asleep. They had been so long drinking and laughing together that it was now night; and it was so dark nobody could see what he was doing.

Then the mason's son went softly to the wall and took down his brother's body, which was hanging on it, and afterward he went to all the soldiers, one by one, and shaved off the whiskers and beard from one side of their faces; and then he returned home to his mother and gave her the body of his brother.

When the morning came the soldiers woke up from their heavy sleep. They felt very dull and stupid, but when they looked at the wall they saw that there was no dead body hanging on it; and when they looked at each other, they knew what a trick the mason's son had played them. They were dreadfully angry and terribly afraid; but there was no help except to go and tell the king.

As they went, a crowd of people gathered round them, and everyone shouted with laughter to see the soldiers who had half their whiskers and beards shaved off. But when King Rhampsinitus heard what the mason's son had done he was quite furious, and he said, "What can I do to find out the man who has done these very wicked and very clever things?"

So he sent a herald all through the country and told him to say with a loud voice that the king would not punish the man who had stolen the money, but would give him his daughter for a wife, if he would only tell him how he had got into his treasure house. Then the son of the old mason came and told Rhampsinitus all the story, and the king looked at him earnestly and said, "I believe that the Egyptians are cleverer than all other men; but you are cleverer than all the Egyptians."

I Ate the Loaf (Spanish)

> Turning the tables is a common theme in folktales. The merchant in "The Mice That Ate Iron" uses a shabby trick to cheat the young man, but the young man turns the tables and fights fire with fire. "I Ate the Loaf" presents a similar situation: those who choose deception may themselves be deceived.

Two citizens and a farmer, going to Mecca, shared provisions till they reached that place, and then their food failed, so that nothing remained save so much flour as would make a single loaf, and that a small one. The citizens, seeing this, said to each other, "We have too little bread, and our companion eats a great deal. Therefore we ought to have a plan to take away from him his share of the loaf and eat it by ourselves alone."

Accordingly they proposed the following plan to him: to make and bake the loaf, and while it was being baked to sleep. Whoever of them saw the most wonderful things in a dream should eat the loaf alone. These words they spake artfully, as they thought the farmer too simple for inventions of the kind.

They made the loaf and baked it, and at length lay down to sleep. But the rustic, more crafty than they thought, while his companions were asleep, took the half-baked loaf, ate it up, and again lay down.

One of the citizens, as if terrified out of his sleep, awoke and called his companion, who thereupon inquired, "What is the matter?"

He said, "I have seen a wondrous vision, for it seemed to me that two angels opened the gates of paradise and let me within."

Then his companion said to him, "This is a wondrous vision you have seen. But I dreamed that two angels took me and, cleaving the earth, led me to the lower regions."

The farmer heard all this and pretended to be asleep; but the citizens, being deceived, and wishing to deceive, called on him to awake. Thereupon the rustic cunningly cried out, as though terrified, "Who are they that call me?"

Then they said, "We are your companions."

"Have you returned already?" he exclaimed.

To this they replied, "Where did we go, that we should return?"

Then the farmer said, "Now it seemed to me that two angels took one of you, opened the gates of heaven and led him within, then two others took the other, opened the earth, and took him to hell. Seeing this, I thought neither of you would return anymore; so I rose and ate the loaf."

VI. Travelers' Tales

"By Allah, I will not kill her until I hear the rest of her story."

This intriguing exclamation by the Sultan Schahriah is near the beginning of one of the greatest collections of folktales: *The Arabian Nights' Entertainment* or *The Thousand and One Nights*. Though the framework of these stories is Persian, the stories are believed to be of many origins: Arabian, Egyptian, Indian, and Jewish.

What made the Sultan utter so extraordinary a line? The explanation is a kind of folktale in itself.

Sultan Schahriah had become embittered, an enemy of all women. He had an unpleasant habit of marrying and then having his brides beheaded shortly after the wedding. Soon all the eligible girls had been killed or had departed in haste. But the Sultan was still eager to be a bridegroom. He ordered his grand vizier to find him another bride. The hapless vizier looked all over in vain, for no one sought the doubtful honor of becoming Schahriah's wife.

Fearing that his own neck would be forfeit if he admitted failure, the vizier fell into profound melancholy. His beautiful daughter Scheherazade noticed his depression and asked its cause. After he had told her, she insisted that she be the Sultan's new bride. The father tried to dissuade her, but she persisted. With a heavy heart the father consented. Before she left him, Scheherazade concocted a plan. Her sister was to ask her, in front of the Sultan, to tell a story.

All went ahead as scheduled. The marriage took place. The sister asked Scheherazade to tell a tale. The Sultan agreed, and Scheherazade told the first of her marvelous stories. At a crucial point in the story Scheherazade stopped.

The listeners complimented her on the telling, but she replied, "What is this in comparison with what I'll tell on the next night, if I live."

The king's reply is at the head of this introduction. And so it went. Each night Scheherazade stopped and was spared to tell the rest. This went on for a thousand and one nights. At the end of that time the Sultan had fallen in love with her and had forgotten his hatred of women. She was spared—and they lived happily ever after.

So much for the framework of the stories. The tales are among the world's greatest. Here are tales of great sultans, jinns, afreets, enchanted maidens, buried treasure, rogues, handsome princes, magicians, sorcerers, and all the personages of great folktales. Here are the tales of Aladdin, of Ali Baba and the Forty Thieves, and above all of Sinbad the Sailor.

The Voyages of Sinbad of the Sea (Arabic)

Sinbad has a series of marvelous voyages, seven in all. On his first voyage Sinbad and his fellow merchants land upon an island. It suddenly starts to submerge, and the unfortunates discover that they have landed upon a huge fish, which has been stirred by the fires they built upon it.

On another voyage he is married to a woman in a strange land. He discovers, to his horror, that the custom of the country requires the husband to be buried alive if his wife dies, and vice versa. His wife dies, and Sinbad is buried alive but manages to escape with great wealth taken from the tombs.

On another voyage his vessel is destroyed by huge stones dropped by gigantic birds called *rocs*. He swims to a desert island, where he meets an old man, who signals to be carried. Sinbad puts the old man on his shoulders but finds to his horror that the old man, called the *Old Man of the Sea*, refuses to get down. He finally is able to shed his tormentor.

On still another voyage, during an elephant hunt, Sinbad hides in a tree to avoid the threatening beasts. One huge elephant uproots the tree—with Sinbad in it—and stalks off.

By now you have guessed that Sinbad escapes his perils, and you realize why Sultan Schahriah was willing to let Scheherazade live to finish her "to be continued" stories.

Among the best of the tales of Sinbad are the second and third voyages. You'll probably find certain familiar situations here, some that will remind you of the *Odyssey*. For example, a monster in the second voyage will remind you of the Cyclops (pages 78–85). It is a source of wonder that many peoples, separated by time and place, have developed stories with similar incidents.

In most of the travel folktales there is a grain of truth—for example, the custom of burying the wife alive with her husband. Isolated examples of this barbaric custom survived as recently as a century ago in India. But the most appealing parts of the Sinbad stories are those of pure fancy, of birds that blot out the sun when they fly and eggs as big as the domes of mosques.

The Second Voyage of Sinbad of the Sea

Know, O my brothers, that I was enjoying a most comfortable life, until it occurred to me one day to travel again in the lands of other people. I felt a longing to see the countries and islands of the world. Having taken from my money a large sum, I purchased with it goods and merchandise suitable for travel and packed them up. Then I went to the bank of the river and found a handsome new vessel. It had a numerous crew and was well equipped. So I embarked my bales in it, and we set sail that day. The voyage was pleasant to us, and we passed from sea to sea and from island to island. At every place where we cast anchor, we sold and bought goods.

Thus we continued to do until we came to a beautiful island abounding with trees bearing ripe fruits. Flowers diffused their fragrance; birds warbled, but there were no inhabitants. The master anchored our vessel at the island, and we went ashore. I wandered about the island with the rest and rested by a spring of pure water among the trees. I had with me some food and sat in that place eating what God had allotted me. The breeze was sweet to us in that place, and the time was pleasant to me. Soon I fell asleep, enjoying that sweet breeze. After I awakened, I found no one left. The vessel had gone with the passengers. Not one of them had remembered me; so they left me on the island.

I looked about it to right and left, and found no one but me. I was thoroughly upset. I had not a thing with me, neither food nor drink. I became desolate, weary in my soul, and despairing of life.

I said, "Not every time does the jar escape unbroken; though I escaped once, there is little chance I'll escape again."

Then I began to weep and wail for myself. I blamed myself for what I had done, and for my having undertaken this voyage after I had been happy at home, enjoying good food and good drink and good apparel. I repented of my having gone forth from the city of

Baghdad and set out on a voyage over the sea, after the fatigue that I had suffered during my first voyage. I felt at the point of destruction, close to madness.

After that, I rose and walked about the island to the right and left, unable to sit in one place. Then I climbed a lofty tree and began to look from it to the right and left. I saw nothing but the sky and water; trees and birds; islands and sands. As I looked sharply, though, there appeared to me on the island a white object, indistinctly seen in the distance, of enormous size. I descended from the tree and went toward it.

When I came to it I found that it was a huge white dome of great height and large circumference. I drew near to it, and walked round it, but found no door to it. I found that I had not strength nor activity to climb it on account of its exceeding smoothness. I made a mark at the place where I stood and went round the dome measuring its circumference. Lo, it was fifty full paces. I tried to think of some way of gaining an entrance into it.

Sunset had now drawn near. Suddenly the sun was hidden, and the sky became dark. The sun was veiled from me. I imagined that a cloud had come over it, but no clouds had formed. I wondered and raised my head. Examining that object attentively, I saw that it was a bird of enormous size, bulky body, and wide wings, flying in the air. This it was that had hidden the sun. At this my wonder increased. I remembered a story which travelers and voyagers had told me long before that there is in certain of the islands, a bird of enormous size called the *roc*. It feeds its young ones with elephants. I was convinced, therefore, that the dome which I had seen was one of the eggs of the roc. While I wondered, that bird alighted upon the dome and brooded over it with its wings. It stretched its legs behind upon the ground and slept over it.

Then I arose and unwound my turban from my head. I folded it and twisted it so that it became like a rope. After this I girded myself with it, binding it tightly round my waist. I tied myself by it to one of the feet of that bird and made the knot fast. I thought, "Perhaps this bird will carry me to a land of cities and inhabitants; and that will be better than remaining on this island."

I passed the night sleepless, fearing that, if I slept, the bird would fly away with me when I was not aware. When the dawn came, and morn appeared, the bird rose from its egg. Uttering a great cry, it drew me up into the sky. It ascended and soared up so high that I imagined it had reached the highest region of the sky. After that, it descended with me gradually until it alighted with me upon the earth and rested upon a lofty spot.

When I reached the earth, I hastily untied the band from its foot, fearing it, though it did not know about me. After I had loosed my turban from it, I walked away. Then it took something from the ground in its talons and soared to the upper region of the sky. I looked attentively at that thing, and, lo, it was a serpent of enormous size.

After this I walked about that place and found myself upon a high ridge. Beneath was a large, wide, deep valley. By its side was a great mountain, very high. No one could see its summit because of its excessive height, and no one had power to ascend it. I therefore blamed myself for what I had done and said, "Would that I had remained on the island, since it is better than this desert place. At least on the island are found fruits that I might have eaten. I might have drunk of its rivers. But here are neither trees nor fruits nor water.

Then I arose and walked into the valley. I found its ground to be composed of diamonds, stones so hard that neither iron nor rock have any effect upon them. All that valley was likewise occupied by serpents and venomous snakes, every one of them like a palm tree. These monsters were large enough to swallow an elephant. They appeared in the night and hid themselves during the day, fearing lest the roc and the vulture should carry them off and after that tear them to pieces. I remained in that valley, repenting of what I had done, and said within myself, "I have hastened my own destruction!"

The day was ending, and I began to walk along that valley, looking for a place in which to pass the night. I feared those serpents and forgot my food and drink, concerned only for my life. There appeared to me a cave nearby, so I walked thither and found its entrance narrow. I therefore entered it. Seeing a large stone by its mouth, I pushed it and stopped with it the mouth of the cave while I was within it. I said to myself, "I am safe now that I have entered this place; when daylight comes I will go forth and see what destiny will do."

Then I looked within the cave and beheld a huge serpent sleeping at the upper end of it over its eggs. At this my flesh quaked, and I raised my head and prayed. I passed all the night sleepless, until the dawn rose and shone. I removed the stone with which I had closed the entrance of the cave and went forth from it, like one intoxicated, giddy from excessive sleeplessness and hunger and fear.

I then walked along the valley. Suddenly a great slaughtered animal fell in front of me, and I found no one. As I wondered, I remembered a story that I had heard long before from certain merchants and travelers. In the mountains of diamonds no one can gain access to the diamonds except through a stratagem. The merchants take a sheep, slaughter it, skin it, and cut up its flesh, which they throw down from the mountain to the bottom of the valley. As it falls fresh and moist, some of the diamonds stick to it. At midday, large birds of the vulture family descend to that meat and take it in their talons. They fly up to the top of the mountains. Then the merchants come to them and cry out at them, and they fly away from the meat. The merchants then go to that meat and take from it the stones sticking to it. After this they leave the meat for the birds and the wild beasts, and carry the stones to their countries.

Therefore when I beheld that slaughtered animal and remembered this story, I arose and went to the slaughtered beast. I selected a great number of the diamonds and put them into my pockets and within my clothes. While I was doing this, lo, another great slaughtered animal fell near me. So I bound myself to it with my turban. Laying myself down on my back, I placed it upon my bosom and grasped it firmly. Thus it was raised high above the ground. Soon a vulture descended upon it, seized it with its talons, and flew up with it into the air with me attached to it. It didn't stop soaring until it had ascended to the summit of the mountain. Then it alighted and was about to tear off some meat. Suddenly there came a great and loud cry from behind that vulture. Something made a clattering with a piece of wood upon the mountain; the vulture flew away in fear and soared into the sky.

I therefore disengaged myself from the slaughtered animal with the blood of which my clothes were polluted, and stood by its side. The merchant who had cried out at the vulture advanced to the slaughtered animal and saw me standing there. He spoke not to me, for he was frightened. But he went to the slaughtered beast and turned it over. Not finding anything upon it, he uttered a loud lament.

I went up to him, and he said to me, "Who are you? Why did you come to this place?"

I answered him, "Fear not; for you shall receive of me what will gladden you. I have with me abundance of diamonds, of which I will give you as much as you need. Every piece that I have is better than all that would come to you by other means. Therefore be not afraid."

Upon this the man thanked me and prayed for me. The other

merchants heard me talking with their companion; so they came to me. Each merchant had thrown down a slaughtered animal. They greeted me and congratulated me on my safety. I told them my whole story.

Then I gave to the owner of the slaughtered animal to which I had attached myself an abundance of what I had brought with me. He was delighted with me and prayed for me and thanked me for that. The other merchants said to me, "By Allah, a new life has been given you. No one has ever arrived at this place before you and escaped from it. But praise be to God for your safety!"

They passed the next night in a pleasant and safe place, and I passed the night with them. I was full of the utmost joy at my escape from the valley of serpents and my arrival in an inhabited country.

When day came, we arose and journeyed over that great mountain. We saw in the valley numerous serpents. At last we arrived at a garden in a great and beautiful island. Here were camphor trees, under each of which a hundred men might shade themselves. In that island too is a kind of wild beast called the rhinoceros, which grazes there like oxen and buffaloes in our country. It is a huge beast with a single thick horn in the middle of its head. The sailors and travelers have told us that this wild beast can lift the great elephant upon its horn and keep grazing without being aware of the elephant. Soon the elephant dies. Its fat, melting by the heat of the sun and flowing upon its head, enters the eyes of the rhinoceros so that it becomes blind. Then it lies down upon the shore, and the roc comes to it and carries it off along with the elephant.

The valley beforementioned contains a great quantity of diamonds such as I carried off and hid in my pockets. For these the people gave me in exchange, goods and commodities belonging to them, as well as pieces of silver and pieces of gold. I traveled about amusing myself with the sight of different countries, until we arrived at the city of El-Basrah.

We remained there a few days, and then I came to the city of Baghdad, the Abode of Peace. I entered my house, bringing with me a great quantity of diamonds and money and commodities and goods in abundance. I met my family and relations, bestowed alms and gifts, made presents to all my family and companions, and began to eat, drink and dress well.

I associated with friends and companions, forgot all that I had suffered, and ceased not to enjoy a pleasant life and joyful heart and dilated bosom, with sport and merriment. Everyone who heard of my arrival came to me and asked me about my voyage and the states of the different countries, so I told what I had experienced and suffered. Everyone wondered at the severity of my sufferings and congratulated me on my safety. —This is the end of the account of the events that befell me during the second voyage.

The Third Voyage of Sinbad of the Sea

Know, O my brothers, and hear from me the story of the third voyage, for it is more wonderful than the preceding stories, hitherto related. When I returned from the second voyage, I resided in the city of Baghdad for a length of time in most perfect prosperity and happiness. Then my soul became desirous of travel and diversion, and I longed for commerce and gain and profits. So I meditated and bought an abundance of goods suited for a sea voyage and packed them up. I departed with them from the city of Baghdad to the city of El-Basrah. There, coming to the bank of the river, I beheld a great vessel, in which were many merchants and other passengers, people of worth and kindness. I therefore embarked with them in that vessel, and we departed in expectation of good fortune and safety. We proceeded from sea to sea, from island to island, and from city to city. At every place we diverted ourselves, selling and buying in the utmost joy and happiness.

We were one day pursuing our course in the midst of the roaring sea, when the master looked at the different quarters of the sea, and then slapped his face, plucked his beard, rent his clothes, and uttered a great cry.

So we said to him, "O master, what is the news?"

He answered, "Know, O passengers that the wind has prevailed against us and driven us out of our course in the midst of the sea. Destiny has cast us, through our evil fortune, towards the Mountain of Apes. No one has ever arrived at this place and escaped, and my heart is oppressed with the conviction of the destruction of us all."

The words of the master were scarcely ended when the apes came to us and surrounded the vessel on every side, numerous as locusts, dispersed about the vessel and on the shore. We feared that if we killed one of them or struck him or drove him away, they would kill us on account of their excessive number. For numbers prevail against courage, and we feared that they would plunder our goods and our commodities. They are the most hideous of beasts, covered with hair like black felt. Their appearance strikes terror. No one understands their language. They shun the society of men. They climbed up the cables and severed them with their teeth. They severed all the ropes of the vessel in every part, so the vessel inclined with the wind and stopped at their mountain and on their coast. Then having seized all the merchants and the other passengers and landed upon the island, they took the vessel with all its contents and went their way with it.

They left us upon the island. The vessel became concealed from us, and we knew not whither they had gone with it. While we were upon that island eating of its fruits and its herbs and drinking of the rivers, there appeared to us an inhabited house in the midst of the island. We therefore walked towards it. It was a pavilion with lofty angles and high walls. It had an entrance with folding doors, which were open. The doors were of ebony. We entered this pavilion, and found in it a wide, open space, like a wide, large court. Around this were many lofty doors, and at its upper end was a high and great bench of stone. There were also in it utensils for cooking, hung over the fire pots, and around them were many bones. But we saw nobody and we wondered at that extremely. We sat in the open space in that pavilion a little while, after which we slept. We slept until sunset.

Suddenly, the earth trembled beneath us, and we heard a confused noise from the upper air. There descended upon us, from the summit of the pavilion, a person of enormous size, in human form. He was of lofty stature, like a great palm tree. He had two eyes like two blazes of fire, tusks like the tusks of swine and a mouth of prodigious size, like the mouth of a well. His lips were like the lips of a camel, hanging down upon his bosom, and he had ears like two mortars, hanging down upon his shoulders. The nails of his hands were like claws of the lion. When we saw him our terror was violent, and through the violence of our fear and dread and terror we became as dead men. And after he had descended upon the ground, he sat a little while upon the bench.

Then he arose and came to us. He seized me by my hands from among my companions the merchants, lifted me up from the ground in his hand, and felt me and turned me over. I was in his hand like a little mouthful. He continued to feel me as the butcher feels the sheep that he is about to slaughter, but he found me lean from excessive fatigue and from the voyage. He therefore let me go from his hand, and took another from among my companions. He turned him over as he had turned me over, and felt him as he had felt me, and let him go. He ceased not to feel us and turn us over, one after another, until he came to the master of our ship. He was a fat, stout, broad-shouldered man, a person of strength and vigor: so he pleased him. The giant seized him as the butcher seizes the animal that he is about to slaughter, and having thrown him on the ground, put his foot upon his neck, which he thus broke. Then he brought a long spit and thrust it into his throat and spitted him.

After this he lighted a fierce fire and placed over it that spit upon which the master was spitted. He turned him round over the burning coals until his flesh was thoroughly roasted. When he took him off from the fire, he separated his joints as a man separates the joints of a chicken, and proceeded to tear his flesh to pieces with his nails and to eat of it. This he continued to do until he had eaten his flesh and gnawed his bones. There remained of him nothing but some bones, which he threw by the side of the pavilion. He then sat a little, and threw himself down, and slept upon that bench, making a noise with his throat like that which is made by a lamb or other beast when slaughtered. He slept uninterruptedly until the morning, when he went his way.

As soon, therefore, as we were sure that he was far from us, we conversed together and wept for ourselves, saying, "Would that we had been drowned in the sea, or that the apes had eaten us; for it were better than the roasting of a man upon burning coals!"

We then arose and went forth upon the island to find a place in which to hide ourselves, or to flee. It had become a light matter to us to die, rather than that our flesh should be roasted with fire. But we found no place in which to hide ourselves; and the evening overtook us. So we turned to the pavilion by reason of the violence of our fear, and sat there a little while. Once again the monster came among us, began to turn us over, one after another, as on the former occasion, and to feel us, until one pleased him. Then he seized the new victim and did with him as he did with the master of the ship the day before. He roasted him and ate him upon the bench. He slept that night, making a noise with his throat like a slaughtered animal. When the day came, he arose and went his way, leaving us as usual.

Upon this we assembled together and said, "By Allah, if we cast ourselves into the sea and die drowned, it will be better than our dying burnt, for this way of being put to death is abominable!"

And one of us said, "Listen. We will plot against him and kill him, and be safe once again."

I said to them, "Hear, O my brothers. If we must kill him, we will carry away this wood, and remove some of this firewood, and make for ourselves rafts, each to bear three men. After this we will go on with our plan to kill him. And if we are not able to kill him, we will put out to sea, and if we are drowned, we shall be preserved from being roasted over the fire and from being slaughtered. If we escape, we escape; and if we are drowned, we die martyrs."

To this they all replied, "By Allah, this is a good plan."

We agreed upon this matter and began the work. We removed the pieces of wood out of the pavilion and constructed rafts. We attached them to the seashore and stowed upon them some provisions. After completing this work, we returned to the pavilion.

When it was evening, the earth trembled beneath us, and the giant came in to us like a snarling dog. He turned us over and felt us, one after another. He took one of us and did with him as he had done with the others before him. He ate him and slept upon the bench, and the noise from his throat was like thunder. Then we arose and took two iron spits, of those which were set up, and put them in the fierce fire until they were red-hot. Then we grasped them firmly and went with them to the monster while he lay asleep snoring. We thrust them into his eyes, all of us pressing upon them with our united strength and force. Thus we pushed them into his eyes as he slept, and his eyes were destroyed.

He uttered a great cry, at which our hearts were terrified. Then he arose resolutely from that bench and began to search for us while we fled from him to the right and left. He saw us not, for his sight was blinded. But we feared him with a violent fear and despaired of safety. He sought the door and went forth from it, crying out. The earth shook beneath us because of the vehemence of his cry. So when he went forth from the pavilion, we followed him, and he went his way searching for us. Then he returned, accompanied by a female, greater than he, and more hideous in form. When we saw him and her who was with him, we were terrified. As soon as the female saw us, we hastily loosed the rafts that we had constructed, embarked on them, and pushed them forth into the sea. But each of the two monsters had a mass of rock which they cast at us until the greater number of us died from the casting. There remained of us only three persons, I and two others. At last the raft brought us to the shores of another island.

We walked forward upon that island until the close of the day. So we slept a little. We awoke from our sleep to find that a serpent of enormous size, of large body and wide belly, had surrounded us. It approached one of us and swallowed him to his shoulders. Then it swallowed the rest of him, and we heard his ribs break in pieces. After this it went its way.

We mourned for our companion and were in the utmost fear for ourselves, saying, "By Allah, this is a horrible thing! Every death that we witness is more horrible than the preceding one. We were rejoiced at our escape from the giant; but our joy is not complete. How shall we escape from this unlucky serpent?"

Then we arose and walked on over the island, eating of its fruits, and drinking of its rivers. We walked till morning, when we found a great, lofty tree. So we climbed up it and slept upon it, but not before I had ascended to the highest of its branches.

When the night arrived, the serpent came, looking to the right and left. It advanced to the tree upon which we were, came up to my companion, and swallowed him to his shoulders. It wound itself round the tree with him, and I heard his bones break in pieces. Then it swallowed him entirely, while I looked on. After this it descended from the tree and went its way.

I remained upon that tree the rest of the night. When the day came, I descended from the tree like one dead through fear and terror. I considered casting myself into the sea that I might be at rest from the world; but it was not a light matter to me to do so, for life is dear. So I tied a wide piece of wood upon the soles of my feet, crosswise. I tied one like it upon my left side, a similar one upon my right side, and a similar one upon the front of my body. I tied one long and wide upon the top of my head, crosswise, like that which was under the soles of my feet. Thus I was in the midst of these pieces of wood, and they enclosed me on every side. I bound them tightly and threw myself with the whole upon the ground. So I lay in the midst of the pieces of wood which enclosed me like a closet.

When the evening arrived, the serpent approached as before. It saw me and drew towards me, but it could not swallow me with the pieces of wood round me on every side. It went round me, but could not come at me. The serpent retired and returned to me. It kept doing this. Every time it desired to get at me to swallow me, the pieces of wood tied upon me on every side prevented it. It continued to do thus from sunset until daybreak. Then it went its way in the utmost vexation and rage. Upon this, I stretched forth my hands and loosed myself from those pieces of wood. I was nearly dead with fright.

I arose and walked along the island until I came to shore. I cast a glance towards the sea and beheld a ship at a distance in the midst of the deep. So I took a great branch of a tree and made a sign with it to the passengers, calling out to them.

When they saw me, they said, "We must see what this is. Perhaps it is a man."

Then they approached me and heard my cries to them. They therefore came to me and took me with them in the ship. They asked me many questions. I informed them of all that had happened to me from beginning to end, and of the troubles that I had suffered. They wondered extremely at all this. They clad me with some of their clothes, attiring me decently. After that they put before me some provisions, and I ate until I was satisfied. They also gave me to drink some cool and sweet water. My heart was revived; my soul became at ease, and I experienced great comfort.

My courage was strengthened so that it seemed to me that all which I then experienced was a dream. We proceeded on our voyage, and the wind was fair to us until we came in sight of an island. There the master anchored the ship. The merchants and other passengers landed and took forth their goods to see and buy.

The owner of the ship then looked towards me and said to me, "Listen to me. You are a stranger and poor, and have informed us that you have suffered many horrors. I therefore desire to help you with something that will aid you to reach your own country, and you will pray for me."

I replied, "So be it; you shall have my prayers."

He answered, "Know that there was with us a man voyaging, whom we lost. We know not whether he is living or dead. I desire to give you his bales that you may sell them in this island. You shall take charge of them, and we will give you something proportionate to your trouble and your services. What remains of them we will take and keep until we return to the city of Baghdad. There we will inquire for the owner's family and give to them the remainder. Will you then take charge of them and land with them upon this island?"

I answered, "I hear and obey you, O my master; you are kind."

And I prayed for him and thanked him for that.

He thereupon ordered the porters and sailors to land those goods upon the island and to deliver them to me. The clerk of the ship said, "O master, what are these bales which these sailors and porters have brought out? What name shall I mark them with?"

He answered, "Write upon them the name Sinbad of the Sea, who was with us and was drowned or left behind at the island of the roc. Since no word of him has come to us, we desire this stranger to sell them and take charge of the price of them. We will give him somewhat of it in payment for his trouble. What remains we will take with us until we return to the city of Baghdad. If we find him, we will give it to him; if we find him not, we will then give it to his family in Baghdad."

So the clerk replied, "Your words are good, and your plan is excellent."

When I heard the words of the master, mentioning that the bales were to be inscribed with my name, I said to myself, "By Allah, *I* am Sinbad of the Sea." I waited till the merchants had landed and had assembled conversing and consulting upon affairs of selling and buying. Then I advanced to the owner of the ship and said to him, "O my master, do you know what manner of man was the owner of the bales which you have committed to me?

He answered me, "I know not his condition, but he was a man of the city of Baghdad, called Sinbad of the Sea. We had cast anchor at one of the islands, where he was lost, and we have no news of him to the present time."

So upon this I uttered a great cry and said to him, "O master, know that I am Sinbad of the Sea. I was not drowned, but when you anchored at the island, and the merchants and other passengers landed, I also landed with the party. I took with me something to eat on the shore of the island and enjoyed myself in sitting in that place. But slumber overtook me. When I awakened the ship had left. Therefore this wealth is my wealth, and these goods are my goods. All the merchants also who deal in diamonds saw me when I was upon the mountain of the diamonds. They will bear witness for me that I am Sinbad of the Sea, as I informed them of my story and of the events that befell me with you in the ship. I informed them that you had forgotten me upon the island, asleep, and that I arose and found no one."

When the merchants and other passengers heard my words, they assembled around me. Some of them believed me, and others disbelieved me. But while we were talking, one of the merchants, when he heard me mention the valley of diamonds, arose and advanced to me. He said to them, "Hear, O company, my words. I related to you the most wonderful thing that I had seen in my travels. I told you that when we cast down the slaughtered animals in the valley of diamonds, there came up with my slaughtered beast a man attached to it. But you didn't believe me. You accused me of falsehood."

They replied, "Yes, you did tell us this thing, and we believed you not."

Then the merchant said to them, "This is the man who attached himself to my slaughtered animal. He gave me some diamonds of high price, rewarding me with more than would have come up with my slaughtered animal. I took him as my companion until we arrived at the city of El-Basrah. From there we returned to our own countries. This is he, and he informed us that his name was Sinbad of the Sea. He told us too of the departure of the ship and of his sitting in that island. All these goods are his property, for he informed us of them at the time of his meeting with us. The truth of his assertion is obvious."

So when the master heard the words of that merchant, he arose and came to me. Having looked at me awhile with a scrutinizing eye, he said, "What is the mark of your goods?"

I answered him, "Know that the mark of my goods is of such and such a kind." And I related to him a circumstance that had occurred between me and him when I embarked with him in the vessel from El-Basrah.

He therefore was convinced that I was Sinbad of the Sea, and he embraced me and congratulated me upon my safety. He said to me, "By Allah, your story is wonderful. But praise be to God who has brought us together, and restored your goods and your wealth to you!"

Upon this I disposed of my goods at a great profit. At this I rejoiced, congratulating myself on my safety and on the restoration of my wealth to me. We kept sailing and buying at the islands many wonders and strange things that cannot be numbered nor calculated. Among the things that I saw there was a fish in the form of a cow. I saw a bird that comes forth from a seashell, lays its eggs and hatches them upon the surface of the water. It never comes forth from the sea upon the face of the earth. After this we continued our voyage until we arrived at El-Basrah, where I remained a few days.

Then I came to the city of Baghdad. I entered my house and saluted my family and companions and friends. I rejoiced at my safety and my return to my country and my family and city and district, and gave alms and presents. I ceased not to live thus, eating and drinking, and sporting and making merry. I ate well and drank well, associating familiarly and mingling in society. I forgot all that had happened to me, and the distress and horrors that I had suffered.

VII. Universal Truths

Folktales reflect human experiences and human hopes. Evil exists in the world and in folktales, but people hope for its ultimate defeat. In folktales villains usually lose out.

Folktales often reflect human daydreams. A beggar becomes

a king. A poor farmer becomes wealthy. A desperately ill
person becomes well again. Sometimes there is an unexpected
twist, and the story ends with the central character back
where he or she started. Folktales can mix realism with
dreams.

Like proverbs, folktales often reflect human wisdom. A
proverb may contain a universal truth compressed into a line
or two, for example—"You never miss the water till the well
runs dry." A folktale may contain a similar bit of wisdom in
more extended story form. We are more likely to remember a
generalized truth if it is illustrated in a delightful tale.

Come Look (Korean)

Do we tend to see life as a reflection of ourselves? Are the
world's smiles and scowls very often a reflection of our own
feelings? In the following folktale an ordinary mirror plays a
crucial role. It suggests the universal truth that each one of us
interprets life by looking into his or her own mirror.

The story opens with a riddle, a common device in folklore.
(See page 7.) Some authorities think that riddles may have
preceded myths, fables, folktales, and proverbs in the development of folk expression. Riddles often contain contradictions,
as in the riddle at the beginning of "Come Look." They are
often humorous, witty, unexpected.

Older riddles usually deal with nature:

> What flies forever
> And rests never?

The answer is *the wind*. The following two describe smoke
and fire.

> A hill full, a hole full,
> But you cannot catch a bowlful.

> The more you feed it
> The more it'll grow high,
> But if you give it water,
> Then it'll go and die.

Riddles cast human observations and generalizations in
puzzle form.

> Look in my face: I am Somebody.
> Scratch my back: I am Nobody.
> *Answer:* Mirror

Long ago in Korea lived a happy young couple. One day the husband said he must go on a journey. "What shall I bring home?" he asked his wife.

"I have heard of a beautiful thing made of metal," said the young wife. "When you look into it you see wonderful sights, and I long to see this thing very much."

So when the husband had finished his business in the city, he began to shop around for the metal thing in which one saw strange sights. He soon found it. "It's called 'a mirror,' " they told him. So he bought one. Quickly he stuffed it into his bag and hurried home without looking at it, for it was late.

When he arrived home, his wife greeted him lovingly. "Have you got it?" she said.

"Yes. It is called 'a mirror.' " And he handed her the little bag which contained it.

She looked into the mirror and saw a lovely woman's face smiling back. "Who is this woman you have brought home?" she cried. "Send her away!"

"What are you talking about?" said the husband. "Let me see! The young husband looked in the mirror and saw a handsome young man scowling fiercely at him. "Who is this man you have brought into the house while I was gone?" he said. "I won't have it!"

The young wife was weeping because she said her husband had brought home a new wife. The husband was furious because he thought a strange man had come to woo his wife while he was gone. They quarreled bitterly.

The young man's mother heard them and came into the room to see what was the trouble.

"Come look!" they said.

So the old mother looked in the mirror and saw an old woman's face looking back at her. "Why that's just an old widow from the neighborhood come to borrow rice," she said. "That's nothing to worry about." And she went out of the room to find the caller.

But the young husband and wife continued to weep and rage and quarrel.

Soon the young man's father came in. "What's all this fuss?" he said.

"Come look!" they told him.

The old father looked in the mirror and saw an old man's face. "Who's that?" he cried. "I don't owe him a penny! Be off!" he yelled. But the old man's face looked angrily back at the old man.

A neighbor was called in. He saw a new face in the mirror. Another came and looked; he saw someone else.

"Send for the magistrate," cried the old man. "We can't have all these people here!"

The magistrate arrived with his young secretary behind him carrying his scrolls.

"Come look!" the people said.

The magistrate looked in the mirror and said nothing. He was completely startled. "Go pack my possessions," he said to the secretary, "for a new magistrate has come to take over my office."

But the secretary, being curious, had looked into the mirror over his master's shoulder and seen his master's face looking back—his master's own face, even to the two hairs in the mole on his nose.

"It is yourself!" he cried, "and that must be me behind you." And so it was.

The magistrate saw that this was true. "This is a marvelous thing," he said, "in which every man can know himself."

Planting a Pear Tree (Chinese)

Folktales often teach kindness, charity, and compassion. Characters who disregard these desirable human qualities may learn a bitter lesson. In the following tale a grower of pears discovers that a callous disregard for a fellow human being can have grievous results. Generosity and sharing are desirable human traits. Selfishness is not.

A country man was one day selling his pears in the market. They were unusually sweet and fine-flavored, and the price he asked was high. A Taoist priest in rags and tatters stopped at the barrow and begged one of them. The country man told him to go away, but when he did not do so the country man began to curse and swear at him. The priest said, "You have several hundred pears on your barrow; I ask for a single one, the loss of which, sir, you would not feel. Why then get angry?"

The lookers-on told the country man to give the man an inferior one and let him go, but this he obstinately refused to do. Thereupon someone, finding the commotion too great, purchased a pear and handed it to the priest. The latter received it with a bow and, turning to the crowd, said, "We who have left our homes and given up all that is dear to us are at a loss to understand selfish conduct in others.

Now I have some exquisite pears which I shall do myself the honor to put before you."

Here somebody asked, "Since you have pears yourself, why don't you eat those?"

"Because, " replied the priest, "I wanted one of these pits to grow them from." So saying, he munched the pear; and when he had finished, took a pit in his hand, unstrapped a pick from his back, and proceeded to make a hole in the ground several inches deep. He deposited the pit, filling in the earth as before. He then asked the bystanders for a little hot water to water it with, and one among them who loved a joke fetched him some boiling water from a neighboring shop.

The priest poured this over the place where he had made the hole, and every eye was turned upon him when sprouts were seen shooting up and gradually growing larger and larger. By and by there was a tree with branches sparsely covered with leaves; then flowers, and last of all fine, large, sweet-smelling pears hanging in great profusion. These the priest picked and handed round to the assembled crowd until all were gone, whereupon he took his pick and hacked away for a long time at the tree, finally cutting it down. This he shouldered, leaves and all, and sauntered quietly away.

Now, from the beginning, our friend the country man had been amongst the crowd, straining his neck to see what was going on and forgetting all about his business. At the departure of the priest he turned round and discovered that every one of his pears was gone. He knew then that those the old fellow had been giving away so freely were really his own pears.

Looking more closely at the barrow, he also found that one of the handles was missing, evidently having newly been cut off. Boiling with rage, he set out in pursuit of the priest, but just as he turned the corner he saw the lost barrow handle lying under the wall, being in fact the very pear tree the priest had cut down. But there were no traces of the priest—much to the amusement of the crowd in the marketplace.

VIII. Origins

A famous painting by Paul Gauguin in the Boston Museum of Fine Arts includes an inscription with three questions:

Where do we come from?
What are we?
Where are we going?

Ever since human beings began to think, they have pondered the meaning of their existence. They have puzzled over questions like those asked by Paul Gauguin. Often their folklore attempted to explain some of these questions.

We have already seen how the Greeks explained the origin of the world (pages 13–14). The Scandinavian example (pages 107–108) provides another explanation. But folktales deal not only with such profound questions as the origin of the universe. They also deal with less grand questions. How did the tiger get his stripes? How did the elephant get his trunk? American Indians, for example, explained why the coyote's nose and tail are black tipped. They told why there is a black mark on the nose of the antelope and how the chipmunk got his stripes.

Explanations like these appear in cultures around the world, explaining how the flounder got a crooked mouth or why the crab's eyes popped up out of his body. The explanations always have a certain logic and demonstrate a great deal of ingenuity.

The stories that follow in this section provide two explanations. One tells how a powerful force of nature came into being. The other explains the appearance and bad temper of a common insect.

The Children of the House of Dawn (South American)

How did the winds come into existence? As the Amazon Indians considered this question, they provided an explanation in terms of what they knew. So do all peoples explain the mysteries of nature in terms they can understand.

This story also contains other ingredients we met before and will meet again. Once again the underdog is triumphant. Once again the despised youngest brother emerges on top. As in the story of the bird on the falcon's back (pages 157–158), an insignificant character attaches himself to the back of a stronger one. In this story, as in many others, trickery wins, but this time there is a difference. The results of trickery are seen to be empty and hollow. The tale seems to be saying that the means do not justify the ends, that selfish actions may at last bring unhappiness. How much human experience entered into such a wise observation?

Far, far away in the wonderful East, where the morning sun appears, there is a great cave lined with mother-of-pearl which is the House of Dawn. Long, long ago, even before the days of Indians and llamas, even longer ago than the time of the Great Flood, there were four brothers who dwelt together in the House of Dawn.

Now the eldest of the four brothers was so huge you would have called him a giant, could you have seen him. And the youngest of the four brothers was so tiny you would have called him a sprite. His name was Coniraya but you may call him Coni for short. The other two brothers were betwixt and between.

The eldest brother was so big and strong that he could travel far away from the beautiful pearl-lined House of Dawn which was his home. One day he went so far and climbed so high that he reached the top of the tallest mountain peak of all.

"This is very wonderful country," said he, as he looked about him at all the little mountains and at all the fleecy clouds. "I am glad I was bold enough to find it."

Admiringly he stroked the muscles of his powerful legs. "By your strength have I traveled from my far-distant home to this high peak. You are the very strongest legs in the whole world."

Then he flexed the muscles of his great arms. "I have the very strongest pair of arms in all the world," he boasted as he looked about him for something upon which to test them.

Soon his eye spied four great rocks balancing themselves on the mountainside. Picking up one of these, he threw it before him with all his might in the direction of the pearly tinted House of Dawn which was his home. Another great rock he threw straight back of him as far as he could throw, in the direction in which the sun disappeared each night. Another of the rocks he threw to the right of him and another to the left of him. These four huge stones became the four points of the compass, East, West, South, and North, and so they remain to this very day.

"These stones shall mark the boundaries of all my lands," said he. "Forever and ever shall they be mine. My legs are the strongest legs in the whole world. My arms are the strongest arms in the whole world. My good legs have brought me to this spot and my good arms have thrown these memorial stones to be the boundaries of my lands. All the world is mine."

You will notice that he did not say a word about having the strongest head in the world. Indeed, he did not have it, for his little brother, Coniraya, the youngest of them all, was the one who had the best head. Coni had very strong lungs, too.

When his big brother came home, boasting that he owned the whole world, Coni laughed at him.

"I know a place you do not own," he chuckled. "Come and see it."

Far away in the mountains the youngest brother had found a deep cave which was as full of darkness as the House of Dawn was full of light. It was a long journey indeed for his short legs, but with a good head one does not tire one's legs. Little Coni danced and pranced along the way beside his big brother until he was tired. Then he hopped on his brother's back and stuck there in the exact place where it was impossible to dislodge him. When at last they reached his cave Coni hopped down.

"How strong you are!" he praised. "Anybody as strong as you can own this cave just as well as he can own the rest of the world."

This speech so pleased his big brother that he forgot to be angry. Very eagerly he pushed his way into the cave. As soon as he was safe inside, little Coni drew in a deep breath with his powerful lungs. Then he blew it out with all his might at the big rock which trembled on the mountainside above the entrance to the cave. Down it fell with a loud crash, completely blocking the entrance. His brother was sealed inside like a rat in a trap. Then Coni danced and pranced up the mountainside until he stood on the top of the tallest peak of all.

Looking to the east, toward his home in the pearl-lined House of Dawn, the tricky sprite shouted at the top of his lungs, "Oh, lands of my brother, you now belong to me!"

Then turning slowly to the south, the west, and the north, where the great memorial stones marked all the points of the compass, Coni shouted at each, "Oh, lands of my brother, you now belong to me! I have the strongest lungs and the best head in the whole world, and the whole world is mine!"

The next day the betwixt and between brother, who was next to the oldest, asked for his brother who was a giant.

"Where is he and why did he not return to the House of Dawn for the night as is his custom?"

"Climb up to the tallest mountain peak with me," replied Coni. "I want to show you something."

Accordingly his brother went up the mountainside with Coni perched on his back in just the spot where he could not be reached.

Jumping down when they had reached the top of the tallest peak, Coni looked up at him admiringly. "How very strong you are!" he flattered. "And how bright your eyes are this morning! You have the best eyes in the world. Lie down and look over the edge of the rock and see what you can see! Don't be afraid to peer over the edge!"

Unsuspectingly his elder brother lay down flat on his stomach and peered over the rocks at the deep abyss which lay below. Little Coni drew in a deep breath and when he blew it out at his brother, he blew him over the edge of the steep precipice. Down he fell over the rocks and stones, turning into a stone himself before he was halfway to the bottom of the deep abyss!

When his two older brothers did not return to their home in the House of Dawn, Coni's remaining brother became deeply troubled. His suspicions grew as the days and weeks passed by until, at last, he became so afraid of Coni's alert mind and powerful lungs that he ran away from home and was drowned by the wild waves of the deep sea. Now Coniraya was monarch of all he surveyed. He owned the whole world and the House of Dawn as well.

But now it was very lonely in the pearl-lined House of Dawn. The great rosy cave was full of grim voices which Coni had never heard when his three older brothers were there to keep him company. At night he tossed upon his bed and could not sleep. By day it was no longer a pleasure to roam over the lands which were now his, for always there was the dread of going home to the grim voices.

At last he could bear it no longer. One night when the grim voices were even louder than ever, he drew in a long, deep breath with his powerful lungs. Then he blew it out again with such force that he drove the voices out of the cave forever. North, south, east and west he blew them, to the four points of the compass which were marked with the big memorial stones. And they became the winds, which even yet bring to us the whisperings of grim voices.

What Makes Brer Wasp Have a Short Patience (North Carolinian)

The following story does not tell the origin of so grand a subject as the wind. It does, however, provide a fanciful explanation of a common problem. Why are wasps so bad-tempered? Anyone who has ever been stung by a wasp remembers that the insect seemed particularly irritated, sometimes attacking without provocation. This folktale provides two explanations: for the wasp's appearance as well as his irritability.

Creatures don't all stay just the way God made them. No sir. With the mistakes made, and accidents, and natural debilitation, and one thing or another, they became different as time goes on, until sometime later they are hardly the same thing at all.

At one time, Brer Wasp looked very different from the way he does today. He was big on company, and he loved to talk, and joke, and cut the fool. He was one person that had to have his laugh.

One day, he was walking on a path, and he met up with Brer Mosquito. Now, Brer Mosquito and his whole family weren't very big at all, but they took themselves mighty seriously. Brer Mosquito and his pa planted a little patch of ground together, but they always called it the plantation. They talked so big about their crops and land and everything that you would have thought that they had a twenty-mile place. Now, Brer Wasp loved to draw Brer Mosquito out on the subject.

That same week, there had been a heavy frost, and all the sweet-potato vines died and turned black and everybody was forced to dig for the early potatoes. And Brer Wasp, after he had passed the time of day with Brer Mosquito, and inquired about his family, asked him about his pa's health and how he had made out with his crop. "We made out fine, Brer Wasp," Brer Mosquito said, "Just too fine. We had the biggest crop you ever have seen!" "The potatoes were big, then?" "They were huge! You have never seen such potatoes!" "How big are they, Brer Mosquito?" Brer Wasp questioned him. "My friend," Brer Mosquito said, puffing out his chest and reaching down and pulling his little britches tight around his little leg, "Most of our crop came up bigger than the calf of my leg!"

Well, sir! Brer Wasp looked at Brer Mosquito's poor little leg, and as he thought about those "huge potatoes," he had to laugh to himself. Now, he tried to mind his manners, but his chest and face swelled up, and his eye water ran out of his eyes, and he burst out laughing right in Brer Mosquito's face. He laughed and he laughed till his sides hurt him. Whenever he thought he would stop, he looked at that ridiculous leg that stood there like a toothpick, and he laughed more than ever. His sides hurt him so much he had to hold them in with both his hands and rock himself back and forth.

"What makes you have to do that?" Brer Mosquito asked him. "You had better explain yourself. That is, if you can act sensible!" Brer Wasp gasped out, "Good lord, Brer Mosquito, looking for the biggest part of your leg is like hunting for the heaviest part of a hair! How big those huge potatoes must be, if you say they are as big as that!" And he laughed again till his sides hurt so bad that it wasn't enough just to press them—he had to grab them in both his hands and squeeze.

Brer Mosquito was so annoyed that he felt like fighting Brer Wasp right on the spot. But then he remembered that Brer Wasp was kind of nasty when he got in a row. So he just drew himself up, and stuck out his mouth, and said, "Laugh, you no-mannered devil! Laugh! But take care that the day doesn't come when somebody laughs at you the same no-mannered way!" And he went away so blistering mad that his two little coattails stuck straight out behind him.

But that didn't stop Brer Wasp. All the way to his house he had been laughing so hard that he had to stop now and then to catch his breath. At last he got home and started to laugh some more and tell his family about Brer Mosquito.

Just then his wife got a good look at him, and she hollered out, "For crying-out-loud, Brer Wasp! What's happened to your stomach?" Brer Wasp looked down where his waist had been and he could hardly see it.

He lost all notion of laughing right then. He looked again and he saw what all the shaking, and pushing, and squeezing had done to him. He was almost in two! Even his little hand could reach around his waist. He remembered how big it had been, and he saw how much he had shrunk up, and he was afraid to so much as sneeze.

Then he remembered what Brer Mosquito had said to him. He remembered all those people he had been joking about and laughing at so hard and for such a long time and he thought about how now the others were going to have their turn to laugh at the little waist he had now. He got so that he couldn't get that shameful thing out of his mind. And that is why he has such a short patience! Everywhere he goes he thinks somebody is ready to laugh at him. If anyone so much as looks at him, he gets so mad that he is ready to fight.

And that isn't the worst, because from that day to this day, he can't laugh anymore, because if he does, he will burst in two!

IX. The Poor Person Triumphant

Throughout history there have been more poor persons than wealthy ones. The poor have dreamed of a better life, but basic changes are rare. If real life does not bring wealth, however, at least folklore can do a better job. In the stories that follow, two poor, downtrodden men reach positions of wealth and power, and make daydreams come true.

Why the Hair on the Head Turns Gray Before the Beard (Jewish)

This tale links the previous section with this. In a sense it is an origin tale. It gives a fanciful explanation for a puzzling phenomenon. Often men with gray hair still have black beards. The folktale goes further, however, and demonstrates another favorite theme. The poor farmer survives by his wits. Threatened with death by the Czar for breaking a promise, he comes up with an inspired explanation and wins himself a place in the palace.

The Czar once went on a journey. On the way he met a poor Jewish farmer who was cultivating his field. The Czar saw that the farmer's hair was gray while his beard was black. At this he was filled with wonder.

"Do explain this mystery to me," the Czar asked him. "Why is the hair on your head gray and your beard black?"

"My beard didn't start growing until after I was Bar Mitzvahed," replied the Jew. "Consequently, since the hair on my head is many years older than the hair in my beard, it turned gray long before."

"How clever of you!" cried the Czar with admiration. "Promise me, on your word of honor, never to repeat this explanation to anyone. I will allow you to reveal the secret only after you have seen me one hundred times."

The Czar then continued on his journey.

Upon his return home he assembled all his ministers, wise men and counsellors.

"I will put to you a very puzzling question," he told them. "See if you can answer it."

"Speak, O King!" cried the wise men.

"Why is it," asked the Czar, "that the hair on the head becomes gray long before the hair in the beard does?"

The wise men remained mute with astonishment. They did not know what to answer.

"Take a month's time to think it over," said the Czar. "Then come back to me with your answer."

The wise men went away and devoted themselves single-mindedly to the solution of the problem the Czar had put to them.

As the month was nearing its end, and still they had not found an answer, they were filled with gloom. But they found a straw of hope to clutch at when one of the ministers recalled that on the day the

Czar had put the puzzling question to them, he had come back from a journey outside the capital. So he undertook to track the matter down to its source.

The minister followed the route the Czar had taken, and he chanced upon the same poor Jewish farmer with whom the Czar had spoken. He recognized him by the fact that the hair on his head was gray and the hair in his beard was black.

"What is the explanation for this strange fact?" he asked the Jew.

The Jewish farmer answered, "Alas, I'm not allowed to give you the answer!"

"I'll pay you well if you'll reveal your secret to me," coaxed the king's counsellor.

The poor Jew hesitated. Then he said, "I'm a poor man. I'm desperately in need of some money. If you will pay me a hundred silver rubles I'll reveal to you my secret."

After he got the hundred silver rubles, he gave him the answer he had given to the Czar.

The minister then returned to St. Petersburg and gave the Czar the answer. But the Czar understood immediately how he had gotten the answer. So he sent for the Jew.

"Do you know what punishment you deserve for breaking your promise to me?" cried the Czar angrily. "Didn't I ask you to keep your answer a secret?"

"Indeed you did!" replied the Jew. "But you must also recall that you gave me permission to talk about it after I had seen you a hundred times."

"Insolent fellow!" cried the Czar. "How dare you lie so brazenly to me! You very well know I only saw you once!"

"I've told you the truth!" persisted the Jew. And he drew out of a bag a hundred silver rubles.

"See for yourself," said he. "On every one of these rubles is graven your image. And, having looked upon them all, I have seen you one hundred times. Was I wrong in giving your minister the answer?"

"What a clever man!" exclaimed the Czar with rapture. "What you deserve is a reward, not punishment! Remain with me here in my palace so that I may always have the benefit of your counsel."

And so the poor Jewish farmer lived with the Czar in his palace in St. Petersburg, and was the first among his counsellors. The Czar never made a decision without consulting him first, and, wherever he went, the Jew went along with him.

The Cobbler Astrologer (Persian)

This Persian story contains many of the most common in-gredients in folktales. First and foremost, a poor man is raised to fame and wealth, partly because of his belief in God and partly because of his inner, spiritual goodness. As in many folktales, luck plays a major role, a good fortune arising from a person's own good qualities. There are the usual three epi-sodes leading to a climax. The tables are turned. Virtue is rewarded and greed, punished.

Though the episodes are fanciful and unlikely, we find the folktale satisfying. "Good for him!" we say. Once again the underdog wins the day.

In the great city of Isfahan lived Ahmed the cobbler, an honest and industrious man, whose wish was to pass through life quietly; and he might have done so, had he not married a handsome wife, who, although she had condescended to accept him as a husband, was far from being contented with his humble sphere of life.

Sittâra, such was the name of Ahmed's wife, was ever forming foolish schemes of riches and grandeur; and though Ahmed never encouraged them, he was too fond a husband to quarrel with what gave her pleasure. An incredulous smile or a shake of the head was his only answer to her often-told daydreams; and she continued to persuade herself that she was certainly destined to great fortune.

It happened one evening, while in this temper of mind, that she went to the *hemmâm* [baths], where she saw a lady retiring dressed in a magnificent robe, covered with jewels and surrounded by slaves. This was the very condition Sittâra had always longed for, and she eagerly inquired the name of the happy person who had so many attendants and such fine jewels. She learned it was the wife of the chief astrologer to the king. With this information she returned home. Her husband met her at the door, but was received with a frown, nor could all his caresses obtain a smile or a word; for several hours she continued silent, and in apparent misery. At length she said: "Cease your caresses, unless you are ready to give me a proof that you do really and sincerely love me."

"What proof of love," exclaimed poor Ahmed, "can you desire which I will not give?"

"Give over cobbling; it is a vile, low trade, and never yields more than ten or twelve dinars a day. Turn astrologer! Your fortune will be made, and I shall have all I wish, and be happy."

"Astrologer!" cried Ahmed, "astrologer! Have you forgotten who I am—a cobbler, without any learning—that you want me to engage in a profession which requires so much skill and knowledge?"

"I neither think nor care about your qualifications," said the enraged wife. "All I know is that if you do not turn astrologer immediately I will be divorced from you tomorrow."

The cobbler remonstrated, but in vain. The figure of the astrologer's wife, with her jewels and her slaves, had taken complete possession of Sittâra's imagination. All night it haunted her; she dreamt of nothing else, and on awakening declared she would leave the house if her husband did not comply with her wishes. What could Ahmed do? He was no astrologer, but he was dotingly fond of his wife, and he could not bear the idea of losing her. He promised to obey, and, having sold his little stock, bought an astrolabe, an astronomical almanac and a table of the twelve signs of the zodiac. Furnished with these he went to the marketplace, crying, "I am an astrologer! I know the sun, and the moon, and the stars, and the twelve signs of the zodiac; I can calculate nativities; I can foretell everything that is to happen!"

No man was better known than Ahmed the cobbler. A crowd soon gathered round him. "What! Friend Ahmed," said one, "have you worked till your head is turned?" "Are you so tired of looking down at your last," cried another, "that you are now looking up at the planets?" These and a thousand other jokes assailed the ears of the poor cobbler, who, notwithstanding, continued to exclaim that he was an astrologer, having resolved on doing what he could to please his beautiful wife.

It so happened that the king's jeweler was passing by. He was in great distress, having lost the richest ruby belonging to the crown. Every search had been made to recover this inestimable jewel, but to no purpose; and as the jeweler knew he could no longer conceal its loss from the king, he looked forward to death as inevitable. In this hopeless state, while wandering about the town, he reached the crowd around Ahmed and asked what was the matter. "Don't you know Ahmed the cobbler?" said one of the bystanders, laughing. "He has been inspired and has become an astrologer."

A drowning man will catch at a broken reed: the jeweler no sooner heard the sound of the word astrologer than he went up to Ahmed, told him what had happened, and said, "If you understand your art, you must be able to discover the king's ruby. Do so, and I will give you two hundred pieces of gold. But if you do not succeed within six hours, I will use all my influence at court to have you put to death as an impostor."

Poor Ahmed was thunderstruck. He stood long without being able to move or speak, reflecting on his misfortunes, and grieving, above all, that his wife, whom he so loved, had, by her envy and selfishness, brought him to such a fearful alternative. Full of these sad thoughts, he exclaimed aloud, "O woman, woman! Thou art more baneful to the happiness of man than the poisonous dragon of the desert!"

The lost ruby had been secreted by the jeweler's wife, who, disquieted by those alarms which ever attend guilt, sent one of her female slaves to watch her husband. This slave, on seeing her master speak to the astrologer, drew near; and when she heard Ahmed, after some moments of apparent abstraction, compare a woman to a poisonous dragon, she was satisfied that he must know everything. She ran to her mistress, and, breathless with fear, cried, "You are discovered, my dear mistress, you are discovered by a vile astrologer. Before six hours are past the whole story will be known, and you will become infamous, if you are even so fortunate as to escape with life, unless you can find some way of prevailing on him to be merciful." She then related what she had seen and heard; and Ahmed's exclamation carried as complete conviction to the mind of the terrified mistress as it had done to that of her slave.

The jeweler's wife, hastily throwing on her veil, went in search of the dreaded astrologer. When she found him she threw herself at his feet, crying, "Spare my honor and my life, and I will confess everything!"

"What can you have to confess to me?" exclaimed Ahmed in amazement.

"Oh, nothing! Nothing with which you are not already acquainted. You know too well that I stole the ruby from the king's crown. I did so to punish my husband, who uses me most cruelly; and I thought by this means to obtain riches for myself, and to have him put to death. But you, most wonderful man, from whom nothing is hidden, have discovered and defeated my wicked plan. I beg only for mercy, and will do whatever you command me."

An angel from heaven could not have brought more consolation to Ahmed than did the jeweler's wife. He assumed all the dignified solemnity that became his new character, and said, "Woman! I know all thou hast done, and it is fortunate for thee that thou has come to confess thy sin and beg for mercy before it was too late. Return to thy house, put the ruby under the pillow of the couch on which thy husband sleeps; let it be laid on the side farthest from the door; and be satisfied thy guilt shall never be even suspected."

The jeweler's wife returned home and did as she was desired. In an hour Ahmed followed her and told the jeweler he had made his calculations, and found by the aspect of the sun and moon, and by the configuration of the stars, that the ruby was at that moment lying under the pillow of his couch, on the side farthest from the door. The jeweler thought Ahmed must be crazy; but as a ray of hope is like a ray from Heaven to the wretched, he ran to his couch, and there, to his joy and wonder, found the ruby in the very place described. He came back to Ahmed, embraced him, called him his dearest friend and the preserver of his life, and gave him the two hundred pieces of gold, declaring that he was the first astrologer of the age.

These praises conveyed no joy to the poor cobbler, who returned home more thankful to God for his preservation than elated by his good fortune. The moment he entered the door his wife ran up to him and exclaimed, "Well, my dear astrologer! What success?"

"There!" said Ahmed, very gravely. "There are two hundred pieces of gold. I hope you will be satisfied now and not ask me again to hazard my life, as I have done this morning." He then related all that had passed. But the recital made a very different impression on the lady from what these occurrences had made on Ahmed. Sittâra saw nothing but the gold, which would enable her to vie with the chief astrologer's wife at the *hemmâm.* "Courage!" she said, "Courage! My dearest husband. This is only your first labor in your new and noble profession. Go on and prosper, and we shall become rich and happy."

In vain Ahmed remonstrated and represented the danger; she burst into tears, and accused him of not loving her, ending with her usual threat of insisting upon a divorce.

Ahmed's heart melted, and he agreed to make another trial. Accordingly, next morning he sallied forth with his astrolabe, his twelve signs of the zodiac and his almanac, explaining, as before, "I am an astrologer! I know the sun, and the moon, and the stars, and the twelve signs of the zodiac; I can calculate nativities; I can foretell everything that is to happen!" A crowd again gathered round him, but it was now with wonder, and not ridicule; for the story of the ruby had gone abroad, and the voice of fame had converted the poor cobbler Ahmed into the ablest and most learned astrologer that was ever seen at Isfahan.

While everybody was gazing at him, a lady passed by veiled. She was the wife of one of the richest merchants in the city, and had just been at the *hemmâm*, where she had lost a valuable necklace and earrings. She was now returning home in great alarm lest her husband should suspect her of having given her jewels to a lover. Seeing the crowd around Ahmed, she asked the reason for their assembling, and was informed of the whole story of the famous astrologer: how he had been a cobbler, was inspired with supernatural knowledge, and could, with the help of his astrolabe, his twelve signs of the zodiac, and his almanac, discover all that ever did or ever would happen in the world. The story of the jeweler and the king's ruby was then told her, accompanied by a thousand wonderful circumstances which had never occurred. The lady, quite satisfied of his skill, went up to Ahmed and mentioned her loss, saying: "A man of your knowledge and penetration will easily discover my jewels; find them, and I will give you fifty pieces of gold."

The poor cobbler was quite confounded, and looked down, thinking only how to escape without a public exposure of his ignorance. The lady, in passing through the crowd, had torn the lower part of her veil. Ahmed's downcast eyes noticed this; and wishing to inform her of it in a delicate manner, before it was observed by others, he whispered to her, "Lady, look down at the rent." The lady's head was full of her loss, and she was at that moment endeavoring to recollect how it could have occurred. Ahmed's speech brought it at once to her mind, and she exclaimed in delighted surprise: "Stay here a few moments, thou great astrologer. I will return immediately with the reward thou so well deservest." Saying this, she left him, and soon returned, carrying in one hand the necklace and earrings, and in the other a purse with the fifty pieces of gold. "There is gold for thee," she said, "thou wonderful man, to whom all the secrets of Nature are revealed! I had quite forgotten where I laid the jewels, and without thee should never have found them. But when thou desiredst me to look at the rent below, I instantly recollected the rent near the bottom of the wall in the bathroom, where, before undressing, I had hid them. I can now go home in peace and comfort; and it is all owing to thee, thou wisest of men!"

After these words she walked away, and Ahmed returned to his home, thankful to Providence for his preservation, and fully resolved never again to tempt it. His handsome wife, however, could not yet rival the chief astrologer's lady in her appearance at the *hemmâm*, so she renewed her entreaties and threats, to make her fond husband continue his career as an astrologer.

About this time it happened that the king's treasury was robbed of forty chests of gold and jewels, forming the greater part of the wealth of the kingdom. The high treasurer and other officers of state used all diligence to find the thieves, but in vain. The king sent for his astrologer, and declared that if the robbers were not detected by a stated time, he, as well as the principal ministers, should be put to death. Only one day of the short period given them remained. All their search had proved fruitless, and the chief astrologer, who had made his calculations and exhausted his art to no purpose, had quite resigned himself to his fate, when one of his friends advised him to send for the wonderful cobbler, who had become so famous for his extraordinary discoveries. Two slaves were immediately dispatched for Ahmed, whom they commanded to go with them to their master. "You see the effects of your ambition," said the poor cobbler to his wife; "I am going to my death. The king's astrologer has heard of my presumption and is determined to have me executed as an impostor."

On entering the palace of the chief astrologer, he was surprised to see that dignified person come forward to receive him, and lead him to the seat of honor, and not less so to hear himself thus addressed: "The ways of Heaven, most learned and excellent Ahmed, are unsearchable. The high are often cast down, and the low are lifted up. The whole world depends upon fate and fortune. It is my turn now to be depressed by fate; it is thine to be exalted by fortune."

His speech was here interrupted by a messenger from the king, who, having heard of the cobbler's fame, desired his attendance. Poor Ahmed now concluded that it was all over with him, and followed the king's messenger, praying to God that he would deliver him from this peril. When he came into the king's presence, he bent his body to the ground and wished his majesty long life and prosperity. "Tell me, Ahmed," said the king, "who has stolen my treasure?"

"It was not one man," answered Ahmed, after some consideration; "there were forty thieves concerned in the robbery."

"Very well," said the king; "but who were they? And what have they done with my gold and jewels?"

"These questions," said Ahmed, "I cannot now answer; but I hope to satisfy your majesty, if you will grant me forty days to make my calculations."

"I grant you forty days," said the king; "but when they are past, if my treasure is not found, your life shall pay the forfeit."

Ahmed returned to his house well pleased; for he resolved to take advantage of the time allowed him to fly from a city where his fame was likely to be his ruin.

"Well, Ahmed," said his wife, as he entered, "what news at court?"

"No news at all," said he, "except that I am to be put to death at the end of forty days, unless I find forty chests of gold and jewels which have been stolen from the royal treasury."

"But you will discover the thieves."

"How? By what means am I to find them?"

"By the same art which discovered the ruby and the lady's necklace."

"The same art!" replied Ahmed. "Foolish woman! Thou knowest that I have no art, and that I have only pretended to it for the sake of pleasing thee. But I have had sufficient skill to gain forty days, during which time we may easily escape to some other city; and with the money I now possess, and the aid of my former occupation, we may still obtain an honest livelihood."

"An honest livelihood!" repeated his lady, with scorn. "Will thy cobbling, thou mean, spiritless wretch, ever enable me to go to the *hemmâm* like the wife of the chief astrologer? Hear me, Ahmed! Think only of discovering the king's treasure. Thou hast just as good a chance of doing so as thou hadst of finding the ruby, and the necklace and earrings. At all events, I am determined thou shalt not escape; and shouldst thou attempt to run away, I will inform the king's officers, and have thee taken up and put to death, even before the forty days are expired. Thou knowest me too well, Ahmed, to doubt my keeping my word. So take courage, and endeavor to make thy fortune, and to place me in that rank of life to which my beauty entitles me."

The poor cobbler was dismayed at this speech; but knowing there was no hope of changing his wife's resolution, he resigned himself to his fate. "Well," said he, "your will shall be obeyed. All I desire is to pass the few remaining days of my life as comfortably as I can. You know I am no scholar, and have little skill in reckoning; so there are forty dates: give me one of them every night after I have said my prayers, that I may put them in a jar, and, by counting them may always see how many of the few days I have to live are gone."

The lady, pleased at carrying her point, took the dates, and promised to be punctual in doing what her husband desired.

Meanwhile the thieves who had stolen the king's treasure, having been kept from leaving the city by fear of detection and pursuit, had received accurate information of every measure taken to discover them. One of them was among the crowd before the palace on the day the king sent for Ahmed; and hearing that the cobbler had immediately declared their exact number, he ran in a fright to his comrades, and exclaimed, "We are all found out! Ahmed, the new astrologer, has told the king that there are forty of us."

"They needed no astrologer to tell that," said the captain of the gang. "This Ahmed, with all his simple good nature, is a shrewd fellow. Forty chests having been stolen, he naturally guessed that there must be forty thieves, and he has made a good hit, that is all; still it is prudent to watch him, for he certainly has made some strange discoveries. One of us must go tonight, after dark, to the terrace of this cobbler's house, and listen to his conversation with his handsome wife; for he is said to be very fond of her, and will, no doubt, tell her what success he has had in his endeavors to detect us."

Everybody approved of this scheme; and soon after nightfall one of the thieves repaired to the terrace. He arrived there just as the cobbler had finished his evening prayers, and his wife was giving him the first date. "Ah!" said Ahmed, as he took it, "there is one of the forty."

The thief, hearing these words, hastened in consternation to the gang, and told them that the moment he took his post he had been perceived by the supernatural knowledge of Ahmed, who immediatedly told his wife that one of them was there. The spy's tale was not believed by his hardened companions; something was imputed to his fears; he might have been mistaken; in short, it was determined to send two men the next night at the same hour. They reached the house just as Ahmed, having finished his prayers, had received the second date, and heard him exclaim, "My dear wife, tonight there are two of them!"

The astonished thieves fled, and told their still incredulous comrades what they had heard. Three men were consequently sent the third night, four the fourth and so on. Being afraid of venturing during the day, they always came as evening closed in, and just as Ahmed was receiving his date; hence they all in turn heard him say that which convinced them he was aware of their presence. On the last night they all went, and Ahmed exclaimed aloud, "The number is complete! Tonight the whole forty are here!"

All doubts were now removed. It was impossible that Ahmed should have discovered them by any natural means. How could he ascertain their exact number? And night after night, without ever once being mistaken? He must have learnt it by his skill in astrology. Even the captain now yielded, in spite of his incredulity, and declared his opinion that it was hopeless to elude a man thus gifted; he therefore advised that they should make a friend of the cobbler, by confessing everything to him, and bribing him to secrecy by a share of the booty.

His advice was approved of, and an hour before dawn they knocked at Ahmed's door. The poor man jumped out of bed, and supposing the soldiers were come to lead him to execution, cried out, "Have patience! I know what you are come for. It is a very unjust and wicked deed."

"Most wonderful man!" said the captain, as the door was opened. "We are fully convinced that thou knowest why we are come, nor do we mean to justify the action of which thou speakest. Here are two thousand pieces of gold, which we will give thee, provided thou wilt swear to say nothing more about the matter."

"Say nothing about it!" said Ahmed. "Do you think it possible I can suffer such gross wrong and injustice without complaining, and making it known to all the world?"

"Have mercy upon us!" exclaimed the thieves, falling on their knees. "Only spare our lives, and we will restore the royal treasure."

The cobbler started, rubbed his eyes to see if he was asleep or awake; and being satisfied that he was awake, and that the men before him were really the thieves, he assumed a solemn tone and said: "Guilty men! Ye are persuaded that ye cannot escape from my penetration, which reaches unto the sun and moon, and knows the position and aspect of every star in the heavens. Your timely repentance has saved you. But ye must immediately restore all that ye have stolen. Go straightway, and carry the forty chests exactly as ye found them, and bury them a foot deep under the southern wall of the old ruined *hemmâm*, beyond the king's palace. If ye do this punctually, your lives are spared; but if ye fail in the slightest degree, destruction will fall upon you and your families."

The thieves promised obedience to his commands and departed. Ahmed then fell on his knees and returned thanks to God for this signal mark of his favor. About two hours after the royal guards came and desired Ahmed to follow them. He said he would attend them as soon as he had taken leave of his wife, to whom he determined not to impart what had occurred until he saw the result. He bade her farewell very affectionately; she supported herself with great fortitude on this trying occasion, exhorting her husband to be of good cheer, and said a few words about the goodness of Providence. But the fact was, Sittâra fancied that if God took the worthy cobbler to himself, her beauty might attract some rich lover, who would enable her to go to the *hemmâm* with as much splendor as the astrologer's lady, whose image, adorned with jewels and fine clothes, and surrounded by slaves, still haunted her imagination.

The decrees of Heaven are just: a reward suited to their merits awaited Ahmed and his wife. The good man stood with a cheerful countenance before the king, who was impatient for his arrival, and immediately said, "Ahmed, thy looks are promising; hast thou discovered my treasure?"

"Does your majesty require the thieves or the treasure? The stars will only grant one or the other," said Ahmed, looking at his table of astrological calculations. "Your majesty must make your choice. I can deliver up either, but not both."

"I should be sorry not to punish the thieves," answered the king; "but if it must be so, I choose the treasure."

"And you give the thieves a full and free pardon?"

"I do, provided I find my treasure untouched."

"Then," said Ahmed, "if your majesty will follow me, the treasure shall be restored to you."

The king and all his nobles followed the cobbler to the ruins of the old *hemmâm*. There, casting his eyes toward Heaven, Ahmed muttered some sounds, which were supposed by the spectators to be magical conjurations, but which are in reality the prayers and thanksgivings of a sincere and pious heart to God for his wonderful deliverance. When his prayer was finished, he pointed to the southern wall, and requested that his majesty would order his attendants to dig there. The work was hardly begun when the whole forty chests were found in the same state as when stolen, with the treasurer's seal upon them still unbroken.

The king's joy knew no bounds; he embraced Ahmed and immediately appointed him his chief astrologer, assigned to him an apartment in the palace and declared that he should marry his only daughter, as it was his duty to promote the man whom God had so singularly favored, and had made instrumental in restoring the treasures of his kingdom. The young princess, who was more beautiful than the moon, was not dissatisfied with her father's choice; for her mind was stored with religion and virtue, and she had learnt to value beyond all earthly qualities that piety and learning which she believed Ahmed to possess. The royal will was carried into execution as soon as formed. The wheel of fortune had taken a complete turn. The morning had found Ahmed in a wretched hovel, rising from a sorry bed, in the expectation of losing his life; in the evening he was the lord of a rich palace, and married to the only daughter of a powerful king. But this change did not alter his character. As he had been meek and humble in adversity, he was modest and gentle in prosperity. Conscious of his own ignorance, he continued to ascribe his good fortune solely to the favor of Providence. He became daily more attached to the beautiful and virtuous princess whom he had married; and he could not help contrasting her character with that of his former wife, whom he had ceased to love, and of whose unreasonable and unfeeling vanity he was now fully sensible.

X. Curiosity

In the myth of Pandora (page 20) curiosity plays an important part. Curiosity is indeed a basic human trait, and folktales provide many examples. Curiosity is one of the motives that sends Sinbad out on his many voyages. Odysseus's curiosity plays a role several times on his homeward journey. His desire to hear the Sirens' song (page 36), for example, causes him to devise a way to hear the song of the Sirens, though his men cannot. Phaëthon's curiosity about driving the chariot of the sun (page 16) leads to his undoing. Curiosity has motivated explorers, inventors, and artists, but sometimes curiosity can have an unexpected outcome.

Folktales examine the range of human weaknesses. Just as curiosity is often a theme of folktales, so greed is sometimes the central point. Greed drove the cobbler astrologer's wife (page 193) to put her husband's life at risk. Midas, King of Phrygia, was once given a wish for anything he might want. He requested that everything he touched might turn to gold. The wish was granted, but Midas found this a deadly boon. Even his food turned to gold, and he asked that the gift be revoked.

Human emotions, like curiosity and greed, need to be kept in check, as the following folktale demonstrates.

The Master and His Pupil (English)

One of the most famous works by the French composer Paul
Dukas is *The Sorcerer's Apprentice.* Walt Disney included this
composition in his masterpiece *Fantasia,* an animated cartoon
version of many great musical works. In the *Fantasia* version,
Mickey Mouse is the magician's apprentice. In his master's
absence Mickey has an idea. Because he considers himself
overworked, he uses one of his master's magic spells to ease
his workload. Buckets of water that he was supposed to carry
are instead carried by brooms. The idea works well—for a
while. Unfortunately, Mickey doesn't know how to cancel the
spell, and the water begins to flood. The folktale suggests that
we should not dabble in something we don't understand and
begin something we cannot stop.

Where did Dukas get his idea for *The Sorcerer's Apprentice?*
Perhaps the following folktale was one of his sources.

Now the master had a pupil who was but a foolish lad, and acted
as servant to the great master, but never was he allowed to look into
the black book, hardly ever to enter the private room.

One day the master was out, and then the lad, impelled by curiosity,
hurried to the chamber where his master kept his wondrous apparatus
for changing copper into gold, and lead into silver, and where was
his mirror in which he could see all that was passing in the world,
and where was the shell which when held to the ear whispered all
the words that were being spoken by anyone the master desired to
know about.

The lad tried in vain with the crucibles to turn copper into gold
and lead into silver. He looked long and vainly into the mirror—
smoke and clouds fleeted over it, but he saw nothing plain, and the
shell to his ear produced only indistinct murmurings, like the breaking
of waves on a distant shore.

"I can do nothing," he said, "as I don't know the right words to
utter, and they are locked up in this book." He looked round, and,
see! the book was unfastened; the master had forgotten to lock it
before he went out. The boy rushed to it and unclosed the volume.
It was written with red and black ink, and much that was in it he
could not understand; but he put his finger on a line and spelled it
through.

At once the room was darkened, and the house trembled; a clap of
thunder rolled through the passage of the old mansion, and there

stood before the terrified youth a horrible form, breathing fire, and with eyes like burning lamps. It was the Evil One, Beelzebub, whom he had called up to serve him.

"Set me a task!" he said with a voice like the roaring of an iron furnace.

The boy only trembled and his hair stood up.

"Set me a task, or I shall strangle you!"

But the lad could not speak. Then the evil spirit stepped toward him and, putting forth his hands, touched his throat. The fingers burned his flesh. "Set me a task!"

"Water that flower," cried the boy in despair, pointing to a geranium which stood in a pot on the floor.

Instantly the spirit left the room, but in another instant he returned with a barrel on his back and poured its contents over the flower; and again and again he went and came, and poured more and more water, till the floor of the room was ankle-deep.

"Enough, enough!" gasped the lad; but the Evil One heeded him not; the lad didn't know the words by which to dismiss him, and still he fetched water.

It rose to the boy's keees, and still more water was poured. It mounted to his waist, and Beelzebub still kept on bringing barrels full. It rose to his armpits, and he scrambled to the tabletop. And over the glass tabletop, it swirled around his feet. It still rose; it reached his breast. In vain he cried; the evil spirit would not be dismissed.

And to this day he would have been pouring water, and would have drowned all Yorkshire, but the master remembered on his journey that he had not locked his book and therefore returned, and, at the moment when the water was bubbling about the pupil's chin, rushed into the room and spoke the words which cast Beelzebub back into his fiery home.

Adam and Eve Again (Italian)

"I'll be gone for an hour. Whatever you do, don't open the oven door."

The mother left her children and proceeded to the store. The children played for a while and then looked at the enticing oven door.

"I wonder why Mom didn't want us to open it. I wonder what's in the oven. Maybe it's chocolate brownies. It can't hurt anything if we take a little peek." So one of the children opened the door, and the cake inside collapsed. Is this far-fetched, or is it all too possible?

The story that follows provides an answer to the question and also reveals a trait of human nature that sometimes leads to trouble.

There was an old couple who earned a poor living by working hard all day in the fields. "See how hard we work all day," said the wife, "and it all comes of the foolish curiosity of Adam and Eve. If it had not been for that, we should have been living now in a beautiful garden with nothing to do all day long."

"Yes," said the husband, "if you and I had been there, instead of Adam and Eve, all the human race would be in Paradise still."

The count, their master, overheard them talking in this way, and he came to them and said, "How would you like it if I took you up into my palazzo there to live and gave you servants to wait on you, and plenty to eat and drink?"

"Oh, that would be delightful indeed! That would be as good as Paradise itself," answered husband and wife together.

"Well, you may come up there if you think so. Only remember, in Paradise there was one tree that was not to be touched; so at my table there will be one dish not to be touched. You mustn't mind that," said the count.

"Oh, of course not," replied the old peasant, "that's just what I say—when Eve had all the fruits in the garden, what did she want with just that one that was forbidden? And if we, who are used to the scantiest victuals, are supplied with enough to live well, what does it matter to us whether there is an extra dish or not on the table?"

"Very well reasoned," said the count. "We quite understand each other, then?"

"Perfectly," replied both husband and wife.

"You come to live at my palace and have everything you can want there, so long as you don't open one dish which there will be in the middle of the table. If you open that, you can go back to your former way of life."

"We quite understand," answered the peasants.

The count went in and called his servant and told him to give the peasants an apartment to themselves, with everything they could want, and a sumptuous dinner, only in the middle of the table was to be an earthen dish into which he was to put a little live bird, so that if one lifted the cover the bird would fly out. He was to stay in the room and wait on them, and report to him what happened.

The old people sat down to dinner and praised everything they saw, so delightful it all seemed.

"Look! that's the dish we're not to touch," said the wife.

"No; better not look at it," said the husband.

"Pshaw! there's no danger of wanting to open it, when we have such a lot of dishes to eat our fill of," returned the wife.

So they set to and made such a repast as they had never dreamed of before. By degrees, however, as the novelty of the thing wore off, they grew more and more desirous for something newer and newer still. Though when they at first sat down, it had seemed that two dishes would be ample to satisfy them, they had now had seven or eight, and they were wishing there might be others coming. There is an end to all things human, and no other came. There only remained the tureen in the middle of the table.

"We might just lift the lid up a little wee bit," said the wife.

"No; don't talk about it," said the husband.

The wife sat still for five minutes, and then she said, "If one just lifted up one corner of the lid, it could scarcely be called opening it, you know."

"Better leave it alone altogether and not think about it at all," said the husband.

The wife sat still another five minutes, and then she said, "If one peeped in just the least in the world, it would not be any harm, surely; and I should so like to know what there can possibly be. Now, what can the count have put in that dish?"

"I'm sure I can't guess in the least," said the husband, "and I must say I can't see what it can signify to him if we did look at it."

"No; that's what I think. And besides, how would he know if we peeped? It wouldn't hurt him," said the wife.

"No; as you say, one could just take a look," said the husband.

The wife didn't want more encouragement than that. But when she lifted one side of the lid the least mite, she could see nothing. She opened it the least mite more, and out flew the bird. The servant ran and told his master, and the count came down and drove them out, bidding them never complain of Adam and Eve anymore.

XI. The Sleeper Wakes

What would it be like to sleep for a certain number of years and then come back to a strange world? Science-fiction stories have often played with this idea. A spaceship goes off on a mission and travels so fast that Einstein's laws operate. Time is relative. The travelers may be away two of their years, but eighty years have passed on earth. The experiences of the space travelers on their return provide some interesting plot possibilities.

Some people believe in cryogenics, arranging to have their bodies frozen at death. Their hope is that science at some future date may be able to revive them. Their experiences and sensations at that time would certainly provide a good story. In the movie *Sleeper*, Woody Allen puts an ordinary man into the future with hilarious results.

Peter Klaus (German)

The long sleep is not new to literature. H.G. Wells used it in *The Sleeper Awakes*. Washington Irving used it in "Rip Van Winkle" and gave a new word to the language. (In a political debate, a candidate may say, "My opponent is a Rip Van Winkle who has been sleeping for the past twenty years and has no idea about what is happening now.") Charles Perrault's "The Sleeping Beauty" (242–250) uses a similar idea. Folktales have toyed with the same idea.

Peter Klaus, a goatherd, follows a straying goat and finds himself in a mysterious cavern. He meets strangely dressed knights playing ninepins. He loses his caution and gets into the spirit of the game, drinking more wine than he should. He falls asleep, and when he awakes, his life has been changed. In a very direct way he realizes the swift passage of time.

In the village of Sittendorf at the foot of a mountain lived Peter Klaus, a goatherd who was in the habit of pasturing his flock upon the nearby Kyffhausen Hills. Toward evening he generally let them browse upon a green plot surrounded by an old ruined wall, from which he could take a muster of his whole flock.

During one period he observed that one of his prettiest goats usually disappeared soon after its arrival at this spot and did not join the fold again until late in the evening. He watched her again and again, and at last found that she slipped through a gap into a passage which widened into a cavern. When he entered the cavern, he found the goat busy picking up oats that fell through some crevices above. He looked up, shook his head at this odd shower, and at first could find no explanation for it.

At length he heard over his head the neighing and stamping of horses; he listened, and concluded that the oats must have fallen through a manger where horses were being fed. The poor goatherd was sadly at a loss to know what horses were doing in that uninhabited part of the mountain, but so it was, for a groom soon made his appearance and, without saying a word, beckoned him to follow.

Peter obeyed and followed him up some steps which led into an open courtyard surrounded by old walls. Next to this was a still more spacious ravine, surrounded by rocky heights and overhung with trees and shrubs which admitted only a kind of twilight. Peter continued on and came at last to a smooth-shaven green, where twelve ancient knights, none of whom spoke a word, were engaged in playing ninepins. His guide now beckoned to Peter to pick up the ninepins and then went his way.

At first, trembling in every limb, Peter did not venture to disobey, but after a time he began to cast stolen glances at the players, and saw at once that their long beards and slashed doublets belonged to a fashion long past. By degrees his looks grew bolder, and, noting among other things a tankard near him filled with wine whose aroma was excellent, he took a draught. It seemed to give him renewed life; and whenever he began to feel tired, he applied with fresh ardor to the tankard. Finally the wine overpowered him, and he fell fast asleep.

When he opened his eyes again, he found himself on the grassy plot once more, in the same old spot where he was in the habit of feeding his goats. He rubbed his eyes and looked round but could see neither dog nor flock. This surprised him, but he was even more surprised at the long, rank grass that grew about him, and at trees and bushes which he had never before seen.

He shook his head and walked a little farther, looking for the old sheep path and the hillocks and road where he used daily to drive his flock; but he could find no trace of them. Yet he saw the village just before him. He hastened down the hill to inquire after his flock.

All the people whom he met going into the village were strangers to him, and all were strangely dressed and spoke in a way different from that of his old neighbors. When he asked about his goats, these people only stared at him and fixed their eyes upon his chin. He put his hand unconsciously to his mouth, and to his great surprise found that he had grown a beard at least a foot long.

He now began to think that both he and all the world around him were in a dream; and yet he knew the mountain he had just come down was the Kyffhausen. And there were the cottages with their gardens and grassy plots, much as he had left them. Besides, when he asked the lads who had collected round him what place it was, they answered that it was Sittendorf.

Still shaking his head, he went farther into the village to look for his own house. He found it, but greatly altered, and for the worse: a strange goatherd in an old tattered frock lay before the door, and near him lay Peter's old dog, which only growled and showed its teeth when Peter tried to call him. He went through the entrance which had once had a door, but all within was empty and deserted. He staggered out of the house like a drunken man, and called for his wife and children again and again by name; but no one listened and no one gave answer.

Soon, however, a crowd of women and children gathered round the stranger with the long hoary beard and asked him what it was he wanted. Peter thought it was such a strange kind of thing to stand before his own house and inquire for his own wife and children, as well as about himself, that, evading these questions he asked for an old neighbor, Kurt Steffen, the blacksmith. Most of the spectators only stared at him blankly, till an old woman at last said, "Why he has been in Sachsenburg these twelve years."

"Where then is Valentine Meier, the tailor?" Peter asked the bystanders.

"The Lord rest his soul!" cried another old woman leaning upon her crutch. "He has been lying more than these fifteen years in a house he will never leave."

Then Peter recognized in these women two who had been young neighbors of his. They seemed to have grown old with incredible suddenness, but he had little inclination to inquire further.

At this moment there appeared, making her way through the crowd of spectators, a sprightly young woman with a year-old baby in her arms and with a girl of about four holding her hand. All three bore a striking resemblance to the wife he was seeking.

"What are your names?" he cried out in surprise.

"Mine is Maria," the woman said.

"And your father's?" continued Peter.

"God rest his soul! Peter Klaus, to be sure. It is now twenty years since we were all looking for him day and night upon the Kyffhausen— after his flock came home without him. I was then," continued the woman, "only seven years old."

The goatherd could no longer contain himself. "I am Peter Klaus," he cried, "Peter and no other." And he took his daughter's child and kissed it. The spectators were struck dumb with astonishment, until first one and then another began to see, "Yes, indeed, that is Peter Klaus! Welcome, good neighbor, after twenty years' absence, welcome home."

XII. Trickster

Tricksters appear in folktales of people around the world. Clever persons have appeared in other myths already read, like the mason in "The Treasures of Rhampsinitus" (page 159) or the farmer in "Why the Hair Turns Gray Before the Beard" (page 191). The trickster is different. He usually appears in a series of tales. He may be a coyote among the North American Indians or a spider on the Gold Coast of Africa. The trickster often seems to be a smaller creature who wins out against stronger adversaries. Just as in the "Poor Person Triumphant" (page 190), we can identify with this lesser creature who lives by his wits.

Sometimes the trickster is more than a folk character. Sometimes he is regarded as the hero who introduced the arts of living. At other times he is on the side of evil, but even then people may benefit by his actions. Often good and evil are combined in the same character.

Trickster tales are so universal and yet so varied that generalizations are difficult. There is one common characteristic, however: the trickster tales are among the most colorful of folktales. Tricksters, like Loki (page 106), are fascinating even when their actions are evil.

Tiger Becomes a Riding Horse (Jamaican)

A good example of a trickster is Anansi in the following folktale. The tale is told in Jamaica, but it had its origin in West Africa in the folklore of Ghana, Liberia, Congo, Angola, and many others. Throughout the West Indies, tales of Anansi flourish. Anansi, crafty and cunning, lives by his wits.

In some stories Anansi appears as a spider. In others he appears as a man. Sometimes he changes from being a man to being a spider, to save himself at a moment of danger. In many ways he is like the clever Brer Rabbit in folktales of the

American South. Like Anansi, Brer Rabbit is an insignificant
creature who must survive by his wits.

Tiger is often the victim of Anansi's tricks. One of the most
famous tales shows Anansi in a characteristically clever role.
He boasts that he can ride Tiger, and in the following story he
shows how.

Once upon a time, long before now, Anansi and Tiger used to go
out romancing those girls together. But as things will happen, one
day they found that they were both courting the same young lady,
and they got very jealous of each other. So you know Anansi, he went
to this lady's yard and he started in on his boasting, claiming that
Tiger was nothing better than his father's old riding horse. Of course,
it wasn't any time before Tiger came by to call upon this girl he
thought was his sweetheart. But the young lady said to him, "Go
along with you now! How can you just come around courting when
I heard that you are nothing but an old riding horse?"

"What do you mean?" asked Tiger. "Who is telling you this? It
looks like somebody has been telling stories about me, and they have
filled your ears with big lies, ma'am. But I tell you what I'll do. I'll
go straight to my friend Anansi, and he'll tell you that all of this is
just something somebody is stirring up. I never have been his father's
old jackass riding horse." So the lady told him to get going.

So Tiger took up his walking stick, and put his pipe in his cheek,
and walking out as respectably as he could, he went straight to
Anansi's yard. He found Anansi lying there on his bed moaning with
fever. So he lifted the latch, and called out, "Brer Anansi! Brer
Anansi!" Anansi heard him very well, but he just said so soft and
sicklike, "Brer Tiger, you call me?" He knew that Brer Tiger was
going to be mad at him, you know.

Tiger said, "Yes, I called you! I came right over to your house
because someone has been telling lies about me and I wanted to find
out if it was you. I want to hear it from your own mouth. If you said
those things, I'm going to make you prove it."

"Oooh," Anansi groaned. "Can't you see I have a fever? My stomach
is hurting me bad, and I have just been to the doctor and taken some
of his medicine!"

"Is that so?" said Tiger. "I don't believe you."

"I just ate two pills, Brer Tiger, so how can you think I could even
get up and go to any lady's yard to prove anything tonight?" "I don't
want to have any argument with you, brother," replied Tiger, "but

I think you better come with me anyhow to tell that lady tonight that I am not your father's old jackass riding horse."

"Oh, Lord!" cried Anansi. "This pain in my breast just won't let me be, it's burning so bad! But if you insist, I could try to go with you to see the lady. But I'm feeling so sick."

Then Tiger said, "Well, since you're so sick maybe I could help you get there. How can I help?" So Brer Anansi said, "Well, just lift me up a little and see how I feel." So Tiger lifted him, and Anansi said, "Oh, Lord, I'm feeling dizzy." So Tiger said, "Just grab on here on my neck, and don't worry; I will carry you on my back." "Wait a minute then, brother, and I will get out of bed here and help out." But he fell back, and he cried out, "Oh, Lord, I just can't get up at all. I beg you, brother, come lift me up again." So Tiger raised him up again, and again Anansi fell back. Now Tiger didn't know what to do. Brer Anansi looked up and said, "Well, why don't you get that saddle up there in the rafters and put it on and I could maybe grab hold of that and you could carry me."

So he went to the rafter, and took down Brer Anansi's saddle. Brer Anansi said, "Now just put that on your back, brother, and I can sit down soft."

Then Anansi got up on his saddle and got his bridle and reins. "Hey!" said Tiger, "what are you going to do with that?" Brer Anansi said, "If you just put that through your mouth, brother, and then I can tell you if you are starting to go too fast and I am going to fall off." "All right then," said Tiger, "put it on."

So Anansi took out his horsewhip. "Hey!" said Tiger. "What are you going to do with that?" "If a fly comes on your ear or back, brother, I will be able to take this whip and lick it off." Tiger said, "Well, O.K." So Anansi put on his spurs. "Hey!" said Tiger. "Now what are you going to do with those?" "If flies come on your side, brother, I can brush them away with my spurs and make them fly away." "O.K., never mind then," said Tiger, "put them on."

Then Anansi moaned, "Well, Brer Tiger, if you stoop down, I can get on." And that way Anansi mounted on his back, and Tiger then began to walk off. But as he went along Anansi pulled him up with the bridle. "Stop, brother! Take your time, will you; my head is hurting me so!"

So Tiger went on about a mile or so, and after a little while, Anansi took his whip out and gave Tiger a lick on the ear. "Hey!" said Tiger. "What's that for?" "Well, there was a stupid fly on your ear! Shoo fly!" "All right, brother," said Tiger, "but next time don't hit so hard."

Tiger went on for another mile or so and Anansi stuck his spur into his side. Tiger jumped and cried out, "Now wait a minute! What is that you're doing?" "Those bothersome flies, brother. They are biting your side hard."

Then Tiger went on for another half-mile, till he came to the lady's yard. Now the lady's house had two doors, a front one and a back one. Just as he came to the entrance of the yard, Anansi rose up in his saddle, just like jockeys run races on the Kingston racecourse, and he took out his whip and he lashed Tiger hard! "Hey!" cried Tiger. "You lick too hard!" But Anansi lashed him more and more until Tiger really started to run. Then Anansi took his spurs and stuck them into Tiger's side and he made him run right up to the lady's door-mouth.

Then Anansi took off his hat and waved it above his head and said to the lady, who was standing at the door, "Good morning, mistress, didn't I tell you the truth that Tiger is nothing but my father's old riding horse?" He leaped off Tiger, and went into the lady's house, and Tiger was so embarrassed that he galloped off, and never was heard of no more.

XIII. The Tall Story

"The report of my death is slightly exaggerated." This is Mark Twain's famous reaction to an obituary notice prematurely announcing his death. "Slightly exaggerated" is an understatement, a frequent source of humor. Another example of understatement is the reaction of a person who goes through all kinds of physical dangers, emerging battered and bruised. Then "I had a bit of bad luck" is classic understatement.

Exaggeration, sometimes called *hyperbole* in language, is the opposite of understatement. The tall talk of Davy Crockett and other American frontiersmen is a good example of this device. Examples of American tall tales are found in Unit VII (pages 273–326). But tall tales are not restricted to the American frontier. They are favorites of people around the world.

That's a Lie (Norse)

"How cold was it?
"It was so cold that . . ."
The speaker goes on to exaggerate, making the cold spell the worst weather in recorded history. The lying tale, often called a *whopper*, is a branch of the tall story. As B.A. Botkin has written, "Outside the realm of both probability and possi-

bility, the world of lies is the world of supermen who perform
miracles midway between nonsense and magic and who inhabit a land of giant vegetables and delightfully preposterous
canny or composite creatures." Botkin then goes on to compare these with travelers' guidebooks and advertisements for
houses and land!

To satisfy our appetite for such tall stories, Liars' Clubs
have been formed, like the Burlington, Wisconsin, Liar's Club.
Members of the clubs outdo each other in dreaming up the
most fantastic, impossible, and creative yarns. Boots, in the
tale that follows, could have been a charter member of any
Liars' Club!

Note that once again we have a princess to be married and
a youngest son as a suitor. Once again there is a special
problem to be solved before the hero can win the princess.
(See also "The Salamanna Grapes," pages 146–151.) This time
the suitors need not go out into the world on difficult quests.
All a successful suitor has to do is outdo the princess in her
favorite activity.

Once on a time there was a king who had a daughter, and she was
such a dreadful teller of fibs that the like of her was not to be found
far or near. So the king gave out that if anyone could tell such a
string of lies as would get her to say, "That's a lie," he should have
her to wife, and half the kingdom besides. Well, many came, as you
may fancy, to try their luck, for everyone would have been very glad
to have the princess, to say nothing of the kingdom; but they all cut
a sorry figure, for the princess was so given to storytelling that all
their lies went in at one ear and out of the other. Among the rest
came three brothers to try their luck, and the two elder went first,
but they fared no better than those who had gone before them. Last
of all the third, Boots, set off and found the princess in the farmyard.

"Good morning," he said, "and thank you for nothing."

"Good morning," said she, "and the same to you."

Then she went on, "You haven't such a fine farmyard as ours, I'll
be bound; for when two shepherds stand, one at each end of it, and
blow their ram's horns, the one can't hear the other."

"Haven't we though!" answered Boots. "Ours is far bigger; for
when a cow begins to go with calf at one end of it, she doesn't get
to the other end before the time to drop her calf is come."

"I dare say!" said the princess. "Well, but you haven't such a big
ox, after all, as ours yonder; for when two men sit one on each horn,
they can't touch each other with a twenty-foot rule."

"Stuff!" said Boots. "Is that all? Why, we have an ox who is so big that when two men sit, one on each horn, and each blows his great mountain trumpet, they can't hear one another."

"I dare say!" said the princess. "But you haven't so much milk as we, I'll be bound; for we milk our kine into great pails and carry them indoors and empty them into great tubs, and so we make great, great cheeses."

"Oh, you do, do you?" said Boots. "Well, we milk ours into great tubs, and then we put them in carts and drive them indoors, and then we turn them out into great brewing vats, and so we make cheeses as big as a great house. We had, too, a dun mare to tread the cheese well together when it was making; but once she tumbled down into the cheese, and we lost her; and after we had eaten at this cheese seven years, we came upon a great dun mare, alive and kicking. Well, once after that I was going to drive this mare to the mill, and her backbone snapped in two; but I wasn't put out, not I, for I took a spruce sapling, and put it into her for a backbone, and she had no other backbone all the while we had her. But the sapling grew up into such a tall tree, that I climbed right up to Heaven by it, and when I got there, I saw the Virgin Mary sitting and spinning the foam of the sea into pig's bristle ropes; but just then the spruce fir broke short off, and I couldn't get down again. So the Virgin Mary let me down by one of the ropes, and down I slipped straight into a fox's hole. And who should sit there but MY MOTHER and YOUR FATHER cobbling shoes. And just as I stepped in, my mother gave your father such a box on the ear that it made his whiskers curl."

"THAT'S A LIE!" shouted the princess. "My father never did any such thing in all his born days!"

So Boots got the princess to wife, and half the kingdom besides.

XIV. The Magic Word

<pre>
A B R A C A D A B R A
A B R A C A D A B R
A B R A C A D A B
A B R A C A D A
A B R A C A D
A B R A C A
A B R A C
A B R A
A B R
A B
A
</pre>

Abracadabra was often considered a magic word of considerable power. A sick person would wear, around the neck, an amulet with the triangular inscription. The belief was that the disease would gradually disappear just as the inscription dwindles to nothing. Ever since the second century this word has had believers in its powers.

We have already seen in "The Master and His Pupil" (page 204) the importance of words. But other words have been assigned great importance, too. In *Macbeth* the three witches cast a charm by saying,

> "Double, double toil and trouble;
> Fire burn and cauldron bubble."

The importance of words varies from society to society. A word considered improper or taboo in one society may be acceptable in another. But in all societies certain words have almost magical properties.

Ali Baba and the Forty Thieves (Arabic)

One of the most popular of all *The Arabian Nights' Entertainments* is the tale of Ali Baba. The power of the words *Open, Sesame!* is another example of word magic, but this story contains other familiar ingredients: Again a poor man becomes rich. Ali Baba's faithful servant, through superior wisdom, outwits the villains and saves him and his family. Unfortunately, his brother is destroyed by his own greed. There is magic in this folktale, but as always in folktales there is realism and the accurate depiction of human emotions.

Once upon a time there was a Persian woodcutter named Ali Baba. As he was cutting wood one day, he spied a band of strange horsemen coming toward him. Afraid of being discovered, he climbed a tree and waited. He held his breath as the band halted beneath him. The leader cried out, "Open, Sesame!" to a nearby rock. A door opened through the hillside, and the men rode into a cave inside, carrying their heavy packs.

Ali Baba waited patiently until the men emerged and rode away. Curious about the cave, he also cried out, "Open, Sesame!" As it did for the thieves, the rock opened and Ali Baba entered the cave. There he discovered treasures that the thieves had stolen and stored away. Ali Baba took a modest amount of gold, too little to be missed, and went home.

Ali Baba and his wife were content with their new and modest fortune, but Ali Baba's brother Cassim was greedy for more wealth. Cassim decided to investigate for himself. Without telling Ali Baba, he went to the cave and cried out, "Open, Sesame!" The cave opened.

At this point greed proved Cassim's undoing. He was so excited seeing the gold and planning to carry off a large part of the treasure, that he couldn't remember the password. The rock would not budge, and Cassim was trapped.

After a time the robbers returned and found Cassim inside. They put him to death, rejoicing that they had trapped him before he could run off with any of their gold. But then they began to worry. If Cassim knew the secret, perhaps others might. They resolved to find Cassim's brother Ali Baba and kill him, to keep safe the secret of their hoard. The leader decided upon a plan. He delivered to Ali Baba's house huge oil jars in which he hid all his men. Ali Baba's beautiful slave, Morgiana, discovered the trick when she went in search of oil. She poured hot oil into the jars and killed the thieves.

The captain, however, was still alive. He came to Ali Baba's house disguised as a merchant. Once again Morgiana proved wiser than the captain. She saw through his disguise and killed him with his own dagger.

Ali Baba rewarded Morgiana by making her a free woman and giving to her his own son in marriage. Ali Baba was the only one left who knew the secret of the cave. He used the treasure little by little, never greedily taking everything at once. He prospered and passed the secret on to his children. So virtue was rewarded.

XV. English and Scottish Ballads

Ballads are folktales in verse. Sometimes they tell about famous people, about popular heroes or great events. Sometimes they just tell stories about knights and ladies and ordinary villagers. In ballads, ghosts and enchantments are commonplace. No matter what the subject matter, though, ballads usually have certain characteristics.

In the ballad the story is usually told through dialog. No words are wasted. The conflict is soon told, and the end is not long in coming. The language is direct. The plot is simple, often tragic. Events follow each other thick and fast. In "Sir Patrick Spens," for example, Sir Patrick is already at sea just after we hear of his reluctance to go.

Some English ballads crossed over into America with the early settlers. These ballads took on a life of their own here. (Refer to page 295 for a discussion of "Barbara Allen" and American folk ballads in general.) Most English ballads can be traced back 500 years or more. No one is quite sure how they originated, but the important thing is that they have a folk quality, just like the folktales you have been reading.

Ballads usually consist of four-line stanzas. In fact, this particular stanza is usually called the *ballad stanza*. Often there is a refrain, a section repeated for effect, as in "Edward." Since ballads were meant to be sung, they have strong rhythm. Try reading them aloud. Most of the dialect and the difficulties of language have been eliminated. However, there is no substitute for the charm of the originals. Perhaps someday you will be able to read these for yourself.

Sir Patrick Spens

One of the most famous of all ballads is "Sir Patrick Spens." Perhaps this commemorated an actual tragedy, but no matter. The story itself is simple, direct, and effective. The plot is complete without a wasted word. The contrast between the king safely drinking his wine and Sir Patrick Spens in the storm is economically presented. The last two stanzas, particularly, bring the tragedy home with force and realism.

> The king sits in Dumferling town,
>   Drinking the blood-red wine:
> "O where will I get good sailor,
>   To sail this ship of mine?"
>
> Up and spake an elder knight,
>   Sat at the king's right knee:
> "Sir Patrick Spens is the best sailor,
>   That sails upon the sea."
>
> The king has written a broad letter,
>   And signed it with his hand,
> And sent it to Sir Patrick Spens,
>   Was walking on the sand.
>
> The first line that Sir Patrick read,
>   A loud laugh laughed he;
> The next line that Sir Patrick read,
>   The tear blinded his ee.*

* eye

"O who is this has done this deed,
  This ill deed done to me,
To send me out this time of the year,
  To sail upon the sea!"

"Make haste, make haste, my merry men all,
  Our good ship sails the morn."
"O say not so, my master dear,
  For I fear a deadly storm."

"Late, late yestreen I saw the new moon,
  Wi' the old moon in her arm,
And I fear, I fear, my dear master,
  That we will come to harm."

O our Scots nobles were right loth
  To wet their cork-heeled shoon,*
But long before all the play were played,
  Their hats they swam aboon.†

O, long, long may their ladies sit,
  Wi' their fans into their hand,
Or ere they see Sir Patrick Spens
  Come sailing to the land.

O, long, long may the ladies stand,
  Wi' their gold combs in their hair,
Waiting for their own dear lords,
  For they'll see them na mair.

Half over, half over to Aberdour,
  Its fifty fathoms deep,
And there lies good Sir Patrick Spens
  Wi' the Scots lords at his feet.

Edward

One of the most powerful and most characteristic of all ballads is "Edward." It is told in the form of a dialog between a mother and her son. As we follow the conversation, we are aware that a tragedy is soon to be told. But we do not know the extent of the tragedy until the very end. It is almost like a detective story, with the real murderer unveiled at the last moment.

* shoes
† above

"Why does your brand so drip with blood,
                Edward, Edward,
Why does your brand so drip with blood,
    And why so sad go ye O?"
"O I have killed my hawk so good,
                Mother, mother,
O I have killed my hawk so good,
    And I had no more but he O."

"Your hawk's blood was never so red,
                Edward, Edward,
Your hawk's blood was never so red,
    My dear son I tell thee O."
"O I have killed my red-roan steed,
                Mother, mother,
O I have killed my red-roan steed,
    That once was so fair and free O."

"Your steed was old, and ye have got more,
                Edward, Edward,
Your steed was old, and ye have got more,
    Some other dule ye dree O."*
"O I have killed my father dear,
                Mother, mother,
O I have killed my father dear,
    Alas, and woe is me O."

"And whatten penance will you do for that,
                Edward, Edward?
And whatten penance will you do for that?
    My dear son, now tell me O."
"I'll set my feet in yonder boat,
                Mother, mother,
I'll set my feet in yonder boat,
    And I'll fare over the sea O."

"And what will you do with your towers and your hall,
                Edward, Edward?
And what will you do with your towers and your hall,
    That were so fair to see O?"
"I'll let them stand till they down fall,
                Mother, mother,
I'll let them stand till they down fall,
    For here never more must I be O."

* Some other grief do you suffer.

"And what will you leave to your bairns* and your wife,
    Edward, Edward?
And what will you leave to your bairns and your wife,
  When you go over the sea O?"
"The world's room, let them beg through life,
    Mother, mother,
The world's room, let them beg through life,
  For them never more will I see O."

"And what will you leave to your own mother dear,
    Edward, Edward?
And what will you leave to your own mother dear?
  My dear son, now tell me O?"
"The curse of hell from me shall you bear,
    Mother, mother,
The curse of hell from me shall you bear,
  Such counsels you gave to me O."

Bonnie George Campbell

    Tragedy is often the subject of the old ballads, and "Bonnie George Campbell" is a typical example. In six short verses we are presented with an unsolved mystery. The repetition heightens the tragedy. There are three characters: George Campbell, his mother, and his bride. In a few lines we meet the distracted mother and the hysterical bride, but we never meet George Campbell. What has happened to him? Why doesn't he come home? How will his work be done? The ballad leaves that answer to us.

High upon Highlands,
  And low upon Tay,
Bonnie George Campbell
  Rode out on a day.
Saddled and bridled
  And gallant rode he:
Home came his good horse,
  But never came he.

Out came his old mother
  Greeting full sair;†
And out came his bonnie bride,
  Tearing her hair.

* children
† sore

Saddled and bridled
  And booted rode he:
Empty home came the saddle,
  But never came he.

"My meadow lies green,
  And my corn is unshorn,
My barn is to build,
  And my babe is unborn."

Saddled and bridled
  And booted rode he:
Empty home came the saddle,
  But never came he.

Get Up and Bar the Door

By now you may be thinking that all ballads deal with
murder, betrayal, and other tragic themes. Not so. Some are
filled with folk humor and fun. One of the finest and funniest
of all ballads is "Get Up and Bar the Door." If you've ever
held out foolishly through stubborn pride, you'll appreciate
the persistence of the good wife, who outlasted her husband in
a contest of wills.

It fell about the Martinmas time,
  And a gay time it was then,
When our goodwife got puddings to make,
  And she's boiled them in the pan.

The wind so cold blew south and north,
  And blew into the floor;
Quoth our goodman to our goodwife,
  "Go out and bar the door."

"My hand is in my hussyfskap,*
  Goodman, as you may see;
If it should not be barred this hundred year,
  It's no be barred for me."

They made a pact between the two,
  They made it firm and sure,
That the first word whoe'er should speak
  Should rise and bar the door.

* kneading-trough

Then by there came two gentlemen,
    At twelve o'clock at night,
And they could neither see house nor hall,
    Nor coal nor candle-light.

"Now whether is this a rich man's house,
    Or whether is it a poor?"
But ne'er a word would one of them speak,
    For barring of the door.

And first they ate the white puddings,
    And then they ate the black;
Though much thought the goodwife to herself,
    Yet ne'er a word she spake.

Then said the one unto the other,
    "Here, man, take you my knife;
Do you take off the old man's beard,
    And I'll kiss the goodwife."

"But there's no water in the house,
    And what shall we do than?"
"What ails thee at* the pudding-broo,
    That boils into the pan?"

O up then started our goodman,
    An angry man was he:
"Will you kiss my wife before my eyes,
    And scald me with pudding-bree?"

Then up and started our goodwife,
    Gave three skips on the floor:
"Goodman, you've spoken the foremost word.
    Get up and bar the door."

READING FOR UNDERSTANDING

Main Idea

1. The main idea of Section II, "Folktales and Literature" (pages 138–139), is that (a) "The Pardoner's Tale" is a greater story than *The Treasure of Sierra Madre* (b) folk heroes appear in a great many different countries (c) writers have used folktales as sources for plot and character ideas (d) *The Taming of the Shrew* may be Shakespeare's funniest play.

* Why not use . . .

Details

2. The first object to talk to the Ashanti gardener (140–142) was a
   (a) palm branch (b) stone (c) fish trap (d) yam.

3. In "Cats Are Queer Articles," the narrator's attitude toward the
   fair was one of (a) fear (b) anticipation (c) disappointment
   (d) satisfaction.

4. In "The Salamanna Grapes" each of the following gifts is mentioned EXCEPT (a) a telescope (b) a book (c) grapes (d) a
   carpet.

5. In "Jack and His Master" Gray Churl is (a) a mysterious pony
   (b) the villain (c) another name for the oldest brother (d) the
   teller of the story.

6. Kunibre (157–158) is the name of a (a) bird (b) coyote (c) tiger
   (d) wasp.

7. Rhampsinitus (159–164) was a king of (a) Syria (b) Persia
   (c) Norway (d) Egypt.

8. The huge white dome discovered by Sinbad (167–179) was really
   (a) an egg (b) the entrance to a secret cave (c) the roof of a
   mosque (d) a natural rock formation.

9. When the magistrate in "Come Look" said, "This is a marvelous
   thing in which every man can know himself," he was referring
   to a (a) book (b) chest (c) mirror (d) magic gemstone.

10. The four points of the compass were created (185–188) by
    (a) huge stones (b) four seas (c) mountains (d) four arrows
    shot into the air.

11. Brer Wasp (188–190) got his narrow waist by too much (a)
    drinking (b) exercising (c) laughing (d) crying.

12. In the story of "Adam and Eve Again," the forbidden object is
    (a) an apple (b) an oven door (c) a door (d) a dish.

13. Another word for Anansi (212–215) is (a) tiger (b) wasp
    (c) trickster (d) farmer.

14. To win the princess, Boots (215–217) has to (a) go on a quest
    (b) choose the right door (c) tell a tall story (d) cure her of a
    mysterious disease.

Inferences

15. The cobbler astrologer's wife (193–203) can best be characterized
    as (a) understanding (b) nagging (c) generous (d) violent.

16. The tragedy in the ballad "Bonnie George Campbell" (a) is
    unexplained (b) arises from the mother's cruelty (c) is played
    out in a storm at sea (d) has a happy ending.

17. "Talk—An Ashanti Tale" can best be described as (a) realistic (b) tragic (c) commonplace (d) humorous.
18. The mice that ate iron (158–159) were (a) robots (b) another name for a furnace (c) fictional (d) magical creatures.
19. To save her life, Scheherazade (165–166) depended upon (a) a magic potion (b) her storytelling ability (c) the Sultan's well-known kindness (d) a strict interpretation of the law.
20. In the folklore of most peoples, words (218) are considered (a) inferior to signs (b) best reserved for the wealthy (c) boring (d) magical.

WORDS IN CONTEXT
GROUP 1

1. "Folklore materials thrive in a society in which there are people of considerable native intelligence, artistic appreciation, memory, imagination and creative urge, who can comprehend, value, remember and recreate their native folklore and thus *propagate* it as living tradition."
   Propagate (137) means (a) understand (b) spread (c) dramatize (d) conceal.
2. The story of Andromeda has its *counterpart* in folktales from ancient Babylon, from Asia, Canada, and Central Europe.
   Counterpart (138) means (a) origin (b) opposite (c) support (d) duplicate.
3. You will notice the *cumulative* repetition of details, as in the old story of "Chicken Little" and the rhyme "This Is the House That Jack Built."
   Cumulative (140) means (a) increasing (b) boring (c) exciting (d) infrequent.
4. The storyteller is a very *prosaic*, no-nonsense farmer.
   Prosaic (142) means (a) poetic (b) handsome (c) ordinary (d) competent.
5. Herself started on me *straightaway*.
   Straightaway (145) means (a) immediately (b) nonstop (c) bitterly (d) warmly.
6. The *hapless* vizier looked all over in vain.
   Hapless (165) means (a) ingenious (b) angry (c) unfortunate (d) lucky.
7. The father tried to *dissuade* her, but she persisted.
   Dissuade (165) means (a) anger (b) quiet (c) stop (d) support.

8. One huge elephant uproots the tree—with Sinbad in it—and *stalks* off.
> *Stalks* (166) means   (a) creeps   (b) strides   (c) rushes (d) gallops.

9. Then my soul became desirous of travel and *diversion*, and I longed for commerce and gain and profits.
> *Diversion* (172) means   (a) danger   (b) amusement   (c) peace (d) food.

10. At every place we *diverted* ourselves, selling and buying in the utmost joy and happiness.
> *Diverted* (172) means   (a) exerted   (b) outdid   (c) surprised (d) entertained.

GROUP 2

11. For numbers *prevail* against courage, and we feared that they would plunder our goods and our commodities.
> *Prevail* (172) means   (a) argue   (b) fail   (c) triumph (d) decrease.

12. They climbed up the cables and *severed* them with their teeth.
> *Severed* (173) means   (a) cut   (b) covered   (c) slid down (d) tested.

13. He had two eyes like two blazes of fire, tusks like the tusks of swine, and a mouth of *prodigious* size, like the mouth of a well.
> *Prodigious* (173) means   (a) enormous   (b) average (c) slightly above average   (d) commonplace.

14. "By Allah, if we cast ourselves into the sea and die drowned, it will be better than our dying burnt, for this way of being put to death is *abominable*."
> *Abominable* (174) means   (a) unusual   (b) merciful   (c) clever (d) detestable.

15. Then it went its way in the utmost *vexation* and rage.
> *Vexation* (176) means   (a) rejoicing   (b) anger (c) thoughtfulness   (d) sensation.

16. "The truth of his *assertion* is obvious."
> *Assertion* (179) means   (a) anecdote   (b) statement   (c) poem (d) repetition.

17. Having looked at me awhile with a *scrutinizing* eye, he said, "What is the mark of your goods?"
> *Scrutinizing* (179) means   (a) examining carefully   (b) doubly suspicious   (c) rapidly blinking   (d) sympathetic.

18. Evil exists in the world and in folktales, but people hope for its *ultimate* defeat.

Ultimate(179) means (a) final (b) effective (c) unexpected
(d) timely.

19. Folktales often teach kindness, charity, and *compassion*.
    Compassion (182) means (a) trickery (b) comprehension
    (c) sympathy (d) cleverness.

20. In the following tale a grower of pears discovers that a *callous*
    disregard for a fellow human being can have grievous results.
    Callous (182) means (a) sympathetic (b) thoughtless
    (c) vital (d) insensitive.

GROUP 3

21. By and by there was a tree with branches sparsely covered with
    leaves; then flowers, and last of all fine, large, sweet-smelling
    pears, hanging in great *profusion*.
    Profusion (183) means (a) abundance (b) beauty
    (c) branches (d) confusion.

22. This he shouldered, leaves and all, and *sauntered* quietly away.
    Sauntered (184) means (a) backed (b) drove (c) hobbled
    (d) strolled.

23. Ever since human beings began to think, they have *pondered* the
    meaning of their existence.
    Pondered (185) means (a) discovered (b) thought about
    (c) solved (d) written about.

24. The youngest of four brothers was so tiny you would have called
    him a *sprite*.
    Sprite (186) means (a) insect (b) small bird (c) elf
    (d) mouse.

25. Anyone who has ever been stung by a wasp remembers that the
    insect seemed particularly irritated, sometimes attacking without
    apparent *provocation*.
    Provocation (188) means (a) reason for anger (b) method
    of attacking (c) effort to calm (d) hope for revenge.

26. "How dare you lie so *brazenly* to me!"
    Brazenly (192) means (a) falsely (b) poetically (c) quietly
    (d) boldly.

27. The cobbler *remonstrated*, but in vain.
    Remonstrated (194) means (a) repeated (b) murmured
    (c) wept (d) protested.

28. He was no astrologer, but he was *dotingly* fond of his wife, and
    he could not bear the idea of losing her.
    Dotingly (194) means (a) excessively (b) cheerfully
    (c) thoughtfully (d) moderately.

29. "O woman, woman! thou art more *baneful* to the happiness of man than the poisonous dragon of the desert."
      Baneful (195) means (a) helpful (b) comforting (c) harmful (d) unyielding.
30. She renewed her *entreaties* and threats, to make her fond husband continue his career as an astrologer.
      Entreaties (198) means (a) wishes (b) reports (c) pleas (d) ideas.

GROUP 4

31. "The king's astrologer has heard of my *presumption* and is determined to have me executed as an impostor."
      Presumption (198) means (a) prescription (b) boldness (c) work (d) thoughtfulness.
32. "He has made a good hit, that is all; still it is *prudent* to watch him."
      Prudent (200) means (a) interesting (b) wise (c) bothersome (d) time-consuming.
33. The thief, hearing these words, hastened in *consternation* to the gang.
      Consternation (200) means (a) increasing speed (b) confused alarm (c) apparent lightheartedness (d) keen curiosity.
34. The spy's tale was not believed by his hardened companions; something was *imputed* to his fears.
      Imputed (200) means (a) uncovered (b) openly discussed (c) fastened (d) attributed.
35. The morning had found Ahmed in a wretched *hovel*, rising from a sorry bed, in the expectation of losing his life.
      Hovel (203) means (a) depressed state (b) kitchen (c) miserable house (d) prison.
36. "If we, who are used to the *scantiest victuals*, are supplied with enough to live well, what does it matter to us whether there is an extra dish or not on the table?"
      Scantiest victuals (206) means (a) poorest foods (b) cheapest accommodations (c) toughest meats (d) dreariest recreations.
37. The count went in and called his servant and told him to give the peasants a *sumptuous* dinner.
      Sumptuous (206) means (a) luxurious (b) satisfactory (c) late (d) unenviable.
38. Soon, however, a crowd of women and children gathered round the stranger with the long *hoary* beard.

Hoary (210) means (a) curly (b) tangled (c) white with age (d) strange in appearance.

39. Ali Baba waited patiently until the men *emerged* and rode away.
    Emerged (218) means (a) cried out (b) came out (c) mounted their horses (d) ran rapidly.

40. Sir Patrick is already at sea just after we hear of his *reluctance* to go.
    Reluctance (219) means (a) eagerness (b) announcement (c) preparation (d) unwillingness.

THINKING IT OVER

1. Which of the folktales seemed to you to display a sense of humor? What is the source of fun in each?

2. Which folktale seemed to you most satisfying? Why?

3. Folktales reveal important human traits, like curiosity, anger, greed, generosity, resourcefulness, deception, fear, obstinacy, impulsiveness, love, hostility, and fickleness. Select three of these traits and select a character who demonstrates each trait.

4. One of the longest sections in this unit is "Cleverness Admired." This is so common a theme in folktales that it appears in several other tales in this section. Can you point them out?

5. "Edward" has been called a condensed detective story. Can you identify the crime, the victim, the actual murderer, the really guilty person, and the result?

SUGGESTED ACTIVITIES

1. What happened to Bonnie George Campbell (223)? What is the hidden story behind his disappearance? Did his wife know more than she seemed to know? Did his mother play a role? What do *you* think? Who can devise the most ingenious explanation? Write your explanation of George's disappearance. Be as imaginative as you like.

2. Have your class act out the ballads "Edward" and "Get Up and Bar the Door." Select appropriate voices for the various roles. For the latter poem you will need a narrator as well as four persons for the four characters.

3. Children's songs are called the oldest folk songs, very similar in countries throughout the world. Skipping and counting rhymes are part of children's possessions everywhere. Nearly everyone knows "London Bridge" and "All Around the Mulberry Bush." There are thousands of others. Perhaps you know one or more.

Write down the words of a counting rhyme or other song you sang in playing children's games. Bring your song to class. Perhaps your class will spend a period comparing different versions and different songs.

4. One of the commonest devices in the detective story is the "locked room" in which a theft or a murder is committed. Edgar Allan Poe is credited with having "invented" this device in "Murders in the Rue Morgue." Actually, though, "The Treasures of Rhampsinitus" uses the trick. Read Poe's story and compare it with the folktale. How does Poe's tale go far beyond the folktale? John Dickson Carr is a skillful modern writer who likes to work with the device of the locked room and the "impossible crime." You may enjoy reading one or more of his novels. G. K. Chesterton's "The Invisible Man" is a unique variation of the same theme.

5. Folk songs and folktales are but a part of folklore. Folk dancing is another part, an increasingly popular part. Indeed, many folk songs are used in folk dances. Perhaps someone in class will be able to demonstrate one or more folk dances; for example, "Road to the Isles" (Scotland), the "Weggis Dance" (Switzerland), "Laces and Graces" (United States). Many schools are incorporating folk dancing and square dancing into the regular course of study.

6. "Get Up and Bar the Door" is sometimes classified in folklore as a "noodle story," a tale in which the characters act foolishly or stubbornly to the point of absurdity. Another illustration, more than 500 years old, tells of the fishermen who want to return to a good spot for fishing. To find the place again they cut a notch in the boat over the spot where they found the fishing best. As they are returning the rented boat to the owner, one of the fishermen has a dismaying thought: "Suppose we don't get the same boat tomorrow!"

A modern "noodle story" tells of the man who lost a quarter in a dark street and went looking under the street light a hundred feet ahead because it was brighter there.

Perhaps you know some modern "noodle stories," in which the humor is based upon the silliness or absurdity of the characters. Modern "shaggy dog" stories are closely related. Many comedians use the device frequently.

WORDS ASSOCIATED WITH FOLKTALES

Word	Definition	Named for
abracadabra	magic spell or formula	the demon Shabriri (possibly)
Midas touch	ability to become wealthy	Midas, King of Phrygia
Old Man of the Sea	unshakable burden	character in Sinbad's Fifth Voyage
Open, Sesame	something that achieves a desired end	the magic words in "Ali Baba"
Rip Van Winkle	a character behind the times	a character in a short story by Washington Irving
Speak of the devil	greeting when person spoken about arrives	belief that uttering a name may bring the spirit called

UNIT · SIX

Fairy Tales and Fables

Imagination is more important than knowledge.

Albert Einstein

This tribute to imagination by one of the world's foremost thinkers suggests the importance of imagination in our lives. In their play, very young children often display active imaginations. Writers, artists, inventors, and experimenters all rely upon imagination for their creative achievements.

Star Wars, Star Trek, E.T.—movies like these leave realism behind and stimulate the imagination of the audience. They travel "where no person has gone before" and open up new worlds. In a sense these movies can be called the fairy tales of the present. A larger-than-life villain like Darth Vader in *Star Wars* resembles supernatural villains in fairy tales. Science-fiction movies are popular with adults as well as young people, proving that stories that stimulate the imagination meet a universal need.

I. Fairy Tales Today

Many of the world's great folktales are fairy tales as well. The story of "The Master and His Pupil" (page 204) brings in a supernatural agency, a demon who can be controlled only by magic. In a sense, then, this chapter is a continuation of the preceding one. However, it rules out the folktale of everyday life and concentrates upon the wonderful and strange. It includes examples by master storytellers like Hans Christian Andersen and Lewis Carroll.

Fairy tales are often assigned to children to read—and rightly so. Any child worth his salt has the kind of imagination that feeds upon tales of the wonderful. Any child who has

235

never heard the story of "Hansel and Gretel," or "Rumpel-
stiltskin," or "The Emperor's New Clothes" has missed a rare
experience. But fairy tales are not merely for children. Many
parents have discovered when reading aloud these wonderful
yarns to their children that they themselves become very
much concerned and interested. Adults may forget for a while
their desire for imaginative writing, but it never altogether
leaves them. It crops out in other forms. The great popularity
in recent years of adult stories of fantasy, science fiction, and
ghosts is traceable to the same impulses at work. The great
popularity of Walt Disney's *Cinderella* and *Snow White* is not
altogether the result of children's interest.

Modern fairy tales still delight both young children and
adults. L. Frank Baum's *The Wizard of Oz* is revived regularly
on television to the delight of old and new audiences. In the
Oz books a scarecrow and a sawhorse come to life. A pumpkin
head has an active, speaking life of its own. Tik-Tok, a windup
mechanical man, anticipates the electronic robots of modern
science fiction. There are many such imaginative classics.
James Stewart's best-known movie, *It's a Wonderful Life*, contains an elflike character, an angel who changes the main
character's life in a supernatural way. This classic is usually
shown at Christmastime on television.

Many of our most famous fairy tales have been circulating
in one form or another for centuries. "Cinderella," for example, is so ancient that its origin cannot be traced. The earliest
known version is Chinese, but there are more than 500 versions in Europe alone! Although Charles Perrault wrote the
tale down and added the fairy godmother, he was merely
refining a tale already known to most people of his day.
Gioacchino Rossini chose Cinderella as the subject of his opera *La Cenerentola*.

In the workaday world people must be bound by the laws of
man and of nature. In our daydreams we would like to fly, to
soar above the limitations of the everyday. Fairy tales enable
us to rise above human limitations. Enchantment is the very
stuff of imaginative writing. Reading that lacks entirely the
imaginative elements of the fairy tale can be very dull.

II. Grimm's Fairy Tales

Jakob Grimm has been called the father of philology, a
branch of language study. A famous principle called *Grimm's
Law* bears his name. It is not as a language scholar that he is

best known, however. With his brother Wilhelm, he began a systematic study and collection of German folktales. Their book, *Grimm's Fairy Tales*, stimulated public interest in folklore and influenced writers and artists for generations to come. Today, the tales are known all over the world, in many tongues and many editions.

The Iron Stove

Perhaps there is no such thing as a "typical" fairy tale. There are certain ingredients, however, which appear and reappear in fairy tales. The enchanted prince or princess is a common theme. Magic charms, often three in number, can be found frequently. A favorite plot is the overcoming of obstacles to find the beloved, who has disappeared. Often a wicked rival seeks to win the beloved by trickery. All these elements are found in "The Iron Stove."

In the old days when wishing was having, a certain King's son was enchanted by an old witch and shut up in a great iron stove which stood in a forest. There he passed many years, for nobody could release him. One day a Princess who had lost herself and could not find her way back to her father's kingdom came, after nine days' wandering, to the spot where the iron stove stood.

As she came near it, she heard a voice say, "Whence do you come and whither are you going?" "I have lost the road to my father's kingdom and am unable to go home," she replied.

"I will help you to get home again and help you most swiftly," said the voice from the iron stove, "if you will consent to what I desire. I am the son of a far greater King than your father, and I will marry you."

The Princess was frightened at this and thought, "What can I do with an iron stove?" But as she was anxious to get home again, she consented to follow his directions. Then the Prince told her that she might go home, but she must return and bring with her a knife with which to cut a hole in the stove. After this he gave her such minute directions as to her road that in two hours she reached her father's palace.

There was great joy in the castle when the Princess returned. The old King fell on her neck and kissed her, but she was sorely troubled and said, "Alas, my dear father, how things have happened! I should never have got home out of the great wildwood had it not been for an iron stove. I have promised to go back, set it free, and marry it."

The King was so frightened when he heard this that he all but fainted, for she was his only daughter. When he recovered, they resolved that the miller's daughter, a very pretty girl, should take her place. So she was led to the spot, furnished with a knife, and told to scrape a hole in the iron stove. For four and twenty hours she scraped and scraped, without making the least bit of a hole. When day broke, the voice out of the stove exclaimed, "It seems to me like daylight."

"Yes," replied the girl, "it seems so to me, too. I think I hear the noise of my father's mill."

"So you are the miller's daughter," said the voice again. "Then go home at once and send the Princess to me."

The girl therefore returned, and told the King the stove would not have her; he demanded the King's daughter. This news frightened the King and made the Princess weep. But the King had also in his service a swineherd's daughter, prettier still than the miller's. He offered to her a piece of gold if she would go to the iron stove instead of the Princess.

This girl, too, went away and scraped for four and twenty hours on the iron with no effect. When day broke, a voice in the stove exclaimed, "It seems to me like daylight."

"Yes, it is so," said the girl, "for I hear my father's horn blowing."

"So you are the swineherd's daughter," said the voice. "Go back and tell the Princess who sent you that it must be as I said. If she does not come to me, everything in the old kingdom shall fall to pieces and not one stone be left upon another anywhere."

As soon as the Princess heard this she began to weep, but it was of no use, for her promise had to be kept. So she took leave of her father and, carrying a knife with her, set out towards the iron stove in the wood. As soon as she reached it, she began to scrape the iron. Before two hours had passed, she had made a small hole. Through this she peeped, and inside the stove she saw a handsome Prince, whose dress glittered with gold and precious stones.

Then she scraped away faster than before and soon made a hole so large that the Prince could get out.

"You are mine, and I am yours," he said, as soon as he stood on the earth. "You are my bride because you have saved me."

He wanted to take her at once to his father's kingdom; but she begged that she might go back to her father to say good-by.

The Prince consented to this, but said she must not speak more than three words and must immediately return. Then the Princess went home, but she spoke more than three words. The iron stove disappeared and was carried far away over many icy mountains and snowy valleys. But the Prince was no longer shut up in his prison.

After a time the Princess bade her father farewell. Taking a little gold, she went back into the wood and searched for the iron stove, but she could find it nowhere. For nine days she sought it; and then her hunger became so great that she knew not how to help herself and thought she must die.

When evening came she climbed a little tree, for she feared the wild beasts that night would bring forth. Just at midnight she saw a little light at a distance. "Ah, there I may find help," thought she; and getting down she went towards the light, saying a prayer as she walked along. She soon came to a hut, surrounded with grass; before the door stood a heap of wood.

"Ah, how did you ever come here?" she thought to herself as she peeped through the window. She saw nothing but fat little toads, a table covered with meat and wine, and dishes made of silver. She took courage and knocked; a toad exclaimed:

> "Little toad with crooked leg
> Open quick the door, I beg
> And see who stands without."

As soon as these words were spoken, a little toad came running up and opened the door. The princess walked in. They all bade her welcome and told her to sit down. They then asked her where she had come from and whither she was going. She told the toads that because she had spoken more than three words, the stove had disappeared as well as the Prince. Now she was about to search over hill and valley till she found him. On hearing this the old toad cried out:

> "Little toad with crooked leg,
> Quickly fetch for me, I beg,
> The basket hanging on the peg."

So the little toad brought the basket to the old one, who took meat and milk from it and gave them to the Princess. After that he showed her a beautiful bed made of silk and velvet in which, under God's protection, she slept soundly.

As soon as day broke the Princess arose, and the old toad gave her three needles to take with her. These would be of great use, since she would have to pass over a mountain of glass, three sharp swords, and a great lake, before she could regain her lover. The old toad gave her, besides, a plough wheel and three nuts. With these the Princess set out.

When she came to the smooth glass mountain, she used the three needles as steps for her feet, and so got over it. When she came to the other side, she placed the needles in a secure place. Soon she came to the three swords, but she rolled over them by means of her plough wheel. At last she came to a great lake, and when she had passed that, she found herself near a fine large castle that belonged to her lost Prince. She entered and offered herself as a servant, saying she was a poor girl, who had rescued a King's son from an iron stove which stood in the forest. After some delay she was hired as a kitchen-maid. She soon found out that the Prince was going to marry another lady because he supposed she was dead.

One evening when she had washed herself and made herself neat, she felt in her pocket and found the three nuts which the old toad had given her. One of them she cracked, and in it she found a fine royal dress instead of a kernel. The bride heard of this and said that she must have the dress, since it was no dress for a servant-maid. But the Princess said she would sell it only on condition that she might be allowed to pass a night outside the chamber of the Prince.

This request was granted, because the bride was anxious to have the dress. When evening came she told the Prince that the silly girl wanted to pass the night outside the room.

"If you are contented, so am I," he replied; but she gave him a glass of wine, into which she had put a sleeping draught. As a result he slept so soundly that the poor Princess could not wake him, although she cried the whole night and kept repeating, "I saved you in the wild forest, and released you from the iron stove. I have sought you and traveled over a mountain of glass and over three swords, and across a wide lake before I found you, and still you will not hear me!"

The servants, however, heard the complaint and told the Prince of it the following morning. That evening, after the Princess had washed herself, she cracked the second nut and found in it a dress more beautiful than the other, and the bride declared she must have it also. But the Princess would not sell it except on the same condition as the first. The Prince again allowed her to sleep outside his door.

The bride, however, gave the Prince another sleeping draught, and he slept too soundly to hear the poor Princess crying as before: "I saved you in the wild forest, and released you from the iron stove. I have sought you and traveled over a mountain of glass, and over three sharp swords, and across a wide lake, before I found you, and you will not hear me!"

The servants heard the crying again, and told the Prince.

On the evening of that day the poor maid broke the third nut and produced a dress starred with gold. The bride declared she must have this at any price. The maid begged for the same privilege as before. This time the Prince threw away the sleeping draught. When the Princess began to cry, "Dearest love, have you forgotten how I saved you in the great, wild wood and released you from the iron stove?" the Prince heard her and jumping up exclaimed, "You are right. I am yours, and you are mine."

Thereupon, while it was still night, he got into a carriage with the Princess, first hiding the clothes of the false bride, that she might not follow them. When they came to the lake they rowed over very quickly and passed the three sharp swords again by means of the plough wheel. Soon they crossed the glass mountain by the aid of the three needles and arrived at last at the little old house, which, as soon as they entered, was changed into a noble castle. At the same moment all the toads were disenchanted and returned to their natural shapes, for they were the sons of the King of the country.

So the wedding took place, and the Prince and Princess remained for some time in his castle. However, because the old King grieved at his daughter's continued absence, they sent for him. They joined the government of the two kingdoms in one, and reigned many years in happiness and prosperity.

III. Charles Perrault's Fairy Tales

Charles Perrault, a French poet of the 18th century, achieved contemporary fame because of a stormy literary quarrel he had with another poet and critic. This disagreement had many consequences in the century to come, stimulating individualism and a breaking away from authority. As with the Grimm brothers, however, his fame now depends upon his retelling of classic folktales, like "Little Red Riding Hood," "Bluebeard," "Puss-in-Boots," and "Hop O' My Thumb." His version of the "Cinderella" story is perhaps the best known.

The Sleeping Beauty in the Wood

Enchantment is an important ingredient of fairy tales. The
enchanted princess appears in Wagner's opera (page 127).
The enchanted prince appears in "The Iron Stove" (page 237).
The following tale introduces perhaps the most famous
enchantment of all, "The Sleeping Beauty in the Wood."
Tchaikovsky's music for the ballet "The Sleeping Beauty"
suggests some of the enchantment of the tale.

There were formerly a King and a Queen who were sorry that they
had no children. They went to all the waters in the world, made
vows and pilgrimages. At last, the Queen had a little daughter. There
was a very fine christening. The Princess had for her godmothers all
the Fairies they could find in the whole kingdom (they found seven),
so that every one of them might give her a gift as was the custom of
Fairies in those days. In this way the Princess might have all the
perfections imaginable.

After the christening ceremony was over, all the company returned
to the King's palace, where a great feast was prepared for the Fairies.
There was placed before every one of them a magnificent cover with
a case of massive gold. Inside each were a spoon, a knife, and a fork,
all of pure gold set with diamonds and rubies. But as they were all
sitting down at table, they saw coming into the hall a very old Fairy
whom they had not invited, because it was more than fifty years
since she had been out of a certain tower. She was believed to be
either dead or enchanted. The King ordered her a cover but could
not furnish her with a case of gold as the others, because they had
made seven only for the Seven Fairies.

The old Fairy fancied she was slighted and muttered some threat
between her teeth. One of the young Fairies, who sat by her, overheard
how she grumbled. Judging that she might give the little Princess
some unlucky gift, she went as soon as they rose from the table and
hid herself behind the hangings. She hoped that she might speak last
and repair, as much as possibly she could, the evil which the old
Fairy might intend to do.

In the meanwhile all the Fairies began to give their gifts to the
Princess. The youngest promised that she should be the most beautiful
person in the world; the next, that she should have the wit of an
angel; the third, that she should have a wonderful grace in everything
she did; the fourth, that she should dance perfectly well; the fifth,

that she should sing like a nightingale; and the sixth, that she should play upon all kinds of music to perfection.

The old Fairy's turn came next. With a head shaking more with spite than with age, she said that the Princess should have her hand pierced with a spindle and die of the wound. This terrible gift made the whole company tremble, and everybody fell a-crying.

At this very instant, the young Fairy came out from behind the hangings and spoke these words aloud:

"Be reassured, O King and Queen; your daughter shall not die of this disaster. It is true I have no power to undo entirely what my elder has done. The Princess shall indeed pierce her hand with a spindle; but instead of dying, she shall only fall into a profound sleep, which shall last a hundred years. At the end of this time a king's son shall come and awaken her."

The King, to avoid the misfortune foretold by the Old Fairy, immediately caused proclamations to be made, forbidding everyone on pain of death to spin with a distaff and spindle or to have so much as one spindle in his house.

About fifteen or sixteen years after, the King and Queen having gone away for a little while, the young Princess happened one day to amuse herself running up and down the palace. Going from one apartment to another, she came into a little room on the top of a tower, where a good old woman was spinning with her spindle. This good woman had never heard of the King's proclamation forbidding the use of spindles.

"What are you doing there, Grandmother?" asked the Princess.

"I am spinning, my pretty child," said the old woman, who did not know who she was.

"Ha!" said the Princess. "This is very pretty. How do you do it? Give it to me that I may see if I can do it."

She had no sooner grasped the spindle in her fingers than it ran into her hand, and she fell down in a faint.

The good old woman, not knowing very well what to do in this affair, cried out for help. People came in from every quarter in great numbers. They threw water upon the Princess's face, struck her on the palms of her hands, and rubbed her temples; but nothing would bring the unfortunate girl to herself.

And now the King, who came up at the noise, remembered the prediction of the Fairies. Realizing that this must necessarily come to pass since Fairies had said it, he caused the Princess to be laid upon a bed all embroidered with gold and silver. One would have taken her for an angel; she was so very beautiful. Her swooning away had not diminished one bit of her complexion. Her cheeks were carnation, and her lips like coral. Indeed her eyes were shut, but she was heard to breathe softly, which satisfied those about her that she was not dead. The King commanded that they should not disturb her, but let her sleep quietly till her hour of awakening came.

The good Fairy, who had saved her life by condemning her to sleep a hundred years, was far away when this accident befell the Princess. But she was instantly informed of it by a little dwarf who had seven-league boots, that is, boots with which he could tread over seven leagues of ground at one stride.

The Fairy came away immediately, and she arrived, about an hour after, in a fiery chariot drawn by dragons. The King handed her out of the chariot, and she approved everything he had done. But as she had very great foresight, she thought, when the Princess should awaken, she might not know what to do with herself, being all alone in the old palace. This was what she did. She touched with her wand everyone in the palace (except the King and Queen): governesses, maids of honor, ladies of the bedchamber, gentlemen, officers, stewards, cooks, under-cooks, guards, pages, and footmen. She likewise touched all the horses which were in the stables, as well as their grooms, the great dogs in the outward court, and pretty little Mopsey too, the Princess's little spaniel, which lay by her on the bed.

Immediately upon her touching them, they all fell asleep, that they might not awaken before their mistress, and that they might be ready to wait upon her when she wanted them. The very spits at the fire, as full as they could hold of partridges and pheasants, did fall asleep, and the fire likewise. All this was done in a moment.

And now the King and the Queen, having kissed their dear child without waking her, went out of the palace and put forth a proclamation that nobody should dare to come near it. This, however, was not necessary; for in a quarter of an hour's time there grew up all around the park such a vast number of trees, bushes, and brambles that neither man nor beast could pass through. Nothing could be seen but the very tops of the towers of the palace; and that too, not unless it was a good way off. Thus the Princess, while she continued sleeping, might have nothing to fear from any curious people.

When a hundred years had passed, the son of the King then reigning, of a different family from that of the sleeping Princess, went hunting on that side of the country. He asked, "What are those towers which I see in the middle of a great thick wood?"

Everyone answered according as they had heard. Some said that it was a ruined old castle, haunted by spirits; others, that all the sorcerers and witches of the country kept there their sabbath or nights' meeting. The common opinion was that an ogre lived there. People believed that he carried there all the little children he could catch, that he might eat them up at his leisure without anybody's being able to follow him, for he only had the power to pass through the wood.

The Prince was puzzled, not knowing what to believe. Then a very old countryman said to him, "May it please your Royal Highness, it is now more than fifty years since I heard my father, who had heard my grandfather, say that there then was in this castle a Princess, the most beautiful ever seen; that she must sleep there a hundred years, and should be awakened by a king's son, for whom she was reserved."

The young Prince was all on fire at these words, believing without a moment's doubt that he could put an end to this rare adventure. Pushed on by love and honor, he resolved that moment to look into it.

As he advanced toward the woods, all the great trees, the bushes and brambles, gave way of themselves to let him pass through. He walked up to the castle which he saw at the end of a large avenue. What surprised him was that he saw none of his people could follow him, because the trees closed again as soon as he had passed through them.

However, he did not cease from continuing his way. He came into a spacious outward court, where everything he saw might have frozen the most fearless person with horror. There reigned over all a most frightful silence; the image of death everywhere showed itself, and there was nothing to be seen but stretched out bodies of men and animals, all seeming to be dead. He, however, very well knew, by the ruby faces and pimpled noses of the servants, that they were only asleep. Their goblets, in which still remained some drops of wine, showed plainly that they had fallen asleep in their cups.

He then crossed a court paved with marble, went up the stairs, and came into the guard chamber, where the guards were standing in their ranks, with their muskets upon their shoulders. After that he went through several rooms full of gentlemen and ladies, all asleep, some standing, others sitting. At last he came into a chamber all gilded with gold, where he saw upon a bed the finest sight he had ever seen: a Princess whose bright and resplendent beauty had something in it divine. He approached with trembling and admiration and fell down before her upon his knees.

And now, as the enchantment was at an end, the Princess awakened and looked on him with eyes more tender than the first view would seem to admit of. "Is it you, my Prince?" she said to him. "You have tarried long."

The Prince, charmed with these words and much more with the manner in which they were spoken, knew not how to show his joy and gratitude. He assured her that he loved her better than he loved himself. His speech was not well connected, but it pleased her all the more: little eloquence, a great deal of love. He was more at a loss than she, and we need not wonder at it. She had had time to think of what to say to him; for it is very probable (though history mentions nothing of it) that the good Fairy, during so long a sleep, had entertained her with pleasant dreams. In short, when the Prince and Princess had talked four hours together, they said not half what they had to say.

In the meanwhile all the palace awakened. Everyone went about his particular business; and as all of them were not in love, they were ready to die of hunger. The chief lady of honor grew very impatient and told the Princess aloud that supper was served. The Prince helped the Princess to rise. She was entirely dressed, and very magnificently, but his Royal Highness took care not to tell her that she was dressed like his great grandmother. She looked not a bit the less beautiful and charming for all that.

They went into the great hall of mirrors, where they supped, and were served by the Princess's officers. The violins and other instruments played old tunes, but very excellent, though it was now a hundred years since they had last been played. After supper, without losing any time, the Prince and Princess were married in the chapel of the castle.

The Prince left her next morning to return into the city, where his father was anxious on his account. The Prince told him that he had lost his way in the forest, as he was hunting, and that he had lain at the cottage of a collier, who gave him cheese and brown bread.

The King, his father, who was of an easy disposition, believed him; but his mother could not be persuaded this was true. Seeing that he went almost every day a-hunting and that he always had some excuse ready when he had stayed away three or four nights at one time, she soon suspected the truth.

The Prince lived with the Princess more than two whole years. They had two children; the elder was a daughter named Dawn. The younger, who was a son, they called Day, because he was even handsomer and more beautiful than his sister.

The Queen tried more than once to get her son to speak freely to her, but he never dared trust her with his secrets. He feared her, though he loved her; for she was of the race of the ogres, and the King would never have married her had it not been for her vast riches. It was even whispered about the court that she had ogreish inclinations, and that, whenever she saw little children passing by, she had all the difficulty in the world to refrain from falling upon them, as the ogres do. And so the Prince would never tell her one word of what had happened.

But when the King died, which happened about two years afterwards, and the Prince saw himself lord and master, he openly declared his marriage; and he went in great ceremony to fetch his Queen from the castle. They made a magnificent entry into the capital city, she riding between her two children.

Some time after, the new King went off on a campaign. He left the government of the kingdom to the Queen his mother, and earnestly recommended that she take care of his wife and children. Since he was expected to be away all summer, as soon as he departed the Queen-mother sent her daughter-in-law and her children to a country-house among the woods, so that she might with the more ease gratify her horrible longing.

Some few days afterwards, she went there herself and said to her cook, "I have a mind to eat little Dawn for my dinner tomorrow."

"Ah! Madam," cried the clerk of the kitchen.

"I will have it so," replied the Queen (and this she spoke in the tone of an ogress who had a strong desire to eat fresh meat), "and will eat her with a special sauce."

The poor man, knowing very well that he must not play tricks with ogresses, took his great knife and went up into little Dawn's chamber. She was then four years old and came up to him jumping and laughing to take him about the neck and ask him for some sugar-candy. Upon this he began to weep; the great knife fell out of his hand, and he went into the backyard and killed a little lamb. He dressed it with such good sauce that his mistress assured him she had never eaten anything so good in her life. He had at the same time taken up little Dawn and carried her to his wife to conceal her in the humble lodging which he had for himself at the end of the courtyard.

About eight days afterwards, the wicked Queen said to the cook, "I will sup upon little Day."

He answered not a word, being resolved to cheat her, as he had done before. He went out to find little Day and saw him with a little foil in his hand with which he was fencing. The child was then only three years of age. He took him up in his arms and carried him to his wife that she might conceal him in her chamber along with his sister. In place of little Day he cooked up a very tender young kid, which the ogress found to be wonderfully good.

This was all quite well, but one evening the wicked Queen-mother said to her clerk of the kitchen, "I will eat the Queen with the same sauce I had with her children."

It was now that the poor clerk of the kitchen despaired of being able to deceive her. The young Queen was just twenty, not reckoning the hundred years she had been asleep. Her skin was somewhat tough, though very fair and white; and how to find in the yard a beast so firm was what puzzled him. To save his own life, he took then a resolution, to cut the young Queen's throat. Going up into her chamber with intent to do it at once, he put himself into as great a fury as he possibly could, and came into the young Queen's room with his dagger in his hand. He would not, however, surprise her, but told her, with a great deal of respect, the orders he had received from the Queen-mother.

"Do it; do it," said she stretching out her neck, "execute your orders, and then I shall go and see my children, my poor children, whom I so much and so tenderly loved," for she thought them dead ever since they had been taken away without her knowledge.

"No, no, Madam," cried the poor cook, all in tears, "you shall not die, and you shall see your children yet again. But it must be in my lodgings, where I have concealed them, and I shall deceive the Queen once more, by giving her in your stead a young deer."

Upon this he immediately conducted her to his chamber. Leaving her to embrace her children and cry along with them, he went and dressed a deer, which the Queen had for her supper. She devoured it with the same appetite as if it had been the young Queen. Exceedingly was she delighted with her cruelty, and she had invented a story to tell the King, at his return, how ravenous wolves had eaten up the Queen his wife, and her two children.

One evening she was, according to her custom, rambling round about the courts and yards of the palace, to see if she could smell any fresh meat. She heard little Day crying in a ground-floor room, for his mamma was going to whip him because he had been naughty. At the same time she heard little Dawn begging pardon for her brother.

The ogress presently knew the voice of the Queen and her children and was quite furious that she had been thus deceived. She commanded next morning by break of day, in a horrible voice, that they should bring into the middle of the great court a large tub, which she caused to be filled with toads, vipers, snakes, and all sorts of serpents. She ordered to have thrown into it the Queen and her children, the cook, his wife, and his maid. She gave orders that all should be brought there with their hands tied behind them.

They were brought out accordingly, and the executioners were just going to throw them into the tub when the King unexpectedly entered the court on horseback. He asked with the utmost astonishment what was the meaning of that horrible spectacle. No one dared to tell him. But the ogress, all enraged to see what had happened, threw herself head-foremost into the tub and was instantly devoured by the ugly creatures she had ordered to be thrown into it for the others. The King could not help but be very sorry, for she was his mother; but he soon comforted himself with his beautiful wife and his pretty children.

IV. Andersen's Fairy Tales

A fairy tale once strengthened an entire people against a conqueror. Does this seem possible in the bitterly practical world of the present? Here is the story.

On April 9, 1940, the Nazi legions of Hitler Germany overran the little country of Denmark. To save the country from devastation, the Danes did not fight actively, but adopted a policy of passive resistance. As the years went by, the Danish underground became more and more effective. At their meetings the Danes would often read aloud a fairy tale. The story was broadcast over the secret radio. The Nazis could do nothing against this weapon. The tale, "The Wicked Prince," by Hans Christian Andersen described a tyrant who had conquered the earth. In his ambition he attempted to conquer the heavens, too, but he was defeated by a single little gnat. Danes had little difficulty in identifying the "prince" with Adolf Hitler. They used another of Andersen's stories to poke fun at the Nazi soldiers. They used the weapon of laughter and satire effectively. And a fairy tale helped them.

The influence of Hans Christian Andersen is strong in times of peace as well. In the harbor of Copenhagen is a statue of

the Little Mermaid, a character in a story by Andersen. It is a
city landmark beloved of natives and tourists alike. Not many
years ago someone stole the head of the Mermaid. The uproar
that followed did not subside till the statue was repaired.

Like many of Andersen's stories, "The Little Mermaid" is
bittersweet. We identify with the Mermaid as she saves the
handsome prince from drowning. We sympathize with the
impossible love she feels. But we rejoice when a new and
better destiny is opened to her.

As you will find, there is something different about the fairy
tales of Hans Christian Andersen. They seem to reflect, more
than most fairy tales, the world of reality. The events in "The
Little Mermaid" are pure fantasy, but the emotions felt by the
main character are real. And in "The Brave Tin Soldier," we
sympathize with the hero almost as if he were a person. The
magic of Andersen is responsible.

Hans Christian Andersen was born in Odense, Denmark, in
1805, but he left for Copenhagen when he was only 14. At first
he tried his hand at poetry, travelogues, sketches, and novels.
In 1835 he published his first book of fairy tales and found his
life's work. He produced about a volume a year and became
instantly famous. Among his most famous and best-loved stories are "The Ugly Duckling," "The Nightingale," "The Snow
Queen," "The Match Girl," and "The Red Shoes."

Andersen's fame has not lessened through the years. In 1950
Odense held its first Andersen Fairy Tale Festival. In 1952
Danny Kaye starred in a movie musical version of the Andersen story. These pay tribute to a man whose work is interna-
tionally known and loved. His stories are among the most
widely translated books in the world.

The Brave Tin Soldier

There are tragic endings to many Andersen stories. "The
Brave Tin Soldier" is characteristically sad, but even in tragedy there is some small consolation in the last two sentences.
These remind us a little of the final lines of "Bonnie Barbara
Allen" (pages 298-299). "The Brave Tin Soldier" proves that a
fairy tale can succeed without the usual ingredients. Here we
find no wicked stepmother, no handsome prince or beautiful
princess, no fairy godmother. True, there is a goblin, but we
cannot be entirely sure whether or not he plays a role. Still
there is an air of enchantment about the story. You will not
soon forget the tin soldier or the dancer.

There were once five-and-twenty tin soldiers, who were all brothers, for they had been made out of the same old tin spoon. They shouldered arms and looked straight before them and wore a splendid uniform, red and blue. The first thing in the world they ever heard were the words, "Tin soldiers!" uttered by a little boy, who clapped his hands with delight when the lid of the box, in which they lay, was taken off. They were given him for a birthday present, and he stood at the table to set them up. The soldiers were all exactly alike, excepting one, who had only one leg. He had been left to the last, and then there was not enough of the melted tin to finish him, so they made him to stand firmly on one leg.

The table on which the tin soldiers stood was covered with other playthings, but the most attractive to the eye was a pretty little paper castle. Through the small windows the rooms could be seen. In front of the castle a number of little trees surrounded a piece of looking-glass, which was intended to represent a transparent lake. Swans, made of wax, swam on the lake, and were reflected in it. All this was very pretty, but the prettiest of all was a tiny little lady, who stood at the open door of the castle. She, also, was made of paper, and she wore a dress of clear muslin, with a narrow blue ribbon over her shoulders just like a scarf. In front of these was fixed a glittering tinsel rose, as large as her whole face. The little lady was a dancer, and she stretched out both her arms and raised one of her legs so high, that the tin soldier could not see it at all; he thought that she, like himself, had only one leg.

"That is the wife for me," he thought; "but she is too grand and lives in a castle, while I have only a box for her. Still I must try and make her acquaintance." Then he laid himself at full length on the table behind a snuffbox that stood upon it, so that he could peep at the little delicate lady, who continued to stand on the one leg without losing her balance. When evening came, the other tin soldiers were all placed in the box, and the people of the house went to bed. Then the playthings began to have their own games together. Soldiers rattled in their box. They wanted to get out and join the amusements, but they could not open the lid. The nutcrackers played at leapfrog, and the pencil jumped about the table. There was such a noise that the canary woke up and began to talk, and in poetry, too. Only the tin soldier and the dancer remained in their places. She stood on tiptoe, with her arms stretched out, as firmly as he did on his one leg. He never took his eyes from her for even a moment. The clock struck twelve, and, with a bounce, up sprang the lid of the snuffbox.

But instead of snuff there jumped up a little black goblin; for the snuffbox was a toy puzzle.

"Tin soldier," said the goblin, "don't wish for what does not belong to you."

But the tin soldier pretended not to hear.

"Very well; wait till tomorrow then," said the goblin.

When the children came in the next morning, they placed the tin soldier in the window. Now whether it was the goblin who did it or the draught is not known, but the window flew open, and out fell the tin soldier, heels over head, from the third story into the street beneath. It was a terrible fall; for he came head downwards. His helmet and his bayonet stuck in between the flagstones, and his one leg was up in the air. The servant maid and the little boy went downstairs directly to look for him; but he was nowhere to be seen, although once they nearly trod upon him. If he had called out, "Here I am," it would have been all right; but he was too proud to cry out for help while he wore a uniform.

Presently it began to rain, and the drops fell faster and faster, till there was a heavy shower. When it was over, two boys happened to pass by, and one of them said, "Look, there is a tin soldier. He ought to have a boat to sail in."

So they made a boat out of a newspaper, placed the tin soldier in it, and sent him sailing down the gutter, while the two boys ran by the side of it and clapped their hands. What large waves arose in that gutter! And how fast the stream rolled on! For the rain had been very heavy. The paper boat rocked up and down and turned itself round sometimes so quickly that the tin soldier trembled; yet he remained firm. His countenance did not change; he looked straight before him. Suddenly the boat shot under a bridge which formed a part of a drain, and then it was as dark as the tin soldier's box.

"Where am I going now?" thought he. "This is the black goblin's fault, I am sure. Ah, well, if the little lady were only here with me in the boat, I should not care for any darkness."

Suddenly there appeared a great rat, who lived in the drain.

"Have you a passport?" asked the rat. "Give it to me at once." But the tin soldier remained silent and held his musket tighter than ever. The boat sailed on, and the rat followed it. How he did gnash his teeth and cry out, "Stop him! stop him! He has not paid toll and has not shown his passport."

But the stream rushed on stronger and stronger. The tin soldier could already see daylight shining where the arch ended. Then he

heard a roaring sound quite terrible enough to frighten the bravest man. At the end of the tunnel the drain fell into a large canal over a steep place, which made it as dangerous for him as a waterfall would be to us. He was too close to it to stop, so the boat rushed on, and the poor tin soldier could only hold himself as stiffly as possible, without moving an eyelid, to show that he was not afraid. The boat whirled round three or four times, and then filled with water to the very edge. Nothing could save it from sinking. He now stood up to his neck in water, while deeper sank the boat, and the paper became soft and loose with the wet, till at last the water closed over the soldier's head. He thought of the elegant little dancer whom he should never see again, and the words of the song sounded in his ears—

> "Farewell, warrior! ever brave,
> Drifting onward to thy grave."

Then the paper boat fell to pieces, and the soldier sank into the water and immediately afterwards was swallowed up by a great fish. Oh, how dark it was inside the fish! It was a great deal darker than in the tunnel, and narrower too, but the tin soldier continued firm and lay at full length shouldering his musket. The fish swam to and fro, but at last he became quite still. After a while, a flash of lightning seemed to pass through him, and then the daylight appeared, and a voice cried out, "I declare, here is the tin soldier."

The fish had been caught, taken to the market and sold to the cook, who took him into the kitchen and cut him open with a large knife. She picked up the soldier, held him by the waist between her finger and thumb, and carried him into the room. They were all anxious to see this wonderful soldier who had traveled about inside a fish; but he was not at all proud. They placed him on the table, and— how many curious things do happen in the world—there he was in the very same room from the window of which he had fallen. There were the same children, the same playthings standing on the table, and the pretty castle with the elegant little dancer at the door.

It touched the tin soldier so much to see her that he almost wept tin tears, but he kept them back. He only looked at her, and they both remained silent. Presently one of the little boys took up the tin soldier and threw him into the stove. He had no reason for doing so; therefore it must have been the fault of the black goblin who lived in the snuffbox. The flames lighted up the tin soldier, as he stood. The heat was very terrible, but whether it proceeded from the real fire or from the fire of love he could not tell. Then he could see that the bright colors were faded from his uniform, but whether they had been washed off during his journey or from the effects of his sorrow, no one could say. He looked at the little lady, and she looked at him. He felt himself melting away, but he still remained firm with his gun on his shoulder.

Suddenly the door of the room flew open, and the draught of air caught up the little dancer. She fluttered like a sylph right into the stove by the side of the tin soldier and was instantly in flames and was gone. The tin soldier melted down into a lump, and the next morning, when the maid servant took the ashes out of the stove, she found him in the shape of a little tin heart. But of the little dancer nothing remained but the tinsel rose, which was burnt black as a cinder.

V. Lewis Carroll and the Alice Stories

"She was grinning like a Cheshire Cat."

Do you know what kind of grin a Cheshire Cat would grin? You do if you've ever read two of the most delightful fantasies ever written: *Alice's Adventures in Wonderland* and its companion volume, *Through the Looking-Glass*. Though the books are considered classics for children, they have won adult readers, too. Indeed, noted mathematicians and philosophers have taken illustrations from the books to explain difficult ideas to the untrained public. Sir Arthur Eddington, to mention but one writer, took examples directly from the book. Much of the nonsense makes amazingly good sense.

Lewis Carroll, the author of these two classics, led a double life. As Charles Lutwidge Dodgson he was a respectable lecturer in mathematics at Oxford. But under his pen name of Lewis Carroll he wrote the two books already mentioned and some famous nonsense verse. One of these poems, "The Hunting of the Snark," is still read and enjoyed.

Perhaps you will recognize some of the Lewis Carroll characters listed below:

the Mock Turtle	the Hatter
the Walrus and the Carpenter	the Dormouse
the Ugly Duchess	the Red Queen
the March Hare	and the White Queen
the Queen of Hearts	Tweedledum and Tweedledee

Alice's Adventures in Wonderland is a dream story. In her dream Alice chases a rabbit who carries a watch. She falls down a rabbit-hole, and her wonderful adventures begin. She grows alternately very tall and very short. She swims in a pool of her own tears and has other amazing adventures. She meets the Ugly Duchess, who sings an odd song to her little boy:

> "Speak roughly to your little boy,
>   And beat him when he sneezes:
> He only does it to annoy,
>   Because he knows it teases."

The little boy promptly turns into a pig. Then she attends a mad tea party with some very odd individuals, plays croquet using flamingoes for mallets, and watches a peculiar dance with a turtle, a lobster, and a gryphon.

The final episode is an upside-down trial to determine who stole the Queen's tarts. After a series of perplexing charges, Alice angrily says to the King, the Queen, and the assembly, "You're nothing but a pack of cards!" They vanish and Alice awakens.

Episodes follow each other in mad sequence as they do in a dream. Fantastic adventures and fantastic characters make up the book.

In the sequel, *Through the Looking-Glass*, Alice wonders what curious world lies on the other side of the mirror. She actually enters the looking-glass house, where everything is turned backward. She sees all her furniture in reverse order. Besides, all the furniture seems to be alive. She looks down upon the hearth and sees the chessmen lying in the ashes. She jumps down and looks at them. They are walking about.

At last she leaves the house and becomes involved in a chess game. She is one of the pawns that must eventually become a queen. She walks along the huge chessboard of fields and brooks. In her travels she meets live flowers, Tweedledum and Tweedledee, Humpty Dumpty, the Lion and the Unicorn, the White Knight, the Red Queen, and the White Queen. The following excerpt describes her meeting with the White Queen.

Alice Learns to Live Backwards*

There is a dream quality to the two Alice books. As in a dream, weird and unexpected things happen without apparent

* From Chapter V of *Through the Looking-Glass*

rhyme or reason. Yet amidst the controlled insanity there are kernels of truth and wisdom. In an episode with Humpty Dumpty (the egg on the wall who had a great fall), Alice gets into a discussion about words. At one point Alice objects to Humpty Dumpty's use of the word *glory*. His famous reply is "When *I* use a word, it means just what I choose it to mean— neither more nor less." This statement is often quoted by language experts. It reminds us that words do not have meanings in themselves. Language users give words their meanings. This is so obvious a truth that it should be a part of everyone's understanding. Yet people feel somehow that words *do* mean something in themselves. Someone once said, "I'm not too amazed when astronomers find out what stars are made of, but how do they discover their names!"

As in the Humpty Dumpty episode, "Alice Learns to Live Backwards" plays with words. It also toys with ideas of time. Is time relative? Let the White Queen provide her topsy-turvy explanation.

In another moment the White Queen came running wildly through the wood, with both arms stretched out wide, as if she were flying, and Alice very civilly went to meet her with the shawl.

"I'm very glad I happened to be in the way," Alice said, as she helped her to put on her shawl again.

The White Queen only looked at her in a helpless, frightened sort of way, and kept repeating something in a whisper to herself that sounded like "Bread-and-Butter, bread-and-butter," and Alice felt that if there was to be any conversation at all, she must manage it herself. So she began rather timidly: "Am I addressing the White Queen?"

"Well, yes, if you call that a-dressing," the Queen said. "It isn't my notion of the thing, at all."

Alice thought it would never do to have an argument at the very beginning of their conversation, so she smiled and said, "If your Majesty will only tell me the right way to begin, I'll do it as well as I can."

"But I don't want it done at all!" groaned the poor Queen. "I've been a-dressing myself for the last two hours."

It would have been all the better, as it seemed to Alice, if she had got someone else to dress her; she was so dreadfully untidy. "Every single thing's crooked," Alice thought to herself, "and she's all over pins!—May I put your shawl straight for you?" she added aloud.

"I don't know what's the matter with it!" the Queen said, in a melancholy voice. "It's out of temper, I think. I've pinned it here, and I've pinned it there, but there's no pleasing it!"

"It can't go straight, you know, if you pin it all on one side," Alice said, as she gently put it right for her; "and dear me, what a state your hair is in!"

"The brush has got entangled in it!" the Queen said with a sigh. "And I lost the comb yesterday."

Alice carefully released the brush, and did her best to get the hair into order. "Come, you look rather better now!" she said, after altering most of the pins. "But really you should have a lady's maid!"

"I'm sure I'll take you with pleasure!" the Queen said. "Two pence a week, and jam every other day."

Alice couldn't help laughing, as she said "I don't want you to hire me—and I don't care for jam."

"It's very good jam," said the Queen.

"Well, I don't want any today, at any rate."

"You couldn't have it if you did want it," the Queen said. "The rule is, jam tomorrow and jam yesterday—but never jam today."

"It must come sometimes to 'jam today.' " Alice objected.

"No, it can't," said the Queen. "It's jam every other day: today isn't any other day, you know."

"I don't understand you," said Alice. "It's dreadfully confusing!"

"That's the effect of living backwards," the Queen said kindly: "it always makes one a little giddy at first—"

"Living backwards!" Alice repeated in great astonishment. "I never heard of such a thing!"

"—but there's one great advantage in it, that one's memory works both ways."

"I'm sure mine only works one way," Alice remarked. "I can't remember things before they happen."

"It's a poor sort of memory that only works backwards," the Queen remarked.

"What sort of things do you remember best?" Alice ventured to ask.

"Oh, things that happened the week after next," the Queen replied in a careless tone. "For instance, now," she went on, sticking a large piece of plaster on her finger as she spoke, "there's the King's Messenger. He's in prison now, being punished: and the trial doesn't even begin till next Wednesday: and of course the crime comes last of all."

"Suppose he never commits the crime?" said Alice.

"That would be all the better, wouldn't it?" the Queen said, as she bound the plaster round her finger with a bit of ribbon.

Alice felt there was no denying that. "Of course it would be all the better," she said: "but it wouldn't be all the better his being punished."

"You're wrong there, at any rate," said the Queen. "Were you ever punished?

"Only for faults," said Alice.

"And you were all the better for it, I know!" the Queen said triumphantly.

"Yes, but then I had done the things I was punished for," said Alice: "that makes all the difference."

"But if you hadn't done them," the Queen said, "that would have been better still; better, and better, and better!" Her voice went higher with each "better," till it got quite to a squeak at last.

Alice was just beginning to say "There's a mistake somewhere—," when the Queen began screaming, so loud that she had to leave the sentence unfinished. "Oh, oh, oh!" shouted the Queen, shaking her hand about as if she wanted to shake it off. "My finger's bleeding! Oh, oh, oh, oh!"

Her screams were so exactly like the whistle of a steam engine, that poor Alice had to hold both her hands over her ears.

"What is the matter?" she said, as soon as there was a chance of making herself heard. "Have you pricked your finger?"

"I haven't pricked it yet," the Queen said, "but I soon shall—oh, oh, oh!"

"When do you expect to do it?" Alice said, feeling inclined to laugh.

"When I fasten my shawl again," the poor Queen groaned out: "the brooch will come undone directly. Oh, oh!" As she said the words the brooch flew open, and the Queen clutched wildly at it, and tried to clasp it again.

"Take care!" cried Alice. "You're holding it all crooked!" And she caught at the brooch; but it was too late; the pin had slipped, and the Queen had pricked her finger.

"That acounts for the bleeding, you see," she said to Alice with a smile. "Now you understand the way things happen here."

"But why don't you scream now?" Alice asked, holding her hands ready to put over her ears again.

"Why, I've done all the screaming already," said the Queen. "What would be the good of having it all over again?"

By this time it was getting light.

"It is so very lonely here!" Alice said in a melancholy voice; and, at the thought of her loneliness, two large tears came rolling down her cheeks.

"Oh, don't go on like that!" cried the poor Queen, wringing her hands in despair. "Consider what a great girl you are. Consider what o'clock it is. Consider anything; only don't cry!"

Alice could not help laughing at this, even in the midst of her tears. "Can you keep from crying by considering things?" she asked.

"That's the way it's done," the Queen said with great decision: "nobody can do two things at once, you know. Let's consider your age to begin with—how old are you?"

"I'm seven and a half, exactly."

"You needn't say 'exactly,'" the Queen remarked. "I can believe it without that. Now I'll give you something to believe. I'm just one hundred and one, five months and a day."

"I can't believe that!" said Alice.

"Can't you?" the Queen said in a pitying tone. "Try again: draw a long breath and shut your eyes."

Alice laughed. "There's no use trying," she said: "one can't believe impossible things."

"I daresay you haven't had much practice," said the Queen. "When I was your age, I always did it for half an hour a day. Why, sometimes I've believed as many as six impossible things before breakfast. There goes the shawl again!"

The brooch had come undone as she spoke, and a sudden gust of wind blew the Queen's shawl across a little brook. The Queen spread out her arms again and went flying after it, and this time she succeeded in catching it herself. "I've got it!" she cried in triumphant tone. "Now you shall see me pin it on again, and by myself!"

"Then I hope your finger is better now?" Alice said very politely, as she crossed the little brook after the Queen.

Alice goes on to more adventures. At last she reaches the eighth square and is made a queen. The dinner in her honor is weird. In the excitement Alice picks up the Red Queen and shakes her. The Red Queen turns into her kitten and Alice awakens.

A summary cannot do justice to books like these. You must read them to see for yourselves whether you too will enjoy them.

VI. Fables

"People often grudge others what they cannot enjoy themselves."

As you read the statement above, it probably made little or no impression upon you. Five minutes from now you will probably have forgotten it—in its present form. Now read this:

The Dog in the Manger

A dog was lying in a manger full of hay. An ox, being hungry, came up to eat the hay. The dog got up and snarled at him. He snapped and growled and kept the ox from eating.

"Miserable creature," said the ox, "you cannot eat the hay yourself; yet you will let no one else eat any."

The Point—People often grudge others what they cannot enjoy themselves.

Notice how the statement has taken on additional meaning. In five minutes or five days or five weeks from now you will be more likely to remember it because it has been made more meaningful to you. What has been done? It has been put into story form. You enjoy stories. You remember stories.

As we have seen, talking animals are not uncommon in folktales (2). In fables animals always talk, but there is an added element. Fables make a point. They express a moral. They teach some general truth. In a sense, they combine the folktale with the proverb. They are, however, usually much shorter than folktales.

In fables, animals talk and act like human beings, but they also keep their animal traits. The fox in "The Fox and the Grapes" may talk like a human being, but he is also a hungry fox.

The earliest examples of animal folktales usually explain origins (184); for example, they tell why the wasp has a narrow waist (188). The fable goes beyond such explanations. It tries to provide a lesson for human beings. If the Brer Wasp story had been cast in the form of a fable, it would be much shorter. It would also have a moral at the end, something like this: "Don't ridicule another or you may be sorry." A fable is more sophisticated than a folktale, though it draws upon the folktale for the story element. Once it has been created, however, a fable usually is taken over by the folk and becomes part of the folklore.

No one is quite sure how fables originated. The oldest surviving fables are those of Greece and India, but experts suggest the origins go back farther into the past.

Parables

Like a fable, a *parable* is a story designed to demonstrate a moral truth. The parable of the "Prodigal Son" is one of the most famous. Both the Old and the New Testaments employ parables frequently to make a point. An *allegory* is similar in many ways, for here in a longer narrative, characters are used to symbolize various qualities. *The Pilgrim's Progress* is a long allegorical narrative in which various characters like Mr. Worldly Wiseman, Faithful, Hopeful, and the Giant Despair help or hinder the Pilgrim in his progress to the Celestial City.

A fable is similar in purpose to a parable or allegory, but it is usually much shorter. Animals or inanimate objects are the usual characters. The point is obvious, as shown in the little tale told about the dog in the manger. The name of Aesop has come to be almost synonymous with that of fable, but there are many other famous tellers of fables: for example, La Fontaine, "Uncle Remus," and Geoffrey Chaucer.

The Fables of Aesop

"Jack says he didn't really want the job, but that's just sour grapes."

There is nothing in the statement itself to tell what it means. But most readers know immediately that Jack is pretending to despise something that he cannot have anyway. They know what the expression *sour grapes* means, even though they may not know where it comes from. Many such expressions have passed into common speech: *the dog in the manger, killing the goose that lays the golden eggs, the tortoise and the hare*, and *a wolf in sheep's clothing*.

Very little is known about Aesop. Some authorities question whether there ever was an Aesop. Indeed, many of the fables ascribed to him are at least 1000 years older than 600 B.C., the period during which he was supposed to have lived.

The usual version of Aesop's life is that he was a slave who lived in Greece. Tradition holds that he was an ugly and impudent fellow who often got himself into trouble, but usually talked himself out of it by telling a story with a point: a fable. Folktales about Aesop abound. In one of them Aesop is supposed to have told the story about "The Frogs Asking for a King" in Athens. This story kept the Greek statesman Pisistratus in power, to the advantage of the Athenians. Another story tells how Aesop went to a neighbor's house to borrow fire. As he was carrying it home in a lantern, a passerby asked what he was looking for with a lantern in broad daylight. Aesop is supposed to have replied, "A man who will mind his own business!"

The half dozen fables that follow include some of the most famous and at least two that are less well-known. Note that not all fables deal exclusively with animals.

The Fox and the Grapes

A hungry fox saw some ripe clusters of grapes hanging from a vine. She jumped at them, but failed to reach them. She tried every trick she knew, but she couldn't reach them. At last she turned away in weary disappointment.

"Just as I thought. The grapes are sour!"

The Point—It is easy to scorn what we cannot have.

The Crow and the Pitcher

A crow was dying of thirst. He came upon a pitcher which he hoped to find full of water. When he reached it, he found that it contained so little water he could not possibly get to it. He tried every trick he knew to get at the water, but all efforts failed. At last he collected a number of stones and dropped them one by one into the pitcher. Soon he brought the water within his reach and saved his life.

The Point—Necessity is the mother of invention.

The Shepherd Boy and the Wolf

A shepherd boy who tended his sheep grew lonely. Thinking to have some fun and pass the time he cried out, "Wolf! Wolf!"

His neighbors rushed over to help him, but of course there was no wolf. He merely laughed at them for coming. Three times he raised a false cry of "Wolf". Three times the neighbors came running.

At last the wolf really did come. The shepherd boy cried out in terror, "Wolf! Wolf! The wolf is killing the sheep."

No one came or paid any attention to his cries. The wolf, having nothing to fear, proceeded to destroy the entire flock.

The Point—No one believes a liar—even when he speaks the truth.

The Chameleon

Two travelers energetically disputed the color of the chameleon. One of the men insisted that it was blue. He had seen it with his very own eyes upon a tree branch in very good light. The other strongly asserted that it was green. He had studied it very closely on a leaf of the fig tree.

Both men were positive. The dispute became louder and angrier. At this moment a third man came along. They agreed to refer the question to him for decision.

"Gentlemen," said the newcomer, "you couldn't have been luckier in your choice. As it happens, I caught a chameleon just last night. Too bad, but you are both mistaken. The creature is wholly black!"

"Impossible!" they cried in unison.

"No," said the newcomer. "We'll soon prove my statement. I caught the chameleon and put him into a little paper box. Here he is."

As he spoke, he drew the box out of his pocket, opened it, and— the chameleon was as white as snow!

The Point—Truth changes with time.

The North Wind and the Sun

The North Wind and the Sun had an argument over who was most powerful. They agreed to settle their disagreement by a contest: whoever could first take the coat off a traveler would be declared the winner.

The North Wind tried first. He blew and blew and blew with all his might, but the harder he blew, the closer the traveler wrapped his coat around him. At last the North Wind gave up. Then the sun had a try.

He shone out in all his warmth. The traveler, feeling the warmth of his rays, began to take off one garment after another. At last, almost overcome by the heat, he took off his clothing and bathed in a stream by the roadside.

The Point—Persuasion is better than force.

The Old Man and Death

A poor old peasant, worn out with age and work, toiled along a country road. He carried a heavy load of firewood over his shoulders. As he walked painfully along toward his distant cottage, he considered his lot and began to despair. He put the burden down and sat beside it.

"What pleasure have I known since I first drew breath? From morning to night it is one round of thankless toil. My cupboards are bare; my wife is discontented; my children are disobedient! If only Death would free me from my troubles."

"Did you call me?" It was Death, the King of Terrors, standing before him. "What request did you make?"

"N-n-nothing," stammered the old man. "Please help me get back on my shoulders the bundle of firewood I let fall."

The Point—We would often be sorry if our wishes were gratified.

READING FOR UNDERSTANDING

Main Idea

1. The main idea of the introduction to this unit (235–236) is that (a) imagination is less important than wisdom (b) imagination plays a major role in the lives of people of all ages (c) modern science-fiction stories are superior to fairy tales (d) adults usually show more creative imagination than do children.

Details

2. A Walt Disney movie that is mentioned in this unit is (a) *Dumbo* (b) *Pinocchio* (c) *The Lady and the Tramp* (d) *Snow White*.

3. Jakob Grimm first made his name famous as (a) a writer of fairy tales (b) a language scholar (c) an opera composer (d) a lawyer.

4. In "The Iron Stove" the prince planned to marry another because he thought his true love (a) had married another (b) was bewitched (c) was dead (d) had changed her mind.

5. In "The Sleeping Beauty in the Wood," the princess falls under the evil spell by (a) pricking her hand with a spindle (b) eating a poisoned apple (c) forgetting the magic charm (d) refusing to marry the man chosen by her parents.

6. In the same tale, the prince's mother is in reality (a) an ogress (b) a fairy godmother (c) an enchanted princess (d) a good witch.

7. The Hans Christian Andersen tale that defied Adolf Hitler during World War II was (a) "The Little Mermaid" (b) "The Ugly Duckling" (c) "The Nightingale" (d) "The Wicked Prince."

8. The first Andersen Fairy Tale Festival was held in Odense, Denmark, in (a) 1848 (b) 1850 (c) 1950 (d) 1952.

9. The brave tin soldier had each of the following experiences EXCEPT (a) being challenged by a rat (b) sailing in a paper boat (c) being swallowed by a fish (d) dancing with the little dancer.

10. As well as being an author, Lewis Carroll was also (a) the editor of a dictionary (b) a lecturer in mathematics (c) an important painter (d) a skilled musician.

11. When the White Queen pricked her finger (260), she didn't cry out because (a) she was courageous (b) she was ashamed to show emotion in front of Alice (c) she had cried out earlier (d) Alice experienced the pain for her.

12. Fables differ from folktales in that (a) fables have a moral (b) human beings never appear in fables (c) fables are always humorous (d) folktales are always sad.

13. Aesop is supposed to have lived (a) in 1600 B.C. (b) around 600 B.C. (c) at the same time as Jakob Grimm (d) a century before Hans Christian Andersen.

14. In the argument between the North Wind and the Sun (a) the North Wind flattered the Sun (b) the Sun was disappointed (c) the Sun won the argument (d) the traveler realized he was the subject of a dispute.

15. The two characters who fell under an evil spell are (a) the Princess in "The Iron Stove" and the Princess in "The Sleeping Beauty" (b) the Little Dancer in "The Brave Tin Soldier" and the Princess in "The Iron Stove" (c) the White Queen in *Through the Looking-Glass* and Alice (d) the Prince in "The Iron Stove" and the Princess in "The Sleeping Beauty."

Inferences

16. The success of the Grimm brothers and Hans Christian Andersen suggests that (a) it is important to be a language scholar to tell fairy tales (b) the appeal of imaginative stories is universal (c) the Germans and the Danes are alike in their respect for authority (d) successful storytellers are usually failures early in life.

17. After her first contact with the iron stove, the Princess returned with (a) joy (b) fear (c) curiosity (d) anger.

18. In "The Sleeping Beauty" the cook was (a) impatient (b) cruel (c) slow-witted (d) kind.

19. A word that might be applied to the romance of the Little Dancer and the Tin Soldier is (a) *doomed* (b) *hasty* (c) *fulfilled* (d) *timely*.

20. The behavior of Alice (258–261) can best be described as (a) excitable and irritable (b) unfriendly but talkative (c) calm and unruffled (d) impatient and cunning.

WORDS IN CONTEXT

1. "She shall only fall into a *profound* sleep, which shall last a hundred years."
   Profound (244) means (a) troubled (b) dreamlike (c) light (d) deep.

2. Her *swooning* away had not diminished one bit of her complexion.
   Swooning (245) means (a) losing weight (b) dying (c) fainting (d) weeping.

3. The common opinion was that an *ogre* lived there.
   Ogre (246) means (a) old man (b) monster (c) genius (d) member of the royal family.

4. He saw a Princess whose bright and *resplendent* beauty had something in it divine.
   Resplendent (246) means (a) shining brightly (b) unusual (c) surprising (d) modest and natural.

5. He went to find out little Day and saw him with a little *foil*, with which he was fencing.
   Foil (249) means (a) glove (b) charm (c) sword (d) toy.

6. The uproar that followed did not *subside* till the statue was repaired.
   Subside (251) means (a) grow worse (b) quiet down (c) become known (d) continue.

7. She fluttered like a *sylph* right into the stove by the side of the tin soldier and was instantly in flames and was gone.
   Sylph (256) means (a) graceful girl (b) arrow (c) witch (d) piece of writing paper.

8. "That's the effect of living backwards: it always makes one a little *giddy* at first."
   Giddy (259) means (a) proud (b) uneasy (c) curious (d) dizzy.

9. Animals or *inanimate* objects are the usual characters.
   Inanimate (263) means (a) cartoon (b) lifeless (c) colorful
   (d) disrespectful.
10. Many folktales about Aesop *abound*.
    Abound (264) means (a) are plentiful (b) conceal the truth
    (c) are hard to find (d) were recently discovered.

THINKING IT OVER

1. Why do people of all ages enjoy stories that depict impossible happenings and fantastic imaginings? What important quality of a good fairy tale is present in adult stories of the supernatural and the "almost possible," like *The Shining* and *The Eyes of the Dragon*, by Stephen King.
2. Why did the White Queen in *Through the Looking-Glass* cry out before she stuck herself? If we grant the whole idea of living backward, is her action logical? Many persons have pointed out that fairy tales are completely logical if we accept a few magical assumptions. Discuss this point further with reference to the stories you have read in this book or another.
3. Benjamin Franklin once wrote, "If a man could have half his wishes, he would double his troubles." What does this mean? Do you agree? To which fable does this apply?
4. Why do writers of fables often use animals instead of people to illustrate the moral or point they wish to demonstrate?
5. "And they lived happily ever after." This is the usual formula for the end of a fairy tale. Which tale clearly violates this rule? Do you consider the ending of this story effective? Do you prefer a story with a happy ending? Explain.

SUGGESTED ACTIVITIES

1. Beginning with the formula "Once upon a time . . . ," write a brief fairy tale of your own, perhaps a modern fantasy in the style of *Peter Pan*, *Mary Poppins*, *The Wizard of Oz*, or a science-fiction movie. Except for a few bits of magic, introduce realistic details to give a feeling of actuality to the story.
2. In *No Dawn* by William A. Krauss, the author describes the reactions of an average man on the morning of a day the sun does not rise. Write a story similar to this in which suddenly some natural law is suspended. Perhaps water flows uphill or fire burns water. The story may be humorous or serious, but it should be imaginative.

3. Select some proverb in general use, like "A stitch in time saves nine" or "Experience is the best teacher." Write a fable to illustrate the point you have chosen. Use animals in the style of Aesop's *Fables.*

4. Read additional fables by Aesop and report to the class. These are some of the better known:

   "The Ants and the Grasshopper"
   "The Cat and the Sparrows"
   "The Crow and the Raven"
   "The Fox and the Crow"
   "The Frogs Who Asked for a King"
   "The Lion and the Fox"
   "The Town Mouse and the Country Mouse"
   "The Wolf in Sheep's Clothing"
   "The Hare and the Tortoise"

5. The following are all morals of Aesop's fables. Some of them have passed into everyday speech. Select two or three. In your own words tell what each means. Tell whether or not you agree with the point and use an illustration to prove or disprove the statement.

   He who condemns is rarely free from fault.
   Small fools are the most quarrelsome.
   Actions speak louder than words.
   Honest enemies cannot do the harm that false friends can do.
   While setting one trap you may step into another.
   The race is not always to the swift.
   Look before you leap.
   People who complain of ingratitude usually deserve it.
   The first swallow does not make a summer.
   A gift reflects the giver.
   It is easy to propose impossible remedies.
   Better a sure morsel than an unsure meal.
   The tyrant will always find pretext for his tyranny.
   When a man asks your opinion of himself, he does not want the truth.

6. Fables often reflect folk wisdom, the result of the combined experiences of many people. Yet because the points are very general, they do not apply in all situations. Sometimes conflicting proverbs reflect the limitations of general statements; for example,

   Look before you leap.
   He who hesitates is lost.

Try to find other conflicting proverbs, or proverbs with which you
do not personally agree.

WORDS ASSOCIATED WITH FAIRY TALES AND FABLES

Name or Phrase	Definition	Named for
blow hot and cold	be changeable, unreliable	situation in one of Aesop's fables
bluebeard	man who marries one wife after another	character in a Charles Perrault fairy tale
Cinderella	person whose fortunes change suddenly for the better	character in a Charles Perrault fairy tale
grin like a Cheshire Cat	obviously happy	character in *Alice in Wonderland*
cry wolf	give false alarms that are finally not believed	Aesop character
dog in the manger	someone who prevents another from enjoying what he cannot	Aesop character
Humpty Dumpty	clumsy person	character in *Through the Looking-Glass*
sour grapes	scorn for something that cannot be gained or achieved anyway	situation in one of Aesop's fables
Tweedledum and Tweedledee	a practically indistinguishable pair	characters in *Through the Looking-Glass*
ugly duckling	person whose beauty comes only with maturity	Andersen character
Who'll bell the cat?	It's easy to suggest impossible solutions.	situation in one of Aesop's fables
wolf in sheep's clothing	evil person who pretends to be good	Aesop character

American Folklore

Though folklore has its roots in the past, it flourishes even today—in cities as well as in rural areas. Indeed, one kind of folktale, called a *modern urban legend*, continues to survive even when disproved. One such persistent story concerns a stalled car on an expressway. The driver flags down a motorist, who volunteers to help. The driver of the stalled car explains that a brief push will start the car, "but you must get up to about 35 miles an hour to turn over the motor." He looks in his rear-view mirror and sees, with horror, the other car bearing down on him at 35 miles an hour! Though this story has never been proved, it appears and reappears as truth. It is kept alive, like a folktale of old, with repetition.

Throughout America a renewed interest in more traditional folklore has kept alive the old stories and crafts that enriched the lives of earlier Americans. Folklore is alive and well.

I. Modern Folk Heroes

The making of legendary heroes did not stop with ancient Greece or Rome. It is going on all the time, even now as you read this. All persons in the public eye are potentially folk heroes, although many are famous for only a short time. Hollywood stars become almost legendary to many moviegoers. Their appearance on a street often provokes more interest and excitement than could the arrival of Zeus himself from Olympus. Their offhand remarks may be exaggerated out of all proportion. Unintentional gestures may be analyzed and weighed by a host of columnists.

Within our own time the name of Babe Ruth has become almost legendary, a permanent fixture in America's folklore. His prowess in baseball is frequently recalled by old-timers, who naturally tell their stories in their own way. One feat often retold describes one of Babe Ruth's most famous home runs. The fans had been "riding" him all day. Then at a crucial moment he had a turn at bat. After more taunting by

the fans, he pointed his bat emphatically in the direction of
the right-field stands. The pitcher wound up, and Babe swung.
The ball sailed high in the air and landed just about in the
spot he had indicated.

Here, in the story of this amazing feat, is the germ of a folktale. Everyone who retells the tale cannot resist the temptation to add a few details here and there. In the next retelling
the achievement may include additional details. So the story
grows. Nowadays the printed page acts as a check on the
growth of a good yarn. Imagine, though, how a story could
grow without a written version to fix it for all time!

Folktales often start with just such a germ of truth. Then as
the people get hold of and retell these stories, they grow,
taking on new details all the time. As pure storytelling the
final version is often a great deal better than the original!

II. Tall Tales

Folk heroes are usually supermen. The heroes of the American frontier were superstrong, unflinchingly brave, and unusually keen—just as we would secretly like to be. Many of
these heroes, like Davy Crockett, lived and helped create some
of the yarns. Some of them, like Paul Bunyan, were pure
invention and inspiration. In any event, all these heroes are
interesting to us. They tell us much about our American past
and display a typically American brand of humor—that of
deliberate exaggeration, or the tall tale.

Some of the tall tales make familiar reading. Many a pres-
ent-day radio or television comedian has gone back to these
picturesque liars for inspiration. No one knows how old some
of the stories are. The tall tales usually run something like
this. A man is pursued by a mountain lion. At the last moment, just as the lion opens his mouth to take a bite, the man
turns and reaches down the lion's throat. He grabs the tail
and pulls the lion inside out. The lion then keeps running in
the opposite direction, and the man is saved.

Out West everything has remarkable tenacity of life. One
evening an argument raged about bedbugs. One imaginative
fellow told how he had boiled one without being able to kill
it. Another said he had soaked one in turpentine for hours
without making him dizzy. A third man won this match easily. He said he took an insect to an iron foundry and dropped
it into a ladle of melted iron. A skillet was made out of the

iron, and the bedbug was sealed into the skillet. Well, sir, his wife used the skillet for six years until she dropped it and broke it. The insect walked out of the hole, shook himself, and made tracks for his old hideout. "But," concluded the story-teller, "he looked mighty pale."

Weather and climate are always popular topics of conversation. Have you ever had the temptation to say, "You think this is hot? I can remember when . . . "? Many of the best tall stories are connected with weather. Some days are so hot the rivers boil over and scald the bridge tenders. Other days are so cold that shadows freeze. Sometimes the fog is so thick two people are needed to walk in it; one holds back the fog while the other walks through. America has even had striped weather: a mile of scorching sunshine alternating with a mile of rain!

Parts of the country take great pride in their healthful climate. In East Texas the wind is so healthful it revives corpses. Florida sunshine has the same effect. Dying persons in less favored regions are revived by air expelled from bicycle tires inflated in Arizona. California climate is so healthful they had to shoot a man to start a cemetery. Arkansas soil is so fruitful that planting is dangerous. The seeds sprout so fast the farmer has to jump back out of the way to avoid a concussion. Cucumber vines grow so fast a man has to hack his way out of them right after sowing the seed.

Not all parts of the country are so favored, alas! Some areas are so poor nine partridges are needed to holler, "Bob White!" Dogs have to lean against a fence to bark. Some areas are so dry, frogs seven years old haven't learned to swim. Farmers must plant potatoes between the rows of onions. The onions make the eyes of the potatoes cry. The weeping irrigates both crops. In some areas there is so much dust that housewives polish their pans by holding them against a keyhole. The sand pouring through scours them. In these lands farmers can tell of the approach of a dust storm. They can hear the sneezing of the rattlesnakes on the prairie.

The exaggeration goes with animals and people as well as places. The Kansas jayhawk flies backward. He doesn't care where he's going, but he likes to know where he's been. Hank Lord, efficiency expert, died after a long and busy life. Six pallbearers started to the hearse with the coffin on their shoulders. This was too much for Hank. He sat up, smashed the glass, and yelled, "What is this? You call this efficiency? Put this thing on wheels! Lay five of these birds off, and cut the other one's wages, cause the work is easy and the hours aren't long and the pace is slow."

They Have Yarns

In his poem, *The People, Yes,* Carl Sandburg gathered together some of the best tall stories. In the following excerpt we meet the larger-than-life Paul Bunyan, as well as his fellow heroes Mike Fink, Pecos Bill, and John Henry. But we also meet the exploits of lesser men like farmers, sailors, travelers, and salesmen. In less than half a dozen pages Carl Sandburg presents a summary of American folklore.

They have yarns
Of a skyscraper so tall they had to put hinges
On the two top stories so to let the moon go by,
Of one corn crop in Missouri when the roots
Went so deep and drew off so much water
The Mississippi riverbed that year was dry,
Of pancakes so thin they had only one side,

Of "a fog so thick we shingled the barn and six feet out on the fog,"
Of Pecos Pete straddling a cyclone in Texas and riding it to the west coast where "it rained out under him,"
Of the man who drove a swarm of bees across the Rocky Mountains and the Desert "and didn't lose a bee,"
Of a mountain railroad curve where the engineer in his cab can touch the caboose and spit in the conductor's eye,
Of the boy who climbed a cornstalk growing so fast he would have starved to death if they hadn't shot biscuits up to him,
Of the old man's whiskers: "When the wind was with him his whiskers arrived a day before he did,"
Of the hen laying a square egg and cackling "Ouch!" and of hens laying eggs with the dates printed on them,
Of the ship captain's shadow; it froze to the deck one cold winter night,
Of mutineers on that same ship put to chipping rust with rubber hammers,
Of the sheep counter who was fast and accurate: "I just count their feet and divide by four,"
Of the man so tall he must climb a ladder to shave himself,
Of the runt so teeny-weeny it takes two men and a boy to see him,
Of mosquitoes: one can kill a dog, two of them a man,

Of a cyclone that sucked cookstoves out of the kitchen, up the chimney flue, and on to the next town,

Of the same cyclone picking up wagon-tracks in Nebraska, and dropping them over in the Dakotas,

Of the hook-and-eye snake unlocking itself into forty pieces, each piece two inches long, then in nine seconds flat snapping itself together again,

Of the watch swallowed by the cow—when they butchered her a year later the watch was running and had the correct time,

Of horned snakes, hoop snakes that roll themselves where they want to go, and rattlesnakes carrying bells instead of rattles on their tails,

Of the herd of cattle in California getting lost in a giant redwood tree that had hollowed out,

Of the man who killed a snake by putting its tail in its mouth so it swallowed itself,

Of railroad trains whizzing along so fast they reach the station before the whistle,

Of pigs so thin the farmer had to tie knots in their tails to keep them from crawling through the cracks in their pens,

Of Paul Bunyan's big blue ox, Babe, measuring between the eyes forty-two ax-handles and a plug of Star tobacco exactly,

Of John Henry's hammer and the curve of its swing and his singing of it as "a rainbow round my shoulder."

"Do tell!"
"I want to know!"
"You don't say so!"
"Gosh all fish-hooks!"
"Tell me some more.
I don't believe a word you say
but I love to listen
to your sweet harmonica
to your chin-music.
Your fish stories hang together
when they're just a pack of lies:
you ought to have a leather medal:
you ought to have a statue
carved of butter: you deserve
a large bouquet of turnips."

"Yessir," the traveler drawled,
"Away out there in the petrified forest
everything goes on the same as usual.
The petrified birds sit in their petrified nests
and hatch their petrified young from petrified eggs."

A high-pressure salesman jumped off the Brooklyn Bridge and was saved by a policeman. But it didn't take him long to sell the idea to the policeman. So together they jumped off the bridge.

One of the oil men in heaven started a rumor of a gusher down in hell. All the other oil men left in a hurry for hell. As he gets to thinking about the rumor he had started he says to himself there might be something in it after all. So he leaves for hell in a hurry.

"The number 42 will win this raffle, that's my number." And when he won they asked him whether he guessed the number or had a system. He said he had a system, "I took up the old family album and there on page 7 was my grandfather and grandmother both on page 7. I said to myself this is easy for 7 times 7 is the number that will win and 7 times 7 is 42."

Once a shipwrecked sailor caught hold of a stateroom door and floated for hours till friendly hands from out of the darkness threw him a rope. And he called across the night, "What country is this?" and hearing voices answer, "New Jersey," he took a fresh hold on the floating stateroom door and called back half-wearily, "I guess I'll float a little farther."

An Ohio man bundled up the tin roof of a summer kitchen and sent it to a motor car maker with a complaint of his car not giving service. In three weeks a new car arrived for him and a letter: "We regret delay in shipment but your car was received in a very bad order."

A Dakota cousin of this Ohio man sent six years of tin can accumulations to the same works, asking them to overhaul his car. Two weeks later came a rebuilt car, five old tin cans, and a letter: "We are also forwarding you five parts not necessary in our new model."

Thus fantasies heard at filling stations in the midwest. Another relates to a Missouri mule who took aim with his heels at an automobile rattling by. The car turned a somersault, lit next a fence, ran right along through a cornfield till it came to a gate, moved onto the road and went on its way as though nothing had happened. The mule hee-hawed with desolation, "What's the use?"

Another tells of a farmer and his family stalled on a railroad crossing, how they jumped out in time to see a limited express knock it into flinders, the farmer calling, "Well, I always did say that car was no shucks in a real pinch."

When the Masonic Temple in Chicago was the tallest building in the United States west of New York, two men who would cheat the eyes out of you if you gave 'em a chance, took an Iowa farmer to the top of the building and asked him, "How is this for high?" They told him that for $25 they would go down in the basement and turn the building around on its turntable for him while he stood on the roof and saw how this seventh wonder of the world worked. He handed them $25. They went. He waited. They never came back.

This is told in Chicago as a folktale, the same as the legend of Mrs. O'Leary's cow kicking over the barn lamp that started the Chicago fire, when the Georgia visitor, Robert Toombs, telegraphed an Atlanta crony, "Chicago is on fire, the whole city burning down, God be praised!"

Nor is the prize sleeper Rip Van Winkle and his scolding wife forgotten, nor the headless horseman scooting through Sleepy Hollow

Nor the sunken treasure-ships in coves and harbors, the hideouts of gold and silver sought by Coronado, nor the Flying Dutchman rounding the Cape doomed to nevermore pound his ear nor ever again take a snooze for himself

Nor the sailor's caretaker Mother Carey seeing to it that every seafaring man in the afterworld has a seabird to bring him news of ships and women, an albatross for the admiral, a gull for the deckhand

Nor the sailor with a sweetheart in every port of the world, nor the ships that set out with flying colors and all the promises you could ask, the ships never heard of again

Nor Jim Liverpool, the riverman who could jump across any river and back without touching land, he was that quick on his feet

Nor Mike Fink along the Ohio and the Mississippi, half wild horse and half cock-eyed alligator, the rest of him snags and snapping turtle. "I can out-run, out-jump, out-shoot, out-brag, out-drink, and out-fight, rough and tumble, no holds barred, any man on both sides of the river from Pittsburgh to New Orleans and back again to St. Louis. My trigger finger itches and I want to go redhot. War, famine and bloodshed puts flesh on my bones, and hardship's my daily bread."

Nor the man so lean he threw no shadow: six rattlesnakes struck at him one time and every one missed him.

III. Paul Bunyan

Up in the deep forests of the Great Lakes and the Pacific Northwest there grew a legend about the most famous hero of them all, Paul Bunyan. Whenever lumberjacks gathered together for a talkfest, someone would tell of a Paul Bunyan exploit. His neighbor, not to be outdone, would tell him one better. Old Baron Munchausen, who formerly held the world's liar title, was soon outclassed. Yarns flew thick and fast, and the guffaws flew faster. What kind of person was this Paul Bunyan?

Well, Paul was really a superman, a bearded giant who could fell a spruce six feet through in ten strokes of the axe. When he yelled, he caused a landslide near Pike's Peak. He combed his beard with a pine tree. Almost as famous was his blue ox, Babe, which measured 42 ax handles and a plug of tobacco between the eyes. Among his noteworthy crew, Paul numbered Sourdough Sam and his son Hot Biscuit Slim, cooks; Johnny Inkslinger, the clerk; Cream Puff Fatty, the baker; and Big Swede, the foreman. What men these were, all built on the same scale as Paul!

Paul was a counterpart of Thor, invincible and indestructible. He had an appetite to go with his size. His cookstove alone covered an acre. Four men skated on the griddle while the cook flipped the pancakes. His achievements have left their mark on America, too. The Grand Canyon, contrary to popular belief, is not the work of the Colorado River. Oh, no! Paul Bunyan created it in one of his adventures. And what adventures he had. One winter was so cold the cuss words froze and didn't thaw out until the following Fourth of July. Then there was a din!

Paul was an inventor, too. He invented the Day-Stretcher so that he'd have more time during the day to catch up on his work. But he found that with days twice as long, he got twice as far behind. He had a number of extra-long days on hand, but being thrifty he sold them to a secondhand dealer in the East. These days are still circulating. The next blue Monday, when the day seems endless, you will realize that one of Paul's extra-long days is being used up.

Life wasn't always clear sailing for Paul. He had his problems, and bigger than man-sized ones, too. Once a tribe of mammoth mosquitoes descended upon the camp. Paul's loggers quit work and ran home, howling in anguish. At last, Paul sent for two giant bees to fight off the mosquitoes. The pesky insects flew off at last, with the bees in full pursuit. Alas, for all planning: the bees and the mosquitoes intermarried. The offspring, combining the weapons of both insects, had stingers on *both* ends. How Paul got rid of these hybrid monsters is a tribute to his ingenuity. He bought a boatload of sugar. The bee-instinct in the giant insects forced them to gorge themselves on sugar. Not being built to carry such a load, the insects fluttered lower and lower, and finally drowned.

The Whistling River

It seems that, some years before the winter of the Blue Snow (which every old logger remembers because of a heavy fall of bright blue snow which melted to ink, giving folks the idea of writing stories like these, so they tell), Ol' Paul was logging on what was then known as the Whistling River. It got its name from the fact that every morning, right on the dot, at nineteen minutes after five, and every night at ten minutes past six, it r'ared up to a height of two hundred and seventy-three feet and let loose a whistle that could be heard for a distance of six hundred and three miles in any direction.

Of course, if one man listening by himself can hear that far, it seems reasonable to suppose that two men listening together can hear it just twice as far. They tell me that even as far away as Alaska, most every camp had from two to four whistle-listeners (as many as were needed to hear the whistle without straining), who got two bits a listen and did nothing but listen for the right time, especially quitting time.

However, it seems that the river was famous for more than its whistling, for it was known as the orneriest river that ever ran between two banks. It seemed to take a fiendish delight in tying whole rafts of good saw logs into more plain and fancy knots than forty-three old sailors even knew the names of. It was an old "side winder" for fair. Even so, it is unlikely that Ol' Paul would ever have bothered with it, if it had left his beard alone.

It happened this way. It seems that Ol' Paul is sitting on a low hill one afternoon, combing his great curly beard with a pine tree, while he plans his winter operations. All of a sudden like, and without a word of warning, the river h'ists itself up on its hind legs and squirts about four thousand five hundred and nineteen gallons of river water straight in the center of Ol' Paul's whiskers.

Naturally Paul's considerably startled, but says nothing, figuring that if he pays it no mind, it'll go 'way and leave him be. But no sooner does he get settled back with his thinking and combing again, than the durn river squirts some more! This time, along with the water, it throws in for good measure a batch of mud turtles, thirteen large carp, a couple of drowned muskrat, and half a raft of last year's saw logs. By this time Ol' Paul is pretty mad, and he jumps up and lets loose a yell that causes a landslide out near Pike's Peak, and startles a barber in Missouri so he cuts half the hair off the minister's toupee, causing somewhat of a stir thereabouts. Paul stomps around waving his arms for a spell, and allows:

"By the Gee-Jumpin' John Henry and the Great Horn Spoon, I'll tame that river or bust a gallus tryin'."

He goes over to another hill and sits down to think out a way to tame a river, forgetting his winter operations entirely. He sits there for three days and forty-seven hours without moving, thinking at top speed all the while, and finally comes to the conclusion that the best thing to do is to take out the kinks. But he knows that taking the kinks out of a river as tricky as this one is apt to be quite a chore, so he keeps on sitting there while he figures out ways and means. Of course, he could dig a new channel and run the river through that, but that was never Paul's way. He liked to figure out new ways of doing things, even if they were harder.

Meanwhile he's gotten a mite hungry, so he hollers down to camp for Sourdough Sam to bring him up a little popcorn, of which he is very fond. So Sam hitches up a four-horse team while his helpers are popping the corn, and soon arrives at Paul's feet with a wagonload.

Paul eats popcorn and thinks. The faster he thinks the faster he eats, and the faster he eats the faster he thinks, until finally his hands are moving so fast that nothing shows but a blur, and they make a wind that is uprooting trees all around him. His chewing sounds like a couple hundred coffee grinders all going at once. In practically no time at all the ground for three miles and a quarter in every direction is covered to a depth of eighteen inches with popcorn scraps, and several thousand small birds and animals, seeing the ground all white and the air filled with what looks like snowflakes, conclude that a blizzard is upon them and immediately freeze to death, furnishing the men with pot pies for some days.

But to get back to Ol' Paul's problem. Just before the popcorn is all gone, he decides that the only practical solution is to hitch Babe, the Mighty Blue Ox, to the river and let him yank it straight.

Babe was so strong that he could pull mighty near anything that could be hitched to. His exact size, as I said before, is not known, for although it is said that he stood ninety-three hands high, it's not known whether that meant ordinary logger's hands, or hands the size of Paul's, which, of course, would be something else again.

However, they tell of an eagle that had been in the habit of roosting on the tip of Babe's right horn, suddenly deciding to fly to the other. Columbus Day, it was, when he started. He flew steadily, so they say, night and day, fair weather and foul, until his wing feathers were worn down to pinfeathers and a new set grew to replace them. In all, he seems to have worn out seventeen sets of feathers on the trip, and from reaching up to brush the sweat out of his eyes so much, had worn all the feathers off the top of his head, becoming completely bald, as are all of his descendants to this day. Finally the courageous bird won through, reaching the brass ball on the tip of the left horn on the seventeenth of March. He waved a wing weakly at the cheering lumberjacks and 'lowed as how he'd of made it sooner but for the head winds.

But the problem is how to hitch Babe to the river, as it's a well-known fact that an ordinary log chain and skid hook will not hold water. So after a light lunch of three sides of barbecued beef, half a wagonload of potatoes, carrots, and a few other odds and ends, Ol' Paul goes down to the blacksmith shop and gets Ole, the Big Swede, to help him look through the big instruction book that came with the woods and tells how to do most everything under the sun. But though Paul reads the book through from front to back twice while Ole reads it from back to front, and they both read it once from bottom to top, they find nary a word about how to hook onto a river. However, they do find an old almanac stuck between the pages and get so busy reading up on the weather for the coming year, and a lot of fancy ailments of one kind and another that it's suppertime before they know it, and the problem's still unsolved. So Paul decides that the only practical thing to do is to invent a rigging of some kind himself.

At any rate he has to do something, as every time he hears the river whistle, it makes him so mad he's fit to be tied, which interferes with his work more than something. No one can do their best under such conditions.

Being as how this was sort of a special problem, he thought it out in a special way. Paul was like that. As he always thought best when he walked, he had the men survey a circle about thirty miles in diameter to walk around. This was so that, if he was quite a while thinking it out, he wouldn't be finding himself way down in Australia when he'd finished.

When everything is ready, he sets his old fur cap tight on his head, clasps his hands behind him, and starts walking and thinking. He thinks and walks. The faster he walks the faster he thinks. He makes a complete circle every half hour. By morning he's worn a path that is knee-deep even on him, and he has to call the men to herd the stock away and keep them from falling in and getting crippled. Three days later he thinks it out, but he's worn himself down so deep that it takes a day and a half to get a ladder built that will reach down that far. When he does get out, he doesn't even wait for breakfast, but whistles for Babe and tears right out across the hills to the north.

The men have no idea what he intends to do, but they know from experience that it'll be good, so they cheer till their throats are so sore they have to stay around the mess hall drinking Paul's private barrel of cough syrup till suppertime. And after that they go to bed and sleep very soundly.

Paul and the Ox travel plenty fast, covering twenty-four townships at a stride, and the wind from their passing raises a dust that doesn't even begin to settle for some months. There are those who claim that the present dust storms are nothing more or less than that same dust just beginning to get back to earth—but that's a matter of opinion. About noon, as they near the North Pole, they begin to see blizzard tracks, and in a short time are in the very heart of their summer feeding grounds. Taking a sack from his shoulder, Paul digs out materials for a box trap, which he sets near a well-traveled blizzard trail, and baits with fresh icicles from the top of the North Pole. Then he goes away to eat his lunch, but not until he's carefully brushed out his tracks—a trick he later taught the Indians.

After lunch he amuses himself for a while by throwing huge chunks of ice into the water for Babe to retrieve, but he soon has to whistle the great beast out, as every time he jumps into the water he causes such a splash that a tidal wave threatens Galveston, Texas, which at that time was inhabited by nobody in particular. Some of the ice he threw in is still floating around the ocean, causing plenty of excitement for the iceberg patrol.

About two o'clock he goes back to his blizzard trap and discovers that he has caught seven half-grown blizzards and one grizzled old nor'wester, which is raising considerable fuss and bids fair to trample the young ones before he can get them out. But he finally manages to get a pair of half-grown ones in his sack and turns the others loose.

About midnight he gets back to camp, and hollers at Ole, the Big Swede:

"Build me the biggest log chain that's ever been built, while I stake out these dadblasted blizzards! We're goin' to warp it to 'er proper, come mornin'."

Then he goes down to the foot of the river and pickets one of the blizzards to a tree on the bank, then crosses and ties the other directly opposite. Right away the river begins to freeze. In ten minutes the slush ice reaches nearly from bank to bank, and the blizzards are not yet really warmed to their work, either. Paul watches for a few minutes, and then goes back to camp to warm up, feeling mighty well satisfied with the way things are working out.

In the morning the river has a tough time r'aring up for what it maybe knows to be its last whistle, for its foot is frozen solid for more than seventeen miles. The blizzards have really done the business.

By the time breakfast is over, the great chain's ready and Babe all harnessed. Paul quick-like wraps one end of the chain seventy-two times around the foot of the river, and hitches Babe to the other. Warning the men to stand clear, he shouts at the Ox to pull. But though the great beast strains till his tongue hangs out, pulling the chain out into a solid bar some seven and a half miles long, and sinks knee-deep in the solid rock, the river stubbornly refuses to budge, hanging onto its kinks like a snake in a gopher hole. Seeing this, Ol' Paul grabs the chain and, letting loose a holler that blows the tarpaper off the shacks in the Nebraska sandhills, he and the Ox together give a mighty yank that jerks the river loose from end to end, and start hauling it out across the prairie so fast that it smokes.

After a time Paul comes back and sights along the river, which now is as straight as a gun barrel. But he doesn't have long to admire his work, for he soon finds he has another problem on his hands. You see, it's this way. A straight river is naturally much shorter than a crooked one, and now all the miles and miles of extra river that used to be in the kinks are running wild out on the prairie. This galls the farmers in those parts more than a little. So it looks like Paul had better figure something out, and mighty soon at that, for already he can see clouds of dust the prairie folks are raising as they come at top speed to claim damages.

After three minutes of extra deep thought he sends a crew to camp to bring his big crosscut saw and a lot of baling wire. He saws the river into nine-mile lengths and the men roll it up like linoleum and tie it with the wire. Some say he used these later when he logged off the desert, rolling out as many lengths as he needed to float his logs. But that's another story.

But his troubles with the Whistling River were not all over. It seems that being straightened sort of took the spirit out of the river, and from that day on it refused to whistle even a bird call. And as Paul had gotten into the habit of depending on the whistle to wake up the men in the morning, things were a mite upset.

First he hired an official getter-upper who rode through the camp on a horse, and beat a triangle. But the camp was so big that it took three hours and seventy-odd minutes to make the trip. Naturally some of the men were called too early and some too late. It's hard to say what might have happened if Squeaky Swanson hadn't showed up about that time. His speaking voice was a thin squeak, but when he hollered he could be heard clear out to Kansas on a still day. So every morning he stood outside the cookshack and hollered the blankets off every bunk in camp. Naturally the men didn't stay in bed long after the blankets were off them, what with the cold wind and all, so Squeaky was a great success and for years did nothing but holler in the mornings.

Whether or not there was once a Paul Bunyan who inspired these tales is unimportant. The important thing is that Paul Bunyan is an American tradition more real than many of the shadowy figures in our histories. His giant form is instantly recognizable in advertising and other illustrations. His name is a symbol of gigantic exploits. There is a magic even in the names of Paul's adventures: the Winter of the Blue Snow, Paul and the Bedcats, the Party for the Seven Axmen, the

Sourdough Drive, Paul and the Whistling River. They remind
us that a fascinating mythology does not belong only to the
older nations of the world.

IV. Davy Crockett

Most of us couple the name of Crockett with the Battle of
the Alamo, but Davy was well known to his countrymen long
before that tragic event. His autobiography had a host of
readers. When he entered politics, he charmed his listeners by
speaking to them in their own language, with all the humorous exaggeration of the frontier. He had a reputation for a
good yarn and never let his constituents down. He was elected
to the state legislature and finally to the Congress of the
United States. A devoted follower of Andrew Jackson, he had
many of the solid virtues of Jackson. When campaigning he
would gather his audience around him and delight them with
speeches like this:

"I'm that same David Crockett, fresh from the backwoods,
half-horse, half-alligator, a little touched with the snapping
turtle; can wade the Mississippi, leap the Ohio, ride upon a
streak of lightning, and slip without a scratch down a honey
locust. I can whip my weight in wildcats—and if any gentle-
man pleases, he may throw in a panther—hug a bear too close
for comfort, and eat any man opposed to Jackson."

Davy loved a fight, but sometimes he bit off more than he
could chew. The following is an account of one of his tougher
fights.

My Fight with Joe Snag

One day as I was sitting in the stern of my boat on the Mississippi,
taking a horn of midshipman's grog, with a tin pot in each hand,
first a draught of whiskey and then one of river water, who should
float down past me but Joe Snag. He was in a snooze with his mouth
wide open. He had been ramsquaddled with whiskey for a fortnight.
As it evaporated, it looked like the steam from a vent pipe.

Knowing the feller would be hard to wake with all this steam on
as he floated past me, I hit him a crack over his knob with my big
steering oar. He waked in a thundering rage.

Says he, "Hallo, stranger, who axed you to crack my head?"

Says I, "Shut up your mouth, or your teeth will get sunburnt."

Upon this he crooked up his neck and neighed like a stallion. I clapped my arms and crowed like a cock.

Says he, "If you are a game chicken, I'll pick all the pin feathers off you."

Says I, "Give us none of your chin music, but set your kickers on land, and I'll give you a severe licking."

The fellow now jumped ashore, and he was so tall he could not tell when his feet were cold. He jumped up a rod.

Says he, "Take care how I light on you," and he gave a real sockdologer that made my very lungs and liver turn to jelly. But he found me a real battler. I broke three of his ribs, and he knocked out five of my teeth and one eye. He was the severest colt that I ever tried to break. I finally got a bite hold that he could not shake off.

We were now parted by some boatmen and so exhausted that it was more than a month before either could have a fight. It seemed to me like a little eternity. And although I didn't come out second best, I took care not to wake up a ring-tailed roarer with an oar again.

V. Mike Fink

Like Davy Crockett, Mike Fink was a real person whose exploits became legendary. Although he made his fame as a keelboatman on the Ohio and Mississippi rivers, not all Mike Fink tales deal with this period in his life. Some deal with his experiences as a wilderness scout.

Mike Fink Wins a Bet

When it came to coolness, Mike Fink was blood brother to William Tell. Morgan Neville, who knew Mike Fink personally in later years, tells some of the Mike Fink legends. In this selection, Neville was traveling down the Ohio River on a steamboat. When the boat came to a stop, Neville saw his old friend Mike Fink. But let Morgan Neville tell his story of how Mike Fink showed his marksmanship.

I recognized an old acquaintance, familiarly known to me from my boyhood. He was leaning carelessly against a large beech. His left arm negligently pressed a rifle to his side. His stature was upwards of six feet, his proportions perfectly symmetrical, and exhibiting the evidence of Herculean powers.

Long exposure to the sun and weather on the lower Ohio and Mississippi had changed his skin; and, but for the fine European cast of his countenance, he might have passed for the principal warrior of some powerful tribe. Although he was at least fifty years of age, his hair was as black as the wing of the raven. Next to his skin he wore a red flannel shirt, covered by a blue capot, ornamented with white fringe. On his feet were moccasins. A broad leathern belt, from which hung a large knife, encircled his waist.

As soon as the steamboat became stationary, the cabin passengers jumped on shore. As I ascended the bank, the figure I have just described advanced to offer me his hand.

"How are you, Mike?" said I.

"How goes it?" replied the boatman—grasping my hand with a squeeze that I can compare to nothing but that of a blacksmith's vise.

"I am glad to see you, Mannee!"—continued he in his abrupt manner. "I am going to shoot at the tin cup for a quart—off hand—and you must be judge."

I understood Mike at once, and on any other occasion should have remonstrated and prevented the daring trial of skill. But I was accompanied by a couple of English tourists, who had scarcely ever been beyond the sound of Bow Bells; and who were traveling post over the United States to make up a book of observation on our manners and customs. There were, also, among the passengers a few bloods from Philadelphia and Baltimore, who could conceive of nothing equal to Chestnut or Howard streets; and who expressed great disappointment at not being able to find terrapins and oysters at every village.

My pride was aroused; and I resolved to give them an opportunity of seeing a Western Lion—for such Mike undoubtedly was—in all his glory.

Mike, followed by several of his crew, led the way to a beech grove some little distance from the landing. I invited my fellow passengers to witness the scene. On arriving at the spot, a stout, bull-headed boatman, dressed in a hunting shirt—but barefooted—in whom I recognized a younger brother of Mike, drew a line with his toe. Stepping off thirty yards, he turned round fronting his brother, took a tin cup, which hung from his belt, and placed it on his head. Although I had seen this feat performed before, I acknowledge I felt uneasy while this silent preparation was going on. But I had not much time for reflection; for the brother exclaimed—

"Blaze away, Mike! and let's have the quart."

My fellow voyagers, as soon as they recovered from the first effect of their astonishment, exhibited a disposition to interfere. But Mike, throwing back his left leg, leveled his rifle at the head of his brother. In this horizontal position the weapon remained for some seconds as immovable as if the arm which held it was affected by no pulsation.

"Elevate your gun a little lower, Mike! or you will pay the corn," cried the imperturbable brother.

I know not if the advice was obeyed or not; but the sharp crack of the rifle immediately followed, and the cup flew off thirty or forty yards—rendered unfit for future service. There was a cry of admiration from the strangers, who pressed forward to see if the foolhardy boatman was really safe. He remained as immovable as if he had been a figure hewn out of stone. He had not even winked when the ball struck the cup within two inches of his skull.

"Mike has won!" I exclaimed; and my decision was the signal which, according to their rules, permitted him of the target to move from his position. No more sensation was exhibited among the boatmen than if a common wager had been won. The bet being decided, they hurried back to their boat, giving me and my friends an invitation to partake of "the treat." We declined, and took leave of the thoughtless creatures.

In a few minutes afterwards, we observed their keelboat wheeling into the current—the gigantic form of Mike bestriding the large steering oar, and the others arranging themselves in their places in front of the cabin, which extended nearly the whole length of the boat, covering merchandise of immense value. As they left the shore, they gave the Indian yell; and broke out into a sort of unconnected chorus—commencing with—

> "Hard upon the beech oar!—
> She moves too slow!
> All the way to Shawneetown,
> Long while ago."

In a few minutes the boat "took the chute" of Letart's Falls and disappeared behind the point with the rapidity of an Arabian courser.

Our travelers returned to the boat, lost in speculation on the scene and the beings they had just beheld; and, no doubt, the circumstance has been related a thousand times with all the necessary amplifications of finished tourists.

VI. Davy Crockett and Mike Fink

Sometimes the legends of two of the heroes would be combined. One story tells of a shooting match between Mike Fink and Davy Crockett.

Crockett shot first, aiming at a cat sitting on a rail 150 yards away. "The ball cut off both the old tom cat's ears close to his head, and shaved the hair off clean across the skull, as slick as if I'd done it with a razor, and the critter never stirred, nor knew he'd lost his ears till he tried to scratch 'em."

Mike aimed next at a sow with a litter of pigs away off in the distance. He kept firing until not one pig had enough tail to make a toothpick with. Crockett bettered these shots by shooting off the tiny stubs.

Mike was temporarily beaten. Then he aimed at his wife as she was going out to the spring for water. He knocked half her comb out of her head without stirring a hair. Then he called her to stand still and give Davy a clear shot at the other half. But Davy's chivalry defeated him here. He confessed that his hand would shake too much if he aimed his gun within 100 miles of a "shemale."

VII. Pecos Bill

What Paul Bunyan is to the loggers, Pecos Bill is to the western cowboys. Bill came from sturdy stock. His mother once killed forty-five people with a broom handle. Bill himself cut his teeth on a bowie knife. His early playmates were bears and wildcats. He grew up with coyotes and thought he was a coyote. He used to kill deer coyote-fashion; he ran them to death.

Bill's appearance must have been imposing. Once when he needed a job, Bill went up to a ranch notorious for the hard-bitten cowboys it employed. Bill walked through a group of rough-looking characters and asked in a loud voice, "Who's boss around here?"

There was a pause. A giant of a man with seven pistols and nine knives stood up, walked over to him, and looked him in the eye. Then he took off his hat to Bill and answered, "I *was*, but you *are*."

Many a tale is told round the campfire of Bill's prodigious strength and courage. Once when Bill met a ten-foot rattle-

snake in his path, he paused—to be fair—and gave the snake
the first three bites. When Bill went to work, the rattler soon
cried out for mercy. Soon after, Bill was using the snake for a
lariat.

At another time Bill rode an Oklahoma cyclone clear across
the state of Texas and two other states. When it reached
Arizona, it finally threw him—but unfairly. When it realized it
couldn't shake Bill, it just rained out under him. According to
one version the washout created the Grand Canyon. This
would seem, alas, to dispute the earlier claim of Paul Bunyan.
A reader does not know which one to believe!

Once a mountain lion jumped Bill. This was no commonplace lion, but one that weighed "more than three steers and
a yearling." In no time at all the fur was flying until it
darkened the sun. In three minutes the lion yelled, "I'll give
up, Bill. Can't you take a joke?" Bill thereupon rode the lion
like a horse.

Naturally, only a mighty beast could be a fit mount for Bill.
His horse was named "Widow-Maker," for Bill was the only
man who could ride him. He had raised him from a colt—on
nitroglycerin and dynamite. Once a friend of his tried to ride
Widow-Maker and was jolted to the top of Pike's Peak. Of
course, Bill roped him down in short order. Bill's lariat was,
according to the leading authorities, as long as the equator.
Some say that's an exaggeration, that it was really two feet
shorter on one end.

Bill had ingenuity as well as strength. He had prairie dogs
digging fence holes for him. He never wasted a good buffalo
by killing it for its hide. His dog would run down a buffalo
and hold him by the ear. Then Bill came along and deftly
skinned him alive. Afterwards he'd turn the buffalo loose to
grow a new hide. Except in the chilly wintertime, the scheme
worked to perfectoin.

Everything Bill did was on the grand scale. He used to rope
a herd of cattle at one throw. To keep his cattle, he staked out
New Mexico and used Arizona for a cow pasture. This incredible hero needed a fitting companion. His great love was Slue-
foot Sue. She won his heart when he saw her riding a catfish
down the Rio Grande, which Bill had dug previously.

Bill had a sense of humor. During idle moments he amused
himself putting thorns on the trees and horns on the toads. He
invented the centipede and the tarantula as a joke on his
friends. In fact, his sense of humor proved his undoing. One
day he met a Boston man wearing a mail-order cowboy outfit.

The Easterner asked so many fool questions about the West that poor old Bill just laughed himself to death.

VIII. Other Folk Heroes

The larger-than-life characters just described may be the most famous of American folk heroes, but they certainly aren't the only ones. Every part of the country created its own. The ballad of Casey Jones pays tribute to a hero of the railroads. Johnny Appleseed started a whole series of legends, for in life he made it his mission to plant apple trees all over the East. Some of these trees are still alive. John Henry, steel driver for the railroads, died in competition with a steam drill (pages 296–297)—after he had thoroughly shown it up. The "wild and woolly West" is represented by names like *Wild Bill Hickok*, *Buffalo Bill*, *Billy the Kid*, and *Jesse James*.

Most of those mentioned were actual persons whose fame spread. In the stories and legends they become almost supermen, as more and more feats are accredited to them. Other names can be mentioned, like Old Stormalong, the deepwater sailor; Bowleg Bill, the seagoing cowboy; and Febold Feboldson, on whose farm popcorn was invented. These were major American heroes, some real and some pure invention. Some were pure comics, like Paul Bunyan and Mike Fink; others were heroes of endurance, with a sense of responsibility to their fellowmen, like John Henry and Johnny Appleseed.

The roll call can go on without pausing for breath: Tony Beaver, Jim Bridger, Sam Houston, Big-Foot Wallace, Jim Liverpool, Joe Magarac, Roy Bean. Even the name of Abraham Lincoln has become enshrined in many legends.

There are many names, indeed. This book can do little more than familiarize you with some of the names, give you the flavor of some of the exploits, and whet your appetite for more.

IX. American Folk Ballads

Many of the folk heroes have been honored in songs and verse. Nearly everyone knows the famous saga of Casey Jones and the wreck of his big "eight-wheeler." However, not all ballads are about famous personages. Some reflect the hardships of a trade or occupation. Others reflect the yearnings of

men for a better world. There are cowboy ballads, miners'
ballads, hobo songs, sea chanteys, songs of the mountaineers,
and spirituals from the old South. How all of these originated,
no one can say for certain. Some, like "Barbara Allen," have
been traced to England. These came here with the settlers.
Others seem wholly American in origin. Often, those that have
been taken from old English or European ballads have become Americanized in the process. Many singers have contributed to the versions that are sung today. Often there are many
versions of the same ballad. "Barbara Allen," for example, is
found all over the United States in a variety of versions.
Virginia alone has 92 different texts and a dozen different
tunes.

Many contemporary folksingers are helping Americans to
rediscover the wealth of folk humor and melody. The revival
of interest in square dancing and other American folk dances
is helping to spread a love and knowledge of ballads.

Some of the finest ballads include "The Blue-Tail Fly,"
"Black Is the Color of My Truelove's Hair," "I Ride an Old
Paint," and "Wayfaring Stranger." Four excellent ballads are
included below. The first tells the story of John Henry, who
performed miraculous feats of strength with the rock-tunnel
gangs that helped build American railroads. It is said that he
died competing against a steam drill. For this reason, he
remains a symbol of man against the machine, of the individual who keeps his dignity and identity in an increasingly
mechanized world. The ballad included here reproduces a few
of the many verses circulating around the magic name of John
Henry. The second, "Barbara Allen," is a typical story of
tragic young love, of pride and devotion and misunderstand-
ing. The sentimental ending is characteristic. The third, "The
Cowboy's Lament," is in the tradition of sad western ballads.
Again, as so often in ballads, there is the note of tragedy. The
last ballad is in another key altogether. Though many ballads
are somber and deal with tragedies, some have the delightful
humor that crops up so often in folklore. The famous hobo
ballad, "The Big Rock Candy Mountains," is a good example
of the humorous folk song, with a touch of wistful longing.

John Henry

When John Henry was a little baby
Sittin' on his mammy's knee,
He picked up a hammer and a piece of steel,

Said, "This hammer'll be the death of me,
Lord, Lord, this hammer'll be the death of me."

Well, the Captain said to John Henry,
"Gonna bring that steam drill 'round.
Gonna bring that steam drill out on the job,
Gonna whup that steel on down,
Gonna whup that steel on down."

John Henry said to the Captain,
"Bring that thirty-pound hammer 'round.
Thirty-pound hammer with a nine-foot handle
Gonna beat your steam drill down,
Gonna beat your steam drill down."

John Henry drove about fifteen feet,
The steam drill drove but nine.
He drove so hard that he broke his heart;
And he laid down his hammer and he died,
And he laid down his hammer and he died.

John Henry had a little woman,
Her name was Mary Ann.
John Henry took sick and went to bed,
Mary Ann drove steel like a man,
Mary Ann drove steel like a man.

John Henry said to his shaker,
"Shaker, why don't you sing?
I'm throwin' thirty pounds from my hips on down;
Just listen to the cold steel ring,
Just listen to the cold steel ring."

They took John Henry to the graveyard,
And they buried him in the sand,
And ev'ry engine comes a-roarin' by
Whistled, "There lies a steel-drivin' man,
There lies a steel-drivin' man."

Barbara Allen©

So early in the month of May,
The green buds they were swelling,
A young man on his death bed lay,
For the love of Barbara Allen.

He called his servant to his bed,
And lowly he said to him;
"Go bring the one that I love best,
And that is Barbara Allen."

Slowly, slowly he got up,
And went to the dwelling;
Saying, "I'm sent for the one that he loves best,
And that is Barbara Allen."

Slowly, slowly she got up,
And slowly she went to him;
The very first word when she got there,
"Young man, I'm afraid you're dying."

"Do you remember the other day,
When we were at the tavern;
You drank a health to the ladies all,
And you slighted Barbara Allen."

"Yes, I remember the other day,
When we were at the tavern;
I drank a health to the ladies all,
And three to Barbara Allen."

"Do you remember the other night,
When we were at the ballroom
    dancing?
You gave your hand to the ladies all,
And slighted Barbara Allen."

"Yes, I remember the other night,
When we were at the ballroom dancing;
I gave my hand to the ladies all,
And my heart to Barbara Allen."

He turned his pale face to the wall,
His back upon the dwelling;
And all his friends cried out, "For
  shame,
Hard-hearted Barbara Allen."

She hadn't got more than a mile from town,
'Til she heard some death bell ringing.
And every knock it seemed to say,
"Hard-hearted Barbara Allen."

She hadn't gone more than another mile
'Til she spied his corpse a-coming,
"Lie down, lie down that cold pale corpse
And let me gaze upon him."

The longer she gazed, the louder she cried,
And all of his friends a-telling,
"The loss of your Sweet William dear,
Was the loving of Barbara Allen."

Sweet William he died like it might be today,
And Barbara died tomorrow;
Sweet William he died out of pure, pure love,
And Barbara died for sorrow.

Sweet William was buried in the new church yard,
And Barbara in another;
And out of his grave there grew a red rose,
From Barbara's grew a briar.

The briar and the rose they grew together,
'Til they could not grow any higher;
They wrapped and they tied in a true lover's knot,
For all true lovers to admire.

The Cowboy's Lament

As I walked out in the streets of Laredo,
As I walked out in Laredo one day,

I spied a poor cowboy wrapped up in white linen,
Wrapped up in white linen as cold as the clay.

"Oh, beat the drum slowly and play the fife lowly,
Play the dead march as you carry me along;
Take me to the green valley; there lay the sod o'er me,
For I'm a young cowboy, and I know I've done wrong.

"I see by your outfit that you are a cowboy"—
These words he did say as I boldly stepped by.
"Come sit down beside me and hear my sad story;
I am shot in the breast and I know I must die.

"Let sixteen gamblers come handle my coffin;
Let sixteen cowboys come sing me a song.
Take me to the graveyard and lay the sod o'er me,
For I'm a poor cowboy, and I know I've done wrong.

"My friends and relations, they live in the Nation;
They know not where their boy has gone.
He first came to Texas and hired to a ranchman;
Oh, I'm a young cowboy and I know I've done wrong.

"It was once in the saddle I used to go dashing;
It was once in the saddle I used to go gay;
First to the dram-house and then to the card-house;
Got shot in the breast and I am dying today.

"Get six jolly cowboys to carry my coffin;
Get six pretty maidens to bear up my pall.
Put bunches of roses all over my coffin;
Put roses to deaden the sods as they fall.

"Then swing your rope slowly and rattle your spurs lowly,
And give a wild whoop as you carry me along;
And in the grave throw me and roll the sod o'er me,
For I'm a young cowboy and I know I've done wrong.

"Oh, bury beside me my knife and six-shooter,
My spurs on my heel, my rifle by my side,
And over my coffin put a bottle of brandy
That the cowboys may drink as they carry me along.

"Go bring me a cup, a cup of cold water,
To cool my parched lips," the cowboy then said;
Before I returned his soul had departed,
And gone to his round-up—the cowboy was dead.

We beat the drum slowly and played the fife lowly,
And bitterly wept as we bore him along;
For we all loved our comrade, so brave, young, and handsome;
We all loved our comrade although he'd done wrong.

The Big Rock Candy Mountains

One ev'ning as the sun went down
And the jungle fire was burning,
Down the track came a hobo, hamming, (walking)
And he said, "Boys, I'm not turning.
I'm headed for a land that's far away,
Beside the crystal fountains.
I'll see you all this coming fall
In the Big Rock Candy Mountains.

Refrain
   "In the Big Rock Candy Mountains,
   There's a land that's fair and bright,
   Where the handouts grow on bushes
   And you sleep out every night,
   Where the boxcars all are empty
   And the sun shines ev'ry day—
   Oh, the birds and the bees and the cigaret trees,
   The rock-and-rye springs where the whangdoodle sings,
   In the Big Rock Candy Mountains.

"In the Big Rock Candy Mountains,
All the cops have wooden legs,
And the bulldogs all have rubber teeth,
And the hens lay softboiled eggs.
The farmers trees are full of fruit,
And the barns are full of hay.
Oh, I'm bound to go where there ain't no snow,
Where the sleet don't fall and the wind don't blow,
In the Big Rock Candy Mountains.

"In the Big Rock Candy Mountains,
You never change your socks,
And little streams of alkyhol
Come trickling down the rocks.
The shacks all have to tip their hats
And the railroad bulls are blind,
There's a lake of stew and of whiskey, too,
You can paddle all around in a big canoe,
In the Big Rock Candy Mountains.

"In the Big Rock Candy Mountains,
The jails are made of tin,
And you can bust right out again
As soon as they put you in.
There ain't no shorthandled shovels,
No axes, saws, or picks—
I'm a-going to stay where you sleep all day—
Oh, they boiled in oil the inventor of toil
In the Big Rock Candy Mountains.

"Oh, come with me, and we'll go see
The Big Rock Candy Mountains."

X. Indian Legends

No mention of American folk heroes and folktales would be complete without reference to the legends of those early Americans, the Indians. In most of these tales there is a poetic quality, an appreciation of nature befitting those who lived close to the land and loved it. Since Indians were mostly hunters and fishermen, their tales were often woven around the earth, the sky, birds, and animals. Each tribe had its local folktales, but many stories seem to be common to widely separated tribes.

As in other mythologies, Indian legends explain the beginnings of the universe, the origins of light and dark, day and night. In one legend about the creation of man all the animals provide suggestions for this new creature. The coyote takes the best qualities of all and creates the first man.

Many Indian myths give beautiful and poetic explanations for natural wonders. The mist in a waterfall recalls a beautiful princess who perished there. The wind in a canyon is the lament of a girl for her lover. A rocky crag on a mountainside is a huge stone canoe that carried a tribe safely through the flood. The star group, the Pleiades, is a band of children dancing in the sky.

Just as the Greeks and Romans and Norsemen explained how things began, so did the Indians. The story of the origin of corn is an explanation that reminds us in some ways of the myths of other peoples.

Mon-Daw-Min

The world owes the Indians of the Americas a debt of gratitude. Some of our most popular and important vegetables originated in the New World. The tomato and the potato, for example, were taken to Europe, where they are now staples of the diet. The following charming legend tells how the Indians were introduced to corn.

In times past, a poor Indian was living with his wife and children in a beautiful part of the country. Unfortunately, he was not too clever in getting food for his family, and his children were all too young to give him assistance. Although poor, he was a man of a kind and contented disposition. He was always thankful to the Great Spirit for everything he received.

At the time of this story his eldest son Wunzh had arrived at the proper age for the fasting ceremony to see what kind of spirit would be his guide and guardian through life. Wunzh was of a pensive and mild disposition and was beloved by the whole family. At the first sign of spring they built, for his fast, the customary little lodge at a secluded spot, far from any possible interruption or disturbance. As soon as it was ready, Wunzh went into the lodge and began the fast. During the first few days he amused himself by walking in the woods, examining the early plants and flowers.

While he rambled through the woods, he wished to know how the plants, herbs, and berries grow. "Why are some good to eat and some poisonous?" he wondered. "True, the Great Spirit made all things, and it is to him that we owe our lives. But could he not make it easier for us to get our food than by hunting animals and taking fish?"

Then Wunzh became weak from the fast and kept to his bed. While lying down, he imagined that he saw a handsome young man coming from the sky toward him. He was richly dressed, having on a great many garments of green and yellow, but differing in their shades. He had a plume of waving feathers on his head, and all his motions were graceful.

"I am sent to you, my friend," said the visitor, "by that Great Spirit who made all things in the sky and on the earth. He knows your motives in fasting and sees that you wish to do good to your people. He knows that you do not seek strength in war. I have been sent to show you how you can help your kindred."

The stranger then told Wunzh to rise and wrestle with him. Though weak from fasting, Wunzh felt his courage rising. He determined to die rather than fail. So Wunzh began the trial. As he was almost exhausted, the stranger said, "That is enough for now. I will come again."

The stranger disappeared and reappeared the next day. Again the two renewed the trial. Wunzh was getting weaker, but his courage seemed stronger than ever.

"Tomorrow will be your last trial," said the stranger. "Be strong and you will obtain the favor you seek."

On the third day the trial was again resumed. After a time, the stranger declared, "You have won." Then he entered the lodge and spoke to Wunzh.

"You have won your favor from the Great Spirit. Tomorrow will be the seventh day of your fasting. I shall meet you then and wrestle you for the last time. As soon as you have conquered me, strip off my garments and throw me down. Clean the earth of roots and weeds, make it soft, and bury me in the spot. When you have done this, leave my body in the earth and do not disturb it. Come occasionally to visit the place to see whether I have come to life. Be careful never to let the grass or weeds grow on my grave. Once a month cover me with fresh earth. If you follow my instructions, you will do good for your family." He then shook Wunzh by the hand and disappeared.

In the morning the youth's father came to him with refreshments, saying, "My son, you have fasted long enough."

"My father," replied the youth, "wait till the sun goes down. I have a reason for extending my fast to that hour."

Once again the sky-visitor returned, and the trial of strength was renewed. Wunzh felt that extra strength had been given to him. He wrestled his antagonist to the ground and followed the directions exactly. He buried his friend but felt confident he would come to life.

He returned to his father's lodge, but he never forgot for a moment the grave of his friend. He carefully visited it throughout the spring. He weeded out the grass, and kept the ground soft. Soon he saw the tops of the green plumes coming through the ground. The more careful he was to keep the ground in order, the faster the plumes grew.

As the summer was drawing to a close, Wunzh invited his father to visit the grave of his heavenly opponent. At that spot stood a tall and graceful plant, with bright-colored silken hair, topped with nodding plumes and leaves. On each side of the plant were golden clusters.

"It is my friend," cried Wunzh. "It is the friend of all mankind. It is *Mon-daw-min*. We need no longer rely on hunting alone, for as long as this gift is cherished and taken care of, the ground will give us a living."

He paused and pulled off an ear from the plant. "See, my father," said he. "This is what I fasted for. The Great Spirit has listened to my voice and has sent us something new. From now on our people will not depend only upon the chase or the waters."

Wunzh then told his father the instructions given by the stranger. He showed how the broad husks must be torn away, as he pulled off the garments in the wrestling match. Then he showed how the ear must be held before the fire till all the outer skin turns brown, while all the milk is retained in the grain. The whole family then united in a feast on the newly grown ears, expressing thanks to the Merciful Spirit who provided it. So corn came into the world.

XI. Stephen Vincent Benét

Not all of America's great legends were created anonymously. Some of our finest writers have contributed to America's legendry. Washington Irving, for example, created the tales of Rip Van Winkle and the Headless Horseman. Mark Twain wrote about "The Celebrated Jumping Frog of Calaveras County." Nathaniel Hawthorne wrote about "The Great Stone Face." Their stories are similar to folktales.

The Devil and Daniel Webster

Before his death in 1943, Stephen Vincent Benét had already risen high in the ranks of those who use native American material for their stories. He loved America deeply, and he loved those who helped build America. He loved the Lin-

colns, the Websters, and all the obscure people who have
labored to make America great. His stories reflect that love.
Perhaps his finest story, "The Devil and Daniel Webster,"
might almost have been a folk legend. Its hero takes his place
among the Paul Bunyans, for not even Paul ever outfaced the
devil!

   Do not ever say, in jest or in earnest, that you would sell
your soul to the devil for two cents. Jabez Stone made such a
statement and lived to regret it. No lawyer ever fought
against such odds as those Daniel Webster faced in the early
morning hours, before a prejudiced jury and an unsympa-
thetic judge—with a man's soul at stake.

It's a story they tell in the border country, where Massachusetts
joins Vermont and New Hampshire.

   Yes, Dan'l Webster's dead—or, at least, they buried him. But every
time there's a thunderstorm around Marshfield, they say you can
hear his rolling voice in the hollows of the sky. And they say that if
you go to his grave and speak loud and clear, "Dan'l Webster—Dan'l
Webster!" the ground'll begin to shiver and the trees begin to shake.
And after a while you'll hear a deep voice saying, "Neighbor, how
stands the Union?" Then you better answer the Union stands as she
stood, rock-bottomed and copper-sheathed, one and indivisible, or
he's liable to rear right out of the ground. At least, that's what I was
told when I was a youngster.

   You see, for a while, he was the biggest man in the country. He
never got to be President, but he was the biggest man. There were
thousands that trusted in him right next to God Almighty, and they
told stories about him that were like the stories of patriarchs and
such. They said, when he stood up to speak, stars and stripes came
right out in the sky, and once he spoke against a river and made it
sink into the ground. They said, when he walked the woods with his
fishing rod, Killall, the trout would jump out of the streams right
into his pockets, for they knew it was no use putting up a fight
against him; and, when he argued a case, he could turn on the harps
of the blessed and the shaking of the earth underground. That was
the kind of man he was, and his big farm up at Marshfield was
suitable to him. The chickens he raised were all white meat down
through the drumsticks, the cows were tended like children, and the
big ram he called Goliath had horns with a curl like a morning-glory
vine and could butt through an iron door. But Dan'l wasn't one of
your gentlemen farmers; he knew all the ways of the land, and he'd

be up by candlelight to see that the chores got done. A man with a mouth like a mastiff, a brow like a mountain, and eyes like burning anthracite—that was Dan'l Webster in his prime. And the biggest case he argued never got written down in the books, for he argued it against the devil, nip and tuck and no holds barred. And this is the way I used to hear it told.

There was a man named Jabez Stone, lived Cross Corners, New Hampshire. He wasn't a bad man to start with, but he was an unlucky man. If he planted corn, he got borers; if he planted potatoes, he got blight. He had good-enough land, but it didn't prosper him; he had a decent wife and children, but the more children he had, the less there was to feed them. If stones cropped up in his neighbor's field, boulders boiled up in his; if he had a horse with the spavins, he'd trade it for one with the staggers and give something extra. There's some folks bound to be like that, apparently. But one day Jabez Stone got sick of the whole business.

He'd been plowing that morning and he'd just broke the plowshare on a rock that he could have sworn hadn't been there yesterday. And, as he stood looking at the plowshare, the off-horse began to cough—that ropy kind of cough that means sickness and horse doctors. There were two children down with the measles, his wife was ailing, and he had a whitlow on his thumb. It was about the last straw for Jabez Stone. "I vow," he said, and he looked around him kind of desperately, "I vow it's enough to make a man want to sell his soul to the devil! And I would, too, for two cents!"

Then he felt a kind of queerness come over him at having said what he'd said; though, naturally, being a New Hampshireman, he wouldn't take it back. But, all the same, when it got to be evening and, as far as he could see, no notice had been taken, he felt relieved in his mind, for he was a religious man. But notice is always taken, sooner or later, just as the Good Book says. And sure enough, next day, about suppertime, a soft-spoken, dark-dressed stranger drove up in a handsome buggy and asked for Jabez Stone.

Well, Jabez told his family it was a lawyer, come to see him about a legacy. But he knew who it was. He didn't like the looks of the stranger, nor the way he smiled with his teeth. They were white teeth, and plentiful—some say they were filed to a point, but I wouldn't vouch for that. And he didn't like it when the dog took one look at the stranger and ran away howling, with his tail between his legs. But having passed his word, more or less, he stuck to it, and they went out behind the barn and made their bargain. Jabez Stone had to prick his finger to sign, and the stranger lent him a silver pin. The wound healed up clean, but it left a little white scar.

After that, all of a sudden, things began to pick up and prosper for Jabez Stone. His cows got fat and his horses sleek, his crops were the envy of the neighborhood, and lightning might strike all over the valley, but it wouldn't strike his barn. Pretty soon, he was one of the prosperous people of the county; they asked him to stand for selectman, and he stood for it; there began to be talk of running him for state senate. All in all, you might say the Stone family was as happy and contented as cats in a dairy. And so they were, except for Jabez Stone.

He'd been contented enough, the first few years. It's a great thing when bad luck turns; it drives most other things out of your head. True, every now and then, especially in rainy weather, the little white scar on his finger would give him a twinge. And once a year, punctual as clockwork, the stranger with the handsome buggy would come driving by. But the sixth year, the stranger lighted, and, after that, his peace was over for Jabez Stone.

The stranger came up through the lower field, switching his boots with a cane—they were handsome black boots, but Jabez Stone never liked the look of them, particularly the toes. And, after he'd passed the time of day, he said, "Well, Mr. Stone, you're a hummer! It's a very pretty property you've got here, Mr. Stone."

"Well, some might favor it and others might not," said Jabez Stone, for he was a New Hampshireman.

"Oh, no need to decry your industry!" said the stranger, very easy, showing his teeth in a smile. "After all, we know what's been done, and it's been according to contract and specifications. So when— ahem—the mortgage falls due next year, you shouldn't have any regrets."

"Speaking of that mortgage, mister," said Jabez Stone, and he looked around for help to the earth and the sky, "I'm beginning to have one or two doubts about it."

"Doubts?" said the stranger not quite so pleasantly.

"Why, yes," said Jabez Stone. "This being the U.S.A. and me always having been a religious man." He cleared his throat and got bolder. "Yes sir," he said, "I'm beginning to have considerable doubts as to that mortgage holding in court."

"There's courts and courts," said the stranger, clicking his teeth. "Still, we might as well have a look at the original document." And he hauled out a big black pocketbook, full of papers. "Sherwin,

Slater, Stevens, Stone," he muttered. " 'I, Jabez Stone, for a term of seven years—' Oh, it's quite in order, I think."

But Jabez Stone wasn't listening, for he saw something else flutter out of the black pocketbook. It was something that looked like a moth, but it wasn't a moth. And as Jabez Stone stared at it, it seemed to speak to him in a small sort of piping voice, terrible small and thin, but terrible human. "Neighbor Stone!" it squeaked. "Neighbor Stone! Help me! For God's sake, help me!"

But before Jabez Stone could stir hand or foot, the stranger whipped out a big bandanna handkerchief, caught the creature in it, just like a butterfly, and started tying up the ends of the bandanna.

"Sorry for the interruption," he said "As I was saying—"

But Jabez Stone was shaking all over like a scared horse.

"That's Miser Stevens' voice!" he said in a croak. "And you've got him in your handkerchief!"

The stranger looked a little embarrassed.

"Yes, I really should have transferred him to the collecting box," he said with a simper, "but there were some rather unusual specimens there and I didn't want them crowded. Well, well, these little contretemps will occur."

"I don't know what you mean by contertan," said Jabez Stone, "but that was Miser Stevens' voice! And he ain't dead! You can't tell me he is! He was just as spry and mean as a woodchuck, Tuesday!"

"In the midst of life—" said the stranger, kind of pious. "Listen!" Then a bell began to toll in the valley and Jabez Stone listened, with the sweat running down his face. For he knew it was tolled for Miser Stevens and that he was dead.

"These long-standing accounts," said the stranger with a sigh; "one really hates to close them. But business is business."

He still had the bandanna in his hand, and Jabez Stone felt sick as he saw the cloth struggle and flutter.

"Are they all as small as that?" he asked hoarsely.

"Small?" said the stranger. " Oh, I see what you mean. Why, they vary." He measured Jabez Stone with his eyes, and his teeth showed. "Don't worry, Mr. Stone," he said. "You'll go with a very good grade. I wouldn't trust you outside the collecting box. Now, a man like Dan'l Webster, of course—well, we'd have to build a special box for him, and even at that, I imagine the wingspread would astonish you. But, in your case, as I was saying—"

"Put that handkerchief away!" said Jabez Stone, and he began to beg and to pray. But the best he could get at the end was a three years' extension, with conditions.

But till you make a bargain like that, you've got no idea of how fast four years can run. By the last months of those years, Jabez Stone's known all over the state and there's talk of running him for governor—and it's dust and ashes in his mouth. For every day, when he gets up, he thinks, "There's one more night gone," and every night when he lies down, he thinks of the black pocketbook and the soul of Miser Stevens, and it makes him sick at heart. Till, finally, he can't bear it any longer, and, in the last days of the last year, he hitches up his horse and drives off to seek Dan'l Webster. For Dan'l was born in New Hampshire, only a few miles from Cross Corners, and it's well known that he has a particular soft spot for old neighbors.

It was early in the morning when he got to Marshfield, but Dan'l was up already, talking Latin to the farmhands and wrestling with the ram, Goliath, and trying out a new trotter and working up speeches to make against John C. Calhoun. But when he heard a New Hampshireman had come to see him, he dropped everything else he was doing, for that was Dan'l's way. He gave Jabez Stone a breakfast that five men couldn't eat, went into the living history of every man and woman in Cross Corners, and finally asked him how he could serve him.

Jabez Stone allowed that it was a kind of mortgage case.

"Well, I haven't pleaded a mortgage case in a long time, and I don't generally plead now, except before the Supreme Court," said Dan'l, "but if I can, I'll help you."

"Then I've got hope for the first time in ten years," said Jabez Stone and told him the details.

Dan'l walked up and down as he listened, hands behind his back, now and then asking a question, now and then plunging his eyes at the floor, as if they'd bore through it like gimlets. When Jabez Stone had finished, Dan'l puffed out his cheeks and blew. Then he turned to Jabez Stone and a smile broke over his face like the sunrise over Monadnock.

"You've certainly given yourself the devil's own row to hoe, Neighbor Stone," he said, "but I'll take your case."

"You'll take it?" said Jabez Stone, hardly daring to believe.

"Yes," said Dan'l Webster. "I've got about seventy-five other things to do and the Missouri Compromise to straighten out, but I'll take your case. For if two New Hampshiremen aren't a match for the devil, we might as well give the country back to the Indians."

Then he shook Jabez Stone by the hand and said, "Did you come down here in a hurry?"

"Well, I admit I made time," said Jabez Stone.

"You'll go back faster," said Dan'l Webster, and he told 'em to hitch up Constitution and Constellation to the carriage. They were matched grays with one white forefoot, and they stepped like greased lightning.

Well, I won't describe how excited and pleased the whole Stone family was to have the great Dan'l Webster for a guest, when they finally got there. Jabez Stone had lost his hat on the way, blown off when they overtook a wind, but he didn't take much account of that. But after supper he sent the family off to bed, for he had most particular business with Mr. Webster. Mrs. Stone wanted them to sit in the front parlor, but Dan'l Webster knew front parlors and said he preferred the kitchen. So it was there they sat, waiting for the stranger, with a jug on the table between them and a bright fire on the hearth—the stranger being scheduled to show up on the stroke of midnight, according to specifications.

Well, most men wouldn't have asked for better company than Dan'l Webster and a jug. But with every tick of the clock Jabez Stone got sadder and sadder. His eyes roved round, and though he sampled the jug you could see he couldn't taste it. Finally, on the stroke of 11:30 he reached over and grabbed Dan'l Webster by the arm.

"Mr. Webster, Mr. Webster!" he said, and his voice was shaking with fear and a desperate courage. "For God's sake, Mr. Webster, harness your horses and get away from this place while you can!"

"You've brought me a long way, neighbor, to tell me you don't like my company," said Dan'l Webster, quite peaceable, pulling at the jug.

"Miserable wretch that I am!" groaned Jabez Stone. "I've brought you a devilish way, and now I see my folly. Let him take me if he wills. I don't hanker after it, I must say, but I can stand it. But you're the Union's stay and New Hampshire's pride! He mustn't get you, Mr. Webster! He mustn't get you!"

Dan'l Webster looked at the distracted man, all gray and shaking in the firelight, and laid a hand on his shoulder.

"I'm obliged to you, Neighbor Stone," he said gently. "It's kindly thought of. But there's a jug on the table and a case in hand. And I never left a jug or a case half finished in my life."

And just at that moment there was a sharp rap on the door.

"Ah," said Dan'l Webster very coolly, "I thought your clock was a trifle slow, Neighbor Stone." He stepped to the door and opened it. "Come in!" he said.

The stranger came in—very dark and tall he looked in the firelight. He was carrying a box under his arm—a black japanned box with little holes in the lid. At the sight of the box Jabez Stone gave a low cry and shrank into a corner of the room.

"Mr. Webster, I presume," said the stranger, very polite, but with his eyes glowing like a fox's deep in the woods.

"Attorney of record for Jabez Stone," said Dan'l Webster, but his eyes were glowing too. "Might I ask your name?"

"I've gone by a good many," said the stranger carelessly. "Perhaps Scratch will do for the evening. I'm often called that in these regions."

Then he sat down at the table and poured himself a drink from the jug. The liquor was cold in the jug, but it came steaming into the glass.

"And now," said the stranger, smiling and showing his teeth, "I shall call upon you, as a law-abiding citizen, to assist me in taking possession of my property."

Well, with that the argument began—and it went hot and heavy. At first Jabez Stone had a flicker of hope, but when he saw Dan'l Webster being forced back at point after point, he just sat scrunched up in his corner, with his eyes on that japanned box. For there wasn't any doubt as to the deed or the signature—that was the worst of it. Dan'l Webster twisted and turned and thumped his fist on the table, but he couldn't get away from that. He offered to compromise the case; the stranger wouldn't hear of it. He pointed out the property had increased in value, and state senators ought to be worth more; the stranger stuck to the letter of the law. He was a great lawyer, Dan'l Webster, but we know who's the King of Lawyers, as the Good Book tells us, and it seemed as if, for the first time, Dan'l Webster had met his match.

Finally, the stranger yawned a little. "Your spirited efforts on behalf of your client do you credit, Mr. Webster," he said, "but if you have no more arguments to adduce, I'm rather pressed for time"—and Jabez Stone shuddered.

Dan'l Webster's brow looked dark as a thundercloud.

"Pressed or not, you shall not have this man!" he thundered. "Mr. Stone is an American citizen, and no American citizen may be forced into the service of a foreign prince. We fought England for that in '12 and we'll fight all hell for it again!"

"Foreign?" said the stranger. "And who calls me a foreigner?"

"Well, I never yet heard of the dev— of your claiming American citizenship," said Dan'l Webster with surprise.

"And who with better right?" said the stranger, with one of his terrible smiles. "When the first wrong was done to the first Indian, I was there. When the first slaver put out for the Congo, I stood on her deck. Am I not in your books and stories and beliefs, from the first settlements on? Am I not spoken of, still, in every church in New England? 'Tis true the North claims me for a Southerner and the South for a Northerner, but I am neither. I am merely an honest American like yourself—and of the best descent—for, to tell the truth, Mr. Webster, though I don't like to boast of it, my name is older in this country than yours."

"Aha" said Dan'l Webster, with the veins standing out in his forehead. "Then I stand on the Constitution! I demand a trial for my client!"

"The case is hardly one for an ordinary court," said the stranger, his eyes flickering. "And, indeed, the lateness of the hour—"

"Let it be any court you choose, so it is an American judge and an American jury!" said Dan'l Webster in his pride. "Let it be the quick or the dead; I'll abide the issue!"

"You have said it," said the stranger, and pointed his finger at the door. And with that, and all of a sudden, there was a rushing of wind outside and a noise of footsteps. They came, clear and distinct, through the night. And yet they were not like the footsteps of living men.

"In God's name, who comes by so late?" cried Jabez Stone in an ague of fear.

"The jury Mr. Webster demands," said the stranger, sipping at his boiling glass. "You must pardon the rough appearance of one or two; they will have come a long way."

And with that the fire burned blue and the door blew open and twelve men entered, one by one.

If Jabez Stone had been sick with terror before, he was blind with terror now. For there was Walter Butler, the loyalist, who spread fire and horror through the Mohawk Valley in the times of the Revolution; and there was Simon Girty, the renegade, who saw white men burned at the stake and whooped with the Indians to see them burn. His eyes were green, like a catamount's, and the stains on his hunting shirt did not come from the blood of the deer. King Philip was there, wild and proud as he had been in life, with the great gash in his head that gave him his death wound, and cruel Governor Dale, who broke men on the wheel. There was Morton of Merry Mount, who so vexed the Plymouth Colony, with his flushed, loose, handsome face and his hate of the godly. There was Teach, the bloody pirate, with his black beard curling on his breast. The Reverend John Smeet, with his strangler's hands and his Geneva gown, walked as daintily as he had to the gallows. The red print of the rope was still around his neck, but he carried a perfumed handkerchief in one hand. One and all, they came into the room with the fires of hell still upon them, and the stranger named their names and their deeds as they came, till the tale of twelve was told. Yet the stranger had told the truth—they had all played a part in America.

"Are you satisfied with the jury, Mr. Webster?" said the stranger mockingly, when they had taken their places.

The sweat stood upon Dan'l Webster's brow, but his voice was clear.

"Quite satisfied," he said. "Though I miss General Arnold from the company."

"Benedict Arnold is engaged upon other business," said the stranger, with a glower. "Ah, you asked for a justice, I believe."

He pointed his finger once more, and a tall man, soberly clad in Puritan garb, with the burning gaze of the fanatic, stalked into the room and took his judge's place.

"Justice Hathorne is a jurist of experience," said the stranger. "He presided at certain witch trials once held in Salem. There were others who repented of the business later, but not he."

"Repent of such notable wonders and undertakings?" said the stern old justice. "Nay, hang them—hang them all!" And he muttered to himself in a way that struck ice into the soul of Jabez Stone.

Then the trial began, and, as you might expect, it didn't look anyways good for the defense. And Jabez Stone didn't make much of a witness in his own behalf. He took one look at Simon Girty and screeched, and they had to put him back in his corner in a kind of swoon.

It didn't halt the trial, though; the trial went on, as trials do. Dan'l Webster had faced some hard juries and hanging judges in his time, but this was the hardest he'd ever faced, and he knew it. They sat there with a kind of glitter in their eyes, and the stranger's smooth voice went on and on. Every time he'd raise an objection, it'd be "Objection sustained," but whenever Dan'l objected, it'd be "Objection denied." Well, you couldn't expect fair play from a fellow like this Mr. Scratch.

It got to Dan'l in the end, and he began to heat, like iron in the forge. When he got up to speak he was going to flay that stranger with every trick known to the law, and the judge and jury too. He didn't care if it was contempt of court or what would happen to him for it. He didn't care any more what happened to Jabez Stone. He just got madder and madder, thinking of what he'd say. And yet, curiously enough, the more he thought about it, the less he was able to arrange his speech in his mind.

Till, finally, it was time for him to get up on his feet, and he did so, all ready to bust out with lightnings and denunciations. But before he started he looked over at the judge and jury for a moment, such being his custom. And he noticed the glitter in their eyes was twice as strong as before, and they all leaned forward. Like hounds just before they get the fox, they looked, and the blue mist of evil in the room thickened as he watched them. Then he saw what he'd been about to do, and he wiped his forehead, as a man might who's just escaped falling into a pit in the dark.

For it was him they'd come for, not only Jabez Stone. He read it in the glitter of their eyes and in the way the stranger hid his mouth with one hand. And if he fought them with their own weapons, he'd fall into their power; he knew that, though he couldn't have told you how. It was his own anger and horror that burned in their eyes; and he'd have to wipe that out or the case was lost. He stood there for a moment, his black eyes burning like anthracite. And then he began to speak.

He started off in a low voice, though you could hear every word. They say he could call on the harps of the blessed when he chose. And this was just as simple and easy as a man could talk. But he didn't start out by condemning or reviling. He was talking about the things that make a country a country and a man a man.

And he began with the simple things that everybody's known and felt—the freshness of a fine morning when you're young, and the taste of food when you're hungry, and the new day that's every day when you're a child. He took them up and he turned them in his hands. They were good things for any man. But without freedom, they sickened. And when he talked of those enslaved, and the sorrows of slavery, his voice got like a big bell. He talked of the early days of America and the men who had made those days. It wasn't a spread-eagle speech, but he made you see it. He admitted all the wrong that had ever been done. But he showed how, out of the wrong and the right, the suffering and the starvations, something new had come. And everybody had played a part in it, even the traitors.

Then he turned to Jabez Stone and showed him as he was—an ordinary man who'd had hard luck and wanted to change it. And, because he'd wanted to change it, now he was going to be punished for all eternity. And yet there was good in Jabez Stone, and he showed that good. He was hard and mean, in some ways, but he was a man. There was sadness in being a man, but it was a proud thing too. And he showed what the pride of it was till you couldn't help feeling it. Yes, even in hell, if a man was a man, you'd know it. And he wasn't pleading for any one person any more, though his voice rang like an organ. He was telling the story and the failures and the endless journey of mankind. They got tricked and trapped and bamboozled, but it was a great journey. And no demon that was ever foaled could know the inwardness of it—it took a man to do that.

The fire began to die on the hearth and the wind before morning to blow. The light was getting gray in the room when Dan'l Webster finished. And his words came back at the end to New Hampshire ground, and the one spot of land that each man loves and clings to. He painted a picture of that, and to each one of that jury he spoke of things long forgotten. For his voice could search the heart, and that was his gift and his strength. And to one, his voice was like the forest and its secrecy, and to another like the sea and the storms of the sea; and one heard the cry of his lost nation in it, and another saw a little harmless scene he hadn't remembered for years. But each saw something. And when Dan'l Webster finished he didn't know whether or not he'd saved Jabez Stone. But he knew he'd done a miracle. For the glitter was gone from the eyes of judge and jury, and, for the moment, they were men again, and knew they were men.

"The defense rests," said Dan'l Webster and stood there like a mountain. His ears were still ringing with his speech, and he didn't hear anything else till he heard Judge Hathorne say, "The jury will retire to consider its verdict."

Walter Butler rose in his place and his face had a dark, gay pride on it.

"The jury has considered its verdict," he said and looked the stranger full in the eye. "We find for the defendant, Jabez Stone."

With that, the smile left the stranger's face, but Walter Butler did not flinch.

"Perhaps 'tis not strictly in accordance with the evidence," he said, "but even the damned may salute the eloquence of Mr. Webster."

With that, the long crow of a rooster split the gray morning sky, and judge and jury were gone from the room like a puff of smoke and as if they had never been there. The stranger returned to Dan'l Webster, smiling wryly.

"Major Butler was always a bold man," he said. "I had not thought him quite so bold. Nevertheless, my congratulations, as between two gentlemen."

"I'll have that paper first, if you please," said Dan'l Webster, and he took it and tore it into four pieces. It was queerly warm to the touch. "And now," he said, "I'll have you!" and his hand came down like a bear trap on the stranger's arm. For he knew that once you bested anybody like Mr. Scratch in fair fight, his power on you was gone. And he could see that Mr. Scratch knew it too.

The stranger twisted and wriggled, but he couldn't get out of that grip. "Come, come, Mr. Webster," he said, smiling palely. "This sort of thing is ridic—ouch!—is ridiculous. If you're worried about the costs of the case, naturally I'd be glad to pay—"

"And so you shall!" said Dan'l Webster, shaking him till his teeth rattled. "For you'll sit right down at that table and draw up a document, promising never to bother Jabez Stone nor his heirs or assigns nor any other New Hampshireman till doomsday! For any hades we want to raise in this state, we can raise ourselves, without assistance from strangers."

"Ouch!" said the stranger. "Ouch! Well, they never did run very big to the barrel, but—ouch!—I agree!"

So he sat down and drew up the document. But Dan'l Webster kept his hand on his coat collar all the time.

"And, now, may I go?" said the stranger, quite humble, when Dan'l'd seen the document was in proper and legal form.

"Go?" said Dan'l, giving him another shake. "I'm still trying to figure out what I'll do with you. For you've settled the costs of the case, but you haven't settled with me. I think I'll take you back to Marshfield," he said kind of reflective. "I've got a ram there named Goliath that can butt through an iron door. I'd kind of like to turn you loose in his field and see what he'd do."

Well, with that the stranger began to beg and to plead. And he begged and he pled so humble that finally Dan'l, who was naturally kindhearted, agreed to let him go. The stranger seemed terrible grateful for that and said, just to show they were friends, he'd tell

Dan'l's fortune before leaving. So Dan'l agreed to that, though he didn't take much stock in fortune-tellers ordinarily. But, naturally, the stranger was a little different.

Well, he pried and he peered at the lines in Dan'l's hands. And he told him one thing and another that was quite remarkable. But they were all in the past.

"Yes, all that's true, and it happened," said Dan'l Webster. "But what's to come in the future?"

The stranger grinned kind of happily, and shook his head.

"The future's not as you think it," he said. "It's dark. You have a great ambition, Mr. Webster."

"I have," said Dan'l firmly, for everybody knew he wanted to be President.

"It seems almost within your grasp," said the stranger, "but you will not attain it. Lesser men will be made President and you will be passed over."

"And, if I am, I'll still be Daniel Webster," said Dan'l. "Say on."

"You have two strong sons," said the stranger, shaking his head. "You look to found a line. But each will die in war and neither reach greatness."

"Live or die, they are still my sons," said Dan'l Webster. "Say on."

"You have made great speeches," said the stranger. "You will make more."

"Ah," said Dan'l Webster.

"But the last great speech you make will turn many of your own against you," said the stranger. "They will call you Ichabod; they will call you other names. Even in New England some will say you have turned your coat and sold your country, and their voices will be loud against you till you die."

"So it is an honest speech, it does not matter what men say," said Dan'l Webster. Then he looked at the stranger and their glances locked.

"One question," he said. "I have fought for the Union all my life. Will I see that fight won against those who would tear it apart?"

"Not while you live," said the stranger grimly, "but it will be won. And after you are dead, there are thousands who will fight for your cause, because of words that you spoke."

"Why, then, you long-barreled, slab-sided, lantern-jawed, fortune-telling note shaver," said Dan'l Webster, with a great roar of laughter, "be off with you to your own place before I put my mark on you! For, by the thirteen colonies, I'd go to the Pit itself to save the Union!"

And with that he drew back his foot for a kick that would have stunned a horse. It was only the tip of his shoe that caught the stranger, but he went flying out of the door with his collecting box under his arm.

"And now," said Dan'l Webster, seeing Jabez Stone beginning to rouse from his swoon, "let's see what's left in the jug, for it's dry work talking all night. I hope there's pie for breakfast, Neighbor Stone."

But they say that whenever the devil comes near Marshfield, even now, he gives it a wide berth. And he hasn't been seen in the state of New Hampshire from that day to this. I'm not talking about Massachusetts or Vermont.

READING FOR UNDERSTANDING

Main Idea

1. The main idea of "Modern Folk Heroes" (page 273) is that (a) folklore really belongs to olden days (b) the printed page does not affect the growth of a good yarn (c) folk heroes and folktales are being created all the time (d) the gods of ancient Greece are still worshiped in parts of Greece.

Details

2. In "Tall Tales" (274–281), the creature with the greatest ability to survive difficult conditions is a (a) Kansas jayhawk (b) mountain lion (c) rattlesnake (d) bedbug.
3. Paul Bunyan (281–288) is compared with (a) Thor (b) Sourdough Sam (c) Big Swede (d) Zeus.
4. Paul Bunyan's popcorn feast (283–284) (a) makes him sick (b) creates a "blizzard" (c) attracts the attention of the Blue Ox (d) is attended by all the loggers in Minnesota.
5. When Paul wants to bait a blizzard trap, he baits it with (a) an icicle (b) a north wind (c) some bear meat (d) a fishhook.
6. Paul finally solved the river problem by (a) letting the river go back into its crooked channels (b) sawing it up into nine-mile lengths (c) giving up and admitting defeat (d) moving the entire river into a different state.
7. Davy Crockett (288) was a devoted follower of (a) Abraham Lincoln (b) Robert E. Lee (c) Stonewall Jackson (d) Andrew Jackson.

8. Mike Fink (289–292) was most famous as a (a) logger (b) scout (c) keelboatman (d) navigator.

9. Mike Fink's marksmanship impressed (a) his son (b) English tourists (c) his bride-to-be (d) a rancher.

10. Pecos Bill (292–295) once rode a (a) cyclone and a lion (b) lion and a rattlesnake (c) cyclone and a deer (d) rattlesnake and a deer.

11. "Widow Maker" is the name of a (a) pistol (b) rifle (c) steer (d) horse.

12. All the following American folk heroes are mentioned (295) EXCEPT (a) Old Stormalong (b) Roy Bean (c) Thomas Jefferson (d) Johnny Appleseed.

13. "Barbara Allen" is a ballad about (a) a child and his grandmother (b) two lovers (c) an engagement in the American Revolution (d) a famous western dancer.

14. The legend "Mon-Daw-Min" explains the origin of (a) the peace pipe (b) the Indian idea of justice (c) corn (d) the teepee.

15. At the end of "The Devil and Daniel Webster," the devil promises never to bother again the citizens of (a) Vermont (b) Massachusetts (c) Maine (d) New Hampshire.

Inferences

16. *Modern urban legends* (273) are closely related to (a) traditional folktales (b) literary short stories (c) ballads (d) epic poems.

17. The best word to describe the feats of the folk heroes mentioned is (a) *exaggeration* (b) *realism* (c) *bitterness* (d) *understatement*.

18. Carl Sandburg's attitude (276–281) toward the tall stories he relates can best be described as one of (a) affectionate admiration (b) scornful disapproval (c) lukewarm interest (d) self-satisfied disbelief.

19. Wunzh (303–305) was especially favored by the Great Spirit because of his (a) strength (b) skill in battle (c) recklessness (d) idealism.

20. Daniel Webster (305–320) won his case by appealing to the jury's (a) greed (b) generosity (c) humanity (d) vanity.

WORDS IN CONTEXT

1. His *prowess* in baseball is frequently recalled by old-timers, who naturally tell their stories in their own way.

   Prowess (273) means (a) superior skill (b) becoming modesty (c) forthright honesty (d) great intelligence.

2. After more *taunting* by the fans, he pointed his bat emphatically in the direction of the right-field stands.
   Taunting (273) means   (a) approval   (b) insulting   (c) whistling   (d) excitement.

3. Yarns flew thick and fast, and the *guffaws* flew faster.
   Guffaws (281) means   (a) murmurs   (b) chuckles   (c) giggles   (d) loud laughs.

4. Paul was a counterpart of Thor, *invincible* and indestructible.
   Invincible (281) means   (a) unconquerable   (b) unteachable   (c) impetuous   (d) unlikable.

5. Paul's loggers quit work and ran home, howling in *anguish*.
   Anguish (282) means   (a) excitement   (b) worry   (c) pain   (d) anger.

6. His stature was upwards of six feet, his proportions perfectly *symmetrical*, and exhibiting the evidence of Herculean powers.
   Symmetrical (289) means   (a) pleasing   (b) measured   (c) visible   (d) balanced.

7. In his horizontal position the weapon remained for some seconds as immovable as if the arm which held it was affected by no *pulsation*.
   Pulsation (291) means   (a) atmospheric pressure   (b) throbbing   (c) interference   (d) distraction.

8. "Elevate your gun a little lower, Mike!" cried the *imperturbable* brother.
   Imperturbable (291) means   (a) unhappy   (b) cool   (c) nervous   (d) disturbed.

9. He remained as immovable as if he had been a figure *hewn* out of stone.
   Hewn (291) means   (a) measured   (b) uncovered   (c) cut   (d) moved.

10. Many a tale is told round the campfire of Bill's *prodigious* strength and courage.
    Prodigious (292) means   (a) enormous   (b) well-advertised   (c) unexpected   (d) admired.

11. "The Big Rock Candy Mountain" is a good example of the humorous folksong, with a touch of *wistful* longing.
    Wistful (296) means   (a) joyous   (b) impossible   (c) cruel   (d) sad.

12. Though many ballads are *somber* and deal with tragedies, some have the delightful humor that creeps up so often in folklore.
    Somber (296) means   (a) gloomy   (b) lighthearted   (c) melodic   (d) repetitious.

13. Wunzh was of a *pensive* and mild disposition and was beloved by the whole family.
    Pensive (303) means   (a) reckless   (b) unpredictable (c) thoughtful (d) harmless.

14. I have been sent to show you how you can help your *kindred*.
    Kindred   (304)   means   (a) friends   (b) family (c) acquaintances (d) farm animals.

15. Jabez told his family it was a lawyer, come to see him about a *legacy*.
    Legacy (307) means (a) something inherited (b) a renewal of a mortgage (c) a lawsuit by a neighbor (d) a decision to run for public office.

16. "Oh, no need to *decry* your industry!" said the stranger, showing his teeth in a smile.
    Decry (308) means (a) describe (b) belittle (c) advertise (d) boast about.

17. "If you have no more arguments to *adduce*, I'm rather pressed for time."
    Adduce means (312) (a) deny (b) advance (c) criticize (d) overlook.

18. When he got up to speak, he was going to *flay* that stranger with every trick known to the law.
    Flay (316) means   (a) irritate   (b) amuse   (c) criticize (d) entertain.

19. Till, finally, it was time for him to get up on his feet, and he did so, all ready to bust out with lightnings and *denunciations*.
    Denunciations (316) means (a) condemnations (b) descriptions (c) anecdotes (d) objections.

20. But he didn't start out by condemning or *reviling*.
    Reviling (316) means (a) pleading (b) pitying (c) approving (d) abusing.

THINKING IT OVER

1. How does Pecos Bill resemble Paul Bunyan? What traits do the folk heroes seem to have in common? How do American folk heroes resemble some of the Greek and Scandinavian gods?

2. How do ballads come into being? How does the growth of a ballad resemble the growth of a folktale?

3. Reread the first page of "The Devil and Daniel Webster." In what ways does it remind you of the tales of Paul Bunyan and the others?

4. Is Webster pictured as a man big enough to win out against the Devil? What touches help to build up his invincibility? What keeps the issue in doubt until the end? What touches of humor can you find?

5. Why is it dramatically important to have a jury of renegades and villains rather than a jury of the just? What is the crucial point that sways the jury? Explain the sentence: "He was telling the story and the failures and the endless journey of mankind. They got tricked and trapped and bamboozled, but it was a great journey. And no demon that was ever foaled could know the inwardness of it—it took a man to do that."

Was this a skillful argument before the villainous jury?
Do you consider it a good picture of man's life on earth?

SUGGESTED ACTIVITIES

1. We have already talked about picturesque liars (page 274). Sometimes they form clubs called *Ananias Clubs*—for Ananias, a biblical character notorious for his lying. One ingenious member described a harrowing experience at sea. Alone in a small rowboat far from shore, he noticed that the boat had sprung a leak. Water was pouring in from a hole in the bottom. Desperately he tried to bail the water out, but with no success. He had just given up and become resigned to drowning when he noticed that the water had begun to subside. The tongues in his shoes were lapping up the water.

Another seagoing storyteller told of running out of fuel at sea. His ingenuity was equal to the occasion. Catching a mess of catfish he showed them to the dogfish, which he had already caught. Naturally, the dogfish began to bark when they saw the catfish. The mariner proceeded to *scrape off the bark* and use it for fuel.

Can you top these? Perhaps your class will enjoy a tall-story contest.

2. The comic books, television, and movies have created individuals with superhuman strength. Select one of the following, or choose an example of your own: Superman, Wonder Woman, Spiderman, the Bionic Woman. Show how the individual you have chosen resembles Paul Bunyan or Pecos Bill.

3. Many place names in the United States are of Indian origin. The Mississippi is "the father of waters." Lake Winnepesaukee is "the smile of the great spirit." Make a list of at least ten Indian names. Use cities, states, lakes, mountains, rivers—any place with an Indian name. Include the meaning of the name, if possible.

4. The Indians have given us many things besides corn. In vegetables they have given us the squash, the potato, the eggplant, the pumpkin, and the sweet potato, among others. They have added many words to the language; for example, *moose, raccoon, opossum, chipmunk, hickory,* and *muskrat.* What do these words reveal about the life of the Indians?

These words, too, are of Indian origin: *wigwam, wampum, toboggan, totem, squaw, mackinaw, moccasin, papoose, tomahawk.* How many of them can you define?

5. Stories about the man who sold his soul to the Devil can be traced far back into medieval times. Christopher Marlowe's *Dr. Faustus* and Goethe's *Faust* (made into an opera) are two of the more famous versions. Washington Irving wrote a story called "The Devil and Tom Walker." A modern version, in which the hero completely outwits the Devil, is "Satan and Sam Shay," by Robert Arthur. Max Beerbohm's *Enoch Soames* gives the bargain with the Devil a new twist altogether. Perhaps you will be able to read one or more of these. If you do, notice the difference in treatment, both of the defendant and of the Devil himself.

WORDS ASSOCIATED WITH THE AMERICAN EXPERIENCE

Word	*Definition*	*Named for*
Annie Oakley	a free ticket or pass	famous American markswoman
Babbitt	a thoughtless conformist	character in a novel by Sinclair Lewis
Benedict Arnold	a traitor	officer during American Revolution
Bronx cheer	a sound of contempt	section of New York City
bunk or bunkum	nonsense	county in North Carolina whose congressman was seldom believed by his fellows
Bunyanesque	huge	the folk hero Paul Bunyan
catch-22	something that makes an enterprise hopeless before it begins	a novel by Joseph Heller
Levis	blue jeans	the inventor, Levi Strauss

WORDS ASSOCIATED WITH THE AMERICAN EXPERIENCE
(Cont.)

Word	Definition	Named for
maverick	a nonconformist	Samuel A. Maverick, who refused to brand his calves
poinsettia	the Christmas flower	Joel R. Poinsett, ambassador to Mexico
Quonset hut	a prefabricated shelter	Quonset, Rhode Island
Rube Goldberg	doing a simple job in a complicated way	cartoonist who specialized in complicated gadgets
Simon Legree	a cruel taskmaster	villain of *Uncle Tom's Cabin*
teddy bear	a stuffed toy bear	President Theodore Roosevelt
Uncle Sam	the United States	Samuel Wilson, Amerian financier during the Revolution
Walter Mitty	an impractical daydreamer	character in a short story by James Thurber

Acknowledgments

Grateful acknowledgment is made to the following sources for permission to reprint copyrighted selections.

"Talk—An Ashanti Tale," page 140. From THE COW-TAIL SWITCH AND OTHER WEST AFRICAN STORIES by Harold Courlander and George Herzog. Copyright © 1947, 1975 by Holt, Rinehart and Winston, Inc. Reprinted by permission of Henry Holt and Company, Inc.

"Cats Are Queer Articles," page 142. Reprinted by permission of the publisher, Devin-Adair Publishers, Greenwich, CT.

"The Salamanna Grapes," page 146. From ITALIAN FOLK-TALES by Italo Calvino, copyright © 1956 by Giulio Einaudi Editore; English translation copyright © 1980 by Harcourt Brace Jovanovich, Inc. Reprinted by permission of Harcourt Brace Jovanovich, Inc.

"The Flying Contest," page 157. From SURINAME FOLKLORE by Melville and Frances Herskovits. Copyright © 1936 Columbia University Press. By permission.

"Come Look," page 180. From THE SOUP STONE by Maria Leach (Thomas Y. Crowell). Copyright © 1954, by Harper & Row, Publishers, Inc. Reprinted by permission of Harper & Row, Publishers, Inc.

"The Children of the House of Dawn," page 185. From TALES FROM THE AMAZON by Elsie Spicer Eells. Reprinted by permission of Thelma M. Eells.

"What Makes Brer Wasp Have a Short Patience," page 188. From AFRO-AMERICAN FOLKTALES: STORIES FROM BLACK TRADITIONS IN THE NEW WORLD, edited by Robert D. Abrahams. Copyright © 1985 by Robert D. Abrahams. Reprinted by permission of Random House, Inc.

"Why the Hair on the Head Turns Gray Before the Beard," page 191. Reprinted from A TREASURY OF JEWISH FOLKLORE by Nathan Ausubel. Copyright © 1948, 1976 by Crown Publishers, Inc. Used by permission of Crown Publishers, Inc.

"The Cobbler Astrologer," page 193. From GREAT FOLKTALES OF WIT AND HUMOR, edited by James R. Foster. Copyright © 1955 by Harper & Row, Publishers, Inc. Reprinted by permission of the publisher.

"Tiger Becomes a Riding Horse," page 212. From AFRO-AMER-ICAN FOLKTALES: STORIES FROM BLACK TRADITIONS IN THE NEW WORLD, edited by Robert D. Abrahams. Copyright © 1985 by Robert D. Abrahams. Reprinted by permission of Random House, Inc.

Index and Pronunciation Guide